Ears of Steel

WITHDRAWN

Ears of Steel

THE REAL MAN'S GUIDE
TO WALT DISNEY WORLD

BART SCOTT

EARS OF STEEL
THE REAL MAN'S GUIDE TO WALT DISNEY WORLD

Published by The Intrepid Traveler, P.O. Box 531, Branford, CT 06405
www.intrepidtraveler.com

First Edition
Printed in the United States of America
Cover design by Lisa Rennie
Interior design by Rachel Reiss
ISBN: 978-1-937011-34-5
Library of Congress Control Number: 2013940371
Distributed to the trade by National Book Network

For my Wendy, who creates the real magic in our little kingdom and holds it all together whenever I fly off to Neverland! You never imagined marrying a man equal parts Pan and pirate, but you hold my heart (and hook!).

Contents

Author's Note
(For Men Only!)

Gentleman . . . Don't worry, it's a generic term. If you're a man, you qualify. This book doesn't really start for a few pages. The next section is for your wife, girlfriend, or the significant female in your life. It's boring chatter. You know, the kind *they* like. I only include it because the lawyers insist. Something about an equal-opportunity travel book, *blah blah blah*!

In a moment, I'm going to have you turn the page and hand her the book.

Don't worry, this isn't a trick. I'm telling her to leave you alone while you read. In fact, I'm telling her to bring you a sandwich and a beer, then leave you alone. See, I'm on your side.

Go ahead, flip the page and hand her the book. I'll instruct her when to give it back (and go to the kitchen to make your snack).

Hello, Ladies!

Hi there! It's your old pal Bart, the Disney Guy. Ok, not **the** Disney Guy. I am one of many. We are a community of grown men who go about our daily lives doing manly things, performing manly tasks, and taking care of manly responsibilities. But inside, we are Disney guys. We're proud Men of The Mouse, and we are legion.

If you're reading this, first off thank you for buying my book. My children thank you, and my wife really thanks you! If you stole it, go back to the store and pay for it or may your thieving hand be bitten off by a tick-tock croc! Trust me, hooks are a bad look for a gal.

If you're reading this (and you shelled out money for it) I think I understand why. You've got a problem. You want to go on a family vacation. Specifically, you want to go to Walt Disney World. Your kids want to go to Walt Disney World. The problem? The hairy-backed knucklehead kicked back in his easy chair with potato chip flakes on his shirt and a remote fused to his palm.

Let me guess. He doesn't want to go to Walt Disney World. He probably uses words like "too expensive" or "nothing for me to do" and "just a bunch of kiddie stuff." Is this sounding familiar? Don't worry. I've heard it all before. These are simply the uneducated ramblings of a prideful man. And you know how *they* are. We men don't ask for directions. We don't read instructions. Our natural instinct is that we **just know**. Even if we know we don't know, we can't let you know that we don't know, even though we know you probably know we don't know. You know?

Maybe he's picturing mouse-shaped balloons. Perhaps somewhere in his life he saw footage of *"it's a small world."* It's even possible there's just a sad little boy inside him that always wanted to go to Walt Disney World but never got the chance. Pardon me while I roll a single tear. I'm sure he would rather spend a week charring animal products, hitting things with sticks, beating his chest, and howling at the moon.

Truth is he's only hurting himself. Fortunately, you've come to the right source. I am going to help you—through this book. I know how to talk to your husband. He's a man. I have experience in this area.

Carefully flip to the introduction and slowly place the book in front of his sloping brow. No sudden movements. We don't want to spook him. Trust me. You just go pack your comfortable shoes and sunscreen. You'll be on your way to the Orlando area before you can wish upon a star. If he refuses to read, tell him he will soon find life around his happy home colder than Minneapolis in late January. The exact room you specify is up to you!

Oh, and just for the sake of reinforcement, you might want to read the rest too! Your husband is about to take in a lot of information. I will keep it interesting and funny, but there are no pictures and it might make him a little dizzy. I can't be in your home to talk him down. Well, I suppose for a nominal fee, but best if you handle the aftercare yourself.

All righty then! Ready to make your Walt Disney World family vacation dreams a reality? Turn the page, hand him back the book, and here . . . we . . . go!

Who Needs a Vacation?

Hi there, pal! Told you I'd be back. I'm sure she'll be shuffling off into that kitchen any minute now. So now that it's just you and me, let's talk. I know, you're trying to watch the race or the news or Oprah (don't worry, I won't tell). Hear me out! This is for the sake of your family. If you're reading this book at all, it's most likely because your lady and your kids want to take a trip to Walt Disney World.

Wait! Don't shut down on me, man!

She's watching. I suggest you keep reading. I said I'd help her, but I'm really on your side. *We* are on the same side. We're like the Band of Brothers! Pals before gals, and all that! Trust me when I say I've got your best interests at heart. You need a vacation. You bust your butt all week long, all year for that matter, in what seems like never-ending monotony, right? What's that? No, not the game with hotels and colorful money. Monotony. It means everything feels the same, never changing, that sort of thing.

I'm kidding! Of course, you knew what it meant! See, you are a smart guy. So my question to you is simple. What do you have against Walt Disney World???

You're denying yourself an incredible vacation. What, too macho to have fun? Afraid the boys down at the gravel pit are going to make fun of you? The brain trust at the pub will question your manhood for going to see Mickey? Guess what, pal? They're morons! Don't deny yourself for those orangutans!

I know what you're thinking. You're a grown man. There's nothing there for you, right? Guess what my friend, you're wrong! I'm going to prove it to you.

Where would you rather go? Someplace hot and tropical? Lay around sweating all day, surrounded by leathery septuagenarians stuffed into European swimwear nature never intended for the human form, sipping overpriced slush with tiny umbrellas? Two words: "cartel wars." Not to mention, are you really going to take your family someplace where kidnapping *gringos* is a national trade? Talk about creating memories. That will be well-remembered come Father's Day.

Las Vegas? Why not? "Hey kids, guess what? You get to stay locked up in the room all night while daddy loses your college fund! Better learn to deal blackjack, Junior! You're gonna need a trade!" Vegas isn't even the deal it used to be. The days of 99-cent buffets are over. The Rat Pack is gone. And do you really want to spend half the trip covering your kids' eyes?

What's that? Europe? Ooh, Mr. Continental! I like it. Eight hours on an airplane followed by 24 hours of jet lag. When you do come out of your time-zone-induced haze, figure out how many dollars equal a single Euro. Then leave your hotel to enjoy the fine, friendly service extended to Americans. Why don't you give me half the money and I'll be rude to you domestically.

All right, I shouldn't knock those other destinations. They are great in their own ways and have wonderful things to offer, I guess. They just don't sound like ideal family vacations, especially if your kids are younger. I'm pretty sure you know I'm right. So where does that leave us? I'll tell you where, the ***Walt Disney World Resort!***

The best parts of those other places can be found at Walt Disney World, without any of that bad stuff! You've got beautiful weather. Amazing pools, water parks, even beaches! Plus incredible resort hotels that treat you like a VIP regardless of your bank account. Four different theme parks featuring state-of-the-art (and classic old school) attractions, shows, and amazing spectacles that are almost impossible to describe. I mean, I'll try. I am writing a book here after all! Disney puts entertainment and technology to mind-blowing use, all in the name of giving you the ultimate vacation experience! And no matter where you live in the continental United States, it's only a short (relatively speaking) plane ride away!

Plus Disney's not as expensive as you think. I'm no travel agent, but I'd almost guarantee you can do Walt Disney World cheaper than a week in Vegas, the Caribbean, or most definitely Europe. I would also bet you'll have way more fun, laugh like crazy, and get much better value for your money.

Still not convinced, huh? Sounds like some travel brochure? You're right. You are a smart man! You're not going to fall for some slick sales pitch. I didn't expect you to. In your mind, Walt Disney World is just for kids. You're a *real man* and us real men need to see something to believe it.

I can't afford to fly you to Florida and show you in person, but I can paint a pretty damn good picture for you. How about a private fishing excursion? How do you feel about playing 18 holes on one of several PGA-rated courses? Ever thought about strapping into a real race car and dropping the hammer? How about catching some Spring Training baseball?

No guy wants to do *that* stuff!

How about dining on the best burgers, the thickest, juiciest steaks, fresh seafood, amazing pastas, gourmet pizzas, and washing it all down with the best beers and cocktails from all over the globe?

Oh, you're right, theme parks only serve chicken fingers and popcorn!

How about being strapped into an elevator 13 stories above the World before some unseen force snaps the cables and you plummet into darkness before being yanked right back up? Or being launched forward faster than you can drop the hammer in your '78 Camaro before looping upside down and twisting and turning at high speeds with classic rock 'n' roll blasting in your eardrums?!? Flying backwards into total darkness on a runaway mountain train?!?

Oops, I forgot. Walt Disney World is just for the little ones.

Could it be you're just scared? That's right. I said I think you're scared. I'm not accusing you of being afraid of fast rides, roller coasters, or falling. I simply wonder if maybe, just maybe, you're afraid to have real fun. I mean God forbid anyone sees you let go and actually enjoy yourself, least of all your family. What good could that possibly do, right?

Well, tough guy, I'm calling you out! I'm throwing down the gauntlet! I challenge you to keep reading this book and let me take you on a guided tour of Walt Disney World, highlighting only the most testosterone-filled, white-knuckling, chest-beating, manly attractions and activities! I will tell you every spot oozing with machismo so you don't have to fear losing your "man card." More importantly, I'll prove you'll have fun. By the time you reach the last page, you will be chomping at the bit to get on Disney property.

So man-up! Come on this adventure with me. I've done the leg work. I shelled out the travel expenses. I am going to take you on a tour of what I consider the best and *manliest* of Walt Disney World! I've even kept a travel journal of my exploits at Disney and I'll be including excerpts along the way. And I'll shoot straight with you. I love Disney. I'm not ashamed to say it. But I'm no *shill*! They didn't pay me to write this book. If something's lame, I'm going to put it right on Front Street! If something's chick-centric, I'm going to tell you to avoid it like the rancid smell wafting out of an Abercrombie & Fitch store!

However, if there's something that might NOT be your cup of vodka, but is something your family will enjoy (and a real man could grit his teeth and tolerate), I'm gonna let you know. The way I see it, that's looking out for your best interests. After all, the key to remaining a loved and respected *Lord of the Manor* is to keep the lady of the house (and the offspring) happy.

So trust me and come along on this adventure! Put your feet up, pause the game, crack open a cold one, and read on. I promise, man-to-man, you won't be disappointed.

For Future Reference (Glossary)

Before we get started, here is an obligatory yet brief list of terms and abbreviations. I'll try not to be a total geek and use every shorthand reference Disney regulars use when talking the parks. From time-to-time, however, I might slip one in mostly because I'm lazy and don't feel like typing out terms like *Advance Dining Reservation*. Yes, as you guessed, that's a time booked in advance to eat. You can see why I'd rather just type **ADR**.

When you're down there, you are likely to hear a few of these in conversation. Most are pretty obvious. I'm not saying memorize them. Keep this as a reference to flip back to if needed.

AA: Audio-Animatronics. Lifelike robotic figures that Walt Disney pioneered, which have since become synonymous with Disney theme parks. Not to be confused with that other *double-A* organization. Given the amount of alcoholic beverages imbibed during the writing of this book, I highly doubt it would be considered among their approved literature.

ADR: We already talked about this one. Just making sure you were paying attention. Advanced Dining Reservation. ADRs can be made 180 days in advance and are easily booked over the phone or online. Except at Le Cellier, the steakhouse in Epcot's Canada pavilion, where you can *never* get a reservation!

CM: Cast Member. Employees of Walt Disney World. Every employee, regardless of position or title is a *Cast Member*. I know, but don't laugh. It's cute.

DTD: Downtown Disney. A waterfront area separate from the parks, filled with retail shops and tons of restaurants and nightlife. You'll like it.

DAK: Disney's Animal Kingdom

DHS: Disney's Hollywood Studios

MK: Guess.

Epcot: Not an abbreviation, but I didn't want it to feel left out. Actually some hardcore nerds refer to it as EP. But come on, you can't type five letters???

DME: Disney's Magical Express. Disney's FREE charter service that picks you up from the airport to shuttle you to your WDW resort and returns you at the end of your trip. Personally, I refer to it as *DMX*, but that confuses hip-hop fans.

EMH: Extra Magic Hours. Each day one of the four parks will either open early or stay open later, exclusively for on-property guests. EMH are your friend. They will make a huge difference to your vacation. You will receive a schedule when you check in at your resort. Learn 'em. Live 'em. Love 'em!

FP: FASTPASS. This one isn't used as commonly, but it's on the maps. Plus, lazy writers like to abbreviate whenever I . . . that is, *they* can. FASTPASS lets you to get a ticket for an attraction with a return time to come back and skip most of the line. Not all attractions offer a FASTPASS.

Quick Service: Also referred to as Counter Service. A restaurant at which you are not waited on by a server. You step up to a counter to order, and carry your food to a table of your choosing. The food is generally good, but don't expect filet mignon or lobster. We're talking burgers, dogs, chicken fingers, pizza, and in some cases roast chicken and barbecue. But don't assume because it's cafeteria-style the food is automatically lunchroom quality. Some of the best meals on property can be found at Quick Service spots. If you know where to go! For instance, the ones you might've read about in a book (ahem!).

Table Service: Pretty self-explanatory. They seat you. A dedicated server takes care of you (ideally). The upside: the selection and quality are generally higher (though not always, so don't be fooled just because you have to wait to be seated). Plus, you can sit back and relax. The downside: the prices are usually higher. There are a number of Table Service restaurants in each park, in all the deluxe resorts, and in a couple of the moderate resorts as well. The Table Service restaurants in Epcot's World Showcase are particularly popular so ADRs (*still with me?*) are recommended.

Character Dining: Also referred to as Character Meals. Special dining experiences at various restaurants around property where costumed Disney characters wander through the dining room, stopping for hugs, handshakes, and photo ops. A great way to make sure your kids get to meet some of their favorites without standing in long lines under the hot sun. One word of advice: If you get the urge to extend a prolonged, inappropriately tight hug to a Disney princess, resist. Don't be creepy over breakfast!

Park Hoppers: This is a big one. At Disney, basic admission is called
a *Magic Your Way* ticket. It enables you to enter one park,
each day of your trip. You can leave at any time and come
back later with no problem. But only to that same park that
day. However, if you choose to upgrade (for an additional
charge) to the *Park Hopper* option, you may enter any of the
four Disney theme parks all day long. You could start your
day at Disney's Hollywood Studios, grab some barbecue at
Disney's Animal Kingdom for lunch, and have pizza for dinner at Epcot's Italy pavilion. With a Park Hopper, you could
literally visit all four parks in one day. Don't! I have and it's
crazy. But you could. I recommend Park Hoppers if you're
staying less than five days.

Imagineers: Anywhere else they'd be called designers and engineers.
But as always, Walt "plussed" it and dubbed the creative gen-
iuses behind everything in the parks Imagineers.

There are more but I'm not going to completely geek out on you.
I don't want to lose you this early in the book. These are the essential ones you're likely to hear.

CHAPTER ONE

The Rules

Yes, *Kemosabe*, there are rules. There are only a few, but they're essential to have the best vacation possible. If you decide to be a hard ass and ignore them, I'm not responsible if your Walt Disney World trip goes awry.

1. **Always stay on property!** Don't take chances with some Orlando roach motel, regardless what brand. Disney resort hotels are the best, they maintain your vacation theme, and there are perks provided specifically to resort guests. It's beyond worth it!

2. **Don't obsess about money!** This is a hard one for guys. I know. We work hard for every dollar. I get it. But if you're going to piss and moan every time you look at a price tag, you're not going to have fun. Neither will the people with you. Accept that it's a vacation and you will pay a premium. I promise you'll get value for your money!

3. **Don't spit!** Do what you gotta do in the room or the head, but nothing pisses me off more than walking behind some goober who feels the need to hock a loogie on the sidewalk.

Just **don't**, all right? While we're at it don't swear out loud either! There are kids everywhere. Got me, *mother@#$%?!?*

4. **Call it Walt Disney World!** Originally, yes, it was going to be called Disney World. After Walt passed away, his brother Roy determined in tribute and respect it should always be called Walt Disney World. When you get a theme park, I'll call it by *your* full name. Respect!

5. **Get Over Yourself!** You're all man, I know. You have that hard exterior to show what a real man you are. Guess what, it's not necessary in Walt Disney World. Be a kid for a few days. Let go and have fun! You'll live longer!

CHAPTER TWO

Disney Resorts

WHERE A KING CAN REST HIS WEARY CROWN

hen primeval man first crawled out of the ooze, he had but one priority. To scratch. But after that, he set about finding shelter. A place to rest his sloping brow. Sure, finding food was on his pea-sized mind, but he knew with predators lurking all about, he'd need a place to hide lest he become food himself. Not much has changed since.

When plotting out a vacation, lodgings are the utmost priority. Gotta have a place to drop your bags so you can head out and have fun. That makes it the perfect place to start.

Now I realize real men don't pack a lot of bags. A man could get by for a month with whatever fit in a backpack. Truth be told, we could probably survive on whatever fits in our pockets. I'm assuming you're coming with your family, which more than likely includes at least one woman. So expect luggage. Lots of luggage. Hair products alone usually get their own suitcase.

Let's talk about where you should stay at Walt Disney World. Remember Rule *Numero Uno*? Always stay on property! Disney has 24 hotels on property, all different and unique. A masculine traveler could get confused and end up in the wrong place if he didn't do his homework. Don't worry, I've done it for you. Besides, it is Disney so you really can't go too wrong. Still, some of the hotels are far more suited to a man's tastes than others.

For instance, the **Grand Floridian** is probably the crown jewel of the Walt Disney World Resort. If any self-proclaimed real man chose to stay there, I might question his jewels. It's a 900-room Victorian-style monster located on the Seven Seas lagoon across from Magic Kingdom. It boasts an AAA Five Diamond restaurant (code for really snooty and expensive) called Victoria & Albert's. It is said to be delicious and elegant. I'll never know. I'm sure if you're a Rockefeller (or a Kardashian) you'll probably love the Grand Floridian. But for men like us, there are better (and more affordable) options.

Resort Tiers

As long as we're talking about affordable versus not-so, at the risk of sounding like a real travel guide, let me explain how the resort tiers work. Disney has three categories:

Deluxe (and Deluxe Villas)
Moderate
Value

Aha! I just saw your eyes light up right through the page. I said the magic word: *Value!* Don't lose track of Rule #2. Don't obsess about money. Still, real men love value! Let's quickly skim over the first two categories and get down to brass tacks.

Deluxe hotels are really nice, obviously. They have the largest rooms and the most amenities. Probably their best feature is proximity to the parks. I once stayed at Disney's Beach Club Resort, which is literally within walking distance of Epcot. More importantly, it's within walking distance of Epcot's International Gateway. That is the side that features all the different countries. In guy-speak, "the side that sells beer." And do they sell it, sir! Being a short ride or even walk to and from the theme parks is not only convenient and gives you more control of your schedule, it might also save your life (or your marriage).

Man's Journal

One particularly hot spring afternoon I was hanging with my buddy Kyle at the Rose & Crown pub, located in Epcot's United Kingdom pavilion. After a few half-yards of ale, one of us had the where-withal to check his watch and realize we needed to get back to the hotel for dinner with the rest of our group. We were minutes from being butt-chewingly late. We made for the gate, but still had a decent amount of beer in our plastic flutes. Is there an indecent amount of beer? A Cast Member stopped us, saying we could not leave with alcohol. Being a good Irishman, I couldn't pour out perfectly good ale. So we found ourselves roaming through the shop at the International exit trying to slam heavy English ale so we could get back to the girls.

As I was absently rifling through T-shirts I felt a frantic tug at my arm. I spun around enraged—I'd almost spilled my beer! It was Kyle. He had a look of terror in his eyes. This was his first trip to Walt Disney World so he wasn't accustomed to some of the things that make it so magical.

"What is it?" I asked.

"Over there," he said, gesturing to the door. "Am I really drunk, or is there some kind of giant animal?"

Over his shoulder I saw Dale, the red-nosed half of Chip 'n' Dale wandering into the store. Remember that for future refer-ence. You'll look smart to your kids. He was soon followed by his friend/brother/I'm not asking, Chip. Living cartoon characters the size of grown men are commonplace at Walt Disney World. Try to keep it in mind, even (especially) after a few pints. Otherwise, as Kyle learned, it can really harsh your mellow.

The friendly forest critters passed through the store and we quickly downed the rest of our drinks so we could leave. Keep that

·in mind as well. Don't order another half-yard until you're certain you don't have anywhere else to be for at least 10 to 15 minutes.

We power-walked down the sidewalk under the hot Florida sun with beer turning (and churning) warm and gaseous in our bellies, but we made it back to the Beach Club just in time. Had we been staying at another hotel, we would've had to walk back to the front entrance, find the correct bus stop, wait for a shuttle, and then take the 15- to 20-minute ride back to the hotel. More importantly, we'd have faced some pretty ticked-off ladies.

There are definite perks to staying in a Deluxe resort. Personally, it's hard for me to justify the price for my needs, i.e. a bed and a commode. You could easily spend north of $5,000 on a week's vacation due largely to your lodgings. Hey, maybe that's how you roll. Some guys splurge on a vacation. You work hard for your money. You want to blow it on a hotel room you'll hardly be in, I'm not judging. If that's really your trip let me suggest a couple of Deluxe resorts suitable for a real man.

Disney's Animal Kingdom Lodge is a great choice! This resort will bring out your inner-adventurer! Right next to Disney's Animal Kingdom park, this amazing resort continues the African safari theme right down (er, up) to the Zulu masks hanging from the chandeliers. This hotel might awaken something primal in you. You are king of your pride, after all. Book a Savannah room and you'll see worthy quarry grazing right outside your window. Live zebras, giraffes, and gazelle roam the hotel property just a few feet from your balcony. Easy Quatermain, they're just for looking! It's a once in a lifetime opportunity to sip your morning coffee with a giraffe peering over your railing. Give him the Arts & Leisure section or he'll just read over your shoulder the whole time!

If you're a morning man, spend the extra bucks to stay on the Club level. Aside from a complimentary continental breakfast and beer and wine at night, you'll be privy to the **Sunrise Safari**. Club level guests have the opportunity to head to Disney's Animal Kingdom at dawn and ride *Kilimanjaro Safaris* long before the gates open. Any medicine man knows the misty morning hours are magical. It's the time many of the animals are most active. There'll be fewer heads in front of your lens, and you'll get great views out there on the Savannah. Animal Kingdom Lodge is definitely manly luxury with some cool extras for the price.

Still, as a guy who grew up in the woods, fishing and camping, if I were going to spring for a Deluxe resort, there's one a bit more my style. **Disney's Wilderness Lodge** is a resort for a *man's man!* Get in touch with your inner mountain man! Surrounded by pine and fir and rock formations, the hotel perfectly captures the mountain lodges of the Pacific Northwest. It will transport you to Yellowstone without the long drive in the back of your old man's station wagon. They've even got their very own geyser erupting hourly. And this is just the outside. Wait until you see the lobby.

Be prepared to be enveloped by a six-story lodge where *rustic* is the word of the day. Stepping into the lobby is like putting on your favorite flannel. Massive hand-carved totem poles stand watch over the room. Wooden rockers sit invitingly before the 82-foot-high stone fireplace. Let me repeat, an *82-foot-high fireplace!*

Unnngh. Fire good!

The rooms are comfortable, spacious, with hand-carved furniture and Native American accents. For the kids, there's even the option of woodsy bunk beds. They'll also love the courtyard swimming pool, surrounded by natural looking rocks and a killer water slide that feels like zipping through rapids. I know, I said it's for the kids, but you know you'll be flying down that thing with your Bermuda shorts riding up your keister!

Bottom line: Wilderness Lodge is a serene, rustic resort of wood, stone, and water where a man feels at home, his ancestral home. Fortunately, it's fun for the kids and comfortable for your lady. There's shopping and concierge service, multiple restaurants, including an amazing steakhouse called Artist Point and a crazy family restaurant called Whispering Canyon. Skip the bus and take a water taxi from the resort to Magic Kingdom. Wilderness Lodge even has a health club. (Health-*what now?*) You know the place where skinny people go in spandex. It doesn't matter because you're going to be on vacation. There'll be plenty of exercise walking the parks. Men don't need stair machines and Pilates. Real men don't even know what Pilates are!

Of the two, Animal Kingdom Lodge is definitely bigger and a bit nicer, but in ways you wouldn't notice or care about anyway. And the restaurants at AKL are more exotic than I'm looking for. The noticeable difference is, while both are Deluxe, you'll save a couple hundred bucks at Wilderness Lodge.

If you do opt for staying at Wilderness Lodge, make sure you stress the name Wilderness *Lodge*. Not to be confused with **Fort Wilderness**. Fort Wilderness is Walt Disney World's campground. Really like getting dirt under your fingernails? This is the spot! You can park your own camper, pitch a tent, or have the sense to reserve an air-conditioned cabin with locking doors. Remember the land where Walt Disney World sits was once murky Florida swampland. Nobody can convince me all the venomous snakes and spiders (and werewolves) moved out just because Mickey Mouse arrived.

There are fans who always camp at Fort Wilderness. They love the forest retreat—sitting around an open fire, watching the stars, the scent of mosquito repellent in the air, all manner of vermin and hockey-mask-wearing, machete-wielding maniacs rustling through the brush. I'm a real man, but I'll stick to a hotel, second floor or higher, thank you.

Honorable mention goes to **Saratoga Springs** resort. A Deluxe *Disney Vacation Club* resort (yes, even Disney has a timeshare program) that would make a gambling man feel right at home if he likes to play the ponies. The resort is decked out in a classy East Coast horse-racing theme. Unfortunately, it has two strikes against it. One, it's right next door to Downtown Disney, which as you'll learn later is an area I love. But that means it's footsteps from shopping. A woman with a credit card could do a lot of damage. Second, although it's a Deluxe resort, it feels about a million miles from the parks. Of course, the plus side of being near Downtown Disney is you're a stone's throw (literally, depending on your arm) from great dining and drinking.

As for Moderate resorts at Walt Disney World, I don't have as strong a recommendation. **Coronado Springs** is a cool, relatively masculine property, designed to represent Mexico and the old Southwest. The main pool area is pretty though, designed like Mayan ruins you'd be driven to on a cruise excursion, but without being pressured to buy blankets or Chiclets. It's also got a decent restaurant called Maya Grill spreading out a good breakfast buffet to fill you up on huevos and frijoles. Throw a rock in the air on Disney property and you'll hit a breakfast buffet. This particular one serves Mexican food sans furry characters hovering over you and your Western omelet.

Some complain that Coronado Springs is too big. It is a massive, sprawling compound much like another Moderate resort, **Caribbean Beach**. At Disney's Moderate and Value resorts you can opt to book a "Preferred room" meaning closer to the main building, food, and amenities. At Coronado Springs, if you don't go Preferred, you might actually find yourself in the real Southwest by time you reach your room. I first stayed at Coronado with my wife years ago and, not knowing any better at the time, I just booked the cheapest room option. After we checked in and walked what felt like 10 minutes to reach our room, I was pretty irritated. Fortunately, that walk was a fair trade to learn our room was just around the corner from a second bus stop. A nice, but not always guaranteed, surprise!

However, I have to give you one major warning about Coronado Springs. Watch your feet! Not to guard against the deadly coral snakes hiding in the sawgrass waiting for an unsuspecting toe to latch onto and pump full of toxic venom. No, I'm talking about something far, far worse. A scourge that before I stayed at Coronado, I thought was only reserved for the airport. I'm talking about the deadly black rolling suitcase!

Coronado Springs is also home to a convention center and meeting facilities, making it a popular choice for conferences, business retreats, etc. For some reason traveling professionals feel the need to drag their stupid roller bags along everywhere! On the way to breakfast. Heading to some team building exercise. Going to the bathroom. They are always pulling that luggage and don't care whose feet get in the way. One hit to the ankle could drive your *inner-ape* to launch some careless exec's Samsonite into the lagoon. Resist that urge, of course. I'm not sure Florida law protects against assaults on yuppies, no matter how justified.

Port Orleans—French Quarter might make an acceptable Moderate resort for guys. Its Mardi Gras theme may awaken memories of that lost weekend in college when you and your buddies piled into a van and drove to New Orleans. Although if you have such memories, it probably never happened. The French Quarter architecture, blooming bougainvillea, and jazz floating on the air might make you forget you're not in Louisiana. Swing by **Scat Cat's Club** and you might even find yourself an ice-cold Hurricane! French Quarter has a sister resort called **Port Orleans—Riverside.** Riverside also follows a southern theme with buildings that resemble plantation houses surrounded by magnolia trees. Architecture aside, POR houses what is considered by many the second-best steakhouse on property, **Boatwright's.**

Speaking of food, let's talk turkey here (mmm, *turkey!*). For a week's stay in a Deluxe resort you could buy a sensible sedan. You can go middle-of-the-road with a Moderate choice like Coronado or either Port Orleans. They're nice, not too far from the parks, and you'll save a couple of bucks. But there is always Door #3—Disney's Value resorts!

A lot of people (women) hear "value" and think cheap. They assume it means *low-quality* as opposed to simply less expensive. When it comes to the Disney Value resorts, only the latter is true (that means the second one—okay, just making sure you're still with me). There are now five Value resorts at Walt Disney World, the newest having just opened while I was writing this book. There are the All-Stars: **All-Star Music**, **All-Star Movies**, and **All-Star Sports**. The fourth and, my favorite, is **Pop Century Resort**. Finally there's the brand new resort, **Art of Animation**.

Tell you what, let's get crazy and look at what may be considered the negatives first. The rooms are small. Two beds, a table, a TV, and a bathroom. It's Disney, so they're clean and cozy, but there are *no frills*, although you can request a refrigerator and/or microwave for a small charge. Value resorts are the farthest from the parks, so you're talking longer rides in sometimes overcrowded buses. This can be especially bad at the three All-Star Resorts.

During peak season each has a dedicated bus service, but during slower months all three share a single route. In other words, pray you're at the one getting picked up first or you could find yourself packed like sweaty sardines all the way to Magic Kingdom—and that's not a short trip!

Pop Century always has its own buses. The reason being it's huge. Having walked the entire Pop Century campus, take it from me, pay for a *preferred room*. It's an upgrade but worth the price! Get stuck in the wrong building and your dogs will be barking before you even get to breakfast. At a vacation destination that already requires more walking than Moses, you want to minimize extraneous steps.

Pop Century represents the last five decades of American Pop culture, with each cluster of buildings themed to a popular era. For instance we had a preferred room in the seventies building right behind a giant 8-track cassette. For younger readers, we'll explain 8-tracks later—hell, we'll explain cassettes! The central rooms are sixties-themed. Not only are they close to the buses and the food court, they surround the Hippy Dippy pool. Yes, it's flower-shaped, but it's also a George Carlin reference, so show respect! It's the biggest of the three pools at Pop, but more importantly, it's the one with the bar!

Being a man, my drinking philosophy is generally simple—browns, clears, or beers. However, when on vacation it's okay to let your proverbial hair down. They make a colorful concoction called a Lava Lamp that's pretty damn tasty. Can't tell you exactly what's in it except it starts off blue and red before it quickly turns purple, as does your tongue. It's the kind of cocktail that one or two are great, but any more and the next morning becomes an epic battle between stomach, porcelain, and sheer will.

The **All-Star Resorts** aren't too terribly different from Pop as far as quality, layout, and design. They're just smaller. As mentioned, they are Movies, Music, and Sports. I'll give you a minute to figure out the themes. As a real man, your eyes should have immediately locked-in on Sports. Imagine walking out of your room to see a four-story football helmet and steel footballs so big they house the stairwells. One pool is actually shaped like a baseball diamond. The main building is even called "the Stadium!"

If you're the kind of guy who considers Shark Week sacred television time (and as a real man, you are) you'll notice the two giant shark fins decorating the Surf's Up building. Those fins are 38 feet high. Meaning they'd be attached to a shark 300 feet long. In other words, a shark that would munch on mega yachts!

The new **Art of Animation** resort has four sections, three of which are strictly family suites. The buildings transform guests into characters in classic Disney and Pixar animated features. There's *The Lion King, Cars*, and *Finding Nemo*. For me, it's all about *Cars* and the Route 66 theme! I'm not against Nemo, or even *The Little Mermaid* building, where you'll find standard guest rooms instead of suites. I just find both themes a little unsettling in a hotel where the food court serves sushi. Just sayin'!

Called "family suites," rooms in Art of Animation's suites' sections cost a bit more than at Pop or All-Stars, but they also sleep up to six guests and include a kitchenette and separate bedroom. Personally I wouldn't mention that to your wife, unless you want to find yourself vacationing with your mother-in-law. The rooms are brand new and the entire resort is beautiful. Life-size characters from each movie decorate the courtyards and common areas. Even the pools look like familiar animated scenes. It's pretty mind-blowing!

Bottom line with the Value resorts is simple. You're rarely in your hotel room, and these have everything you actually need. I know Rule #2 was to have a Hakuna Matata attitude about money. That doesn't mean you shouldn't weigh the costs and value. At the Value resorts you'll save a ton of cash and, between you and me, they're way more fun!

Look there's no such thing as a bad resort at Walt Disney World. All the hotels uphold the Disney standard of quality, comfort, and service. Some just make you feel like you need to keep your pinky up when you sip your coffee. You're on vacation. Why feel out of place in someone else's idea of comfort? I highlighted the ones that make a real man feel comfortable and right at home. And your wife will approve of them anyway!

Whatever tier you choose, pick any one of the resorts I've recommended and you'll be surrounded by manly comfort and a little boyhood whimsy, too! There are pools, water slides, tons of amenities (beyond the bars), and that amazing Disney Guest Service. Even if your budget only affords a standard room, you will be treated like royalty from the moment that lobby a/c blasts you in the face. Here you are a King. Enjoy it.

CHAPTER THREE

Epcot: Future World

FUN WITH TECHNOLOGY!

The Magic Kingdom, with its big blue castle and flying elephant ride, may be the first thing to spring to your mind when you hear the words "Walt Disney World." What you may not know is building a larger Disneyland in Orlando was almost a means to an end for Walt. His real dream for the "Florida project" was his Experimental Prototype City of Tomorrow, EPCOT. Walt imagined a functioning community where great minds in technology, science, engineering, and the arts would create a functioning city of the future in the middle of the twentieth century. EPCOT would showcase American ingenuity and imagination before the entire world. Kind of warms your patriotic cockles, doesn't it?

Walt never saw his Florida dreams come to fruition. He died before Disney World (the original name) broke ground. Work on the Magic Kingdom eventually resumed and the park opened in 1971, as much in tribute to Walt's undying spirit as anything else.

Fortunately, he'd left his trusted executives and Imagineers a pretty damn good blueprint in Anaheim. When it came time to figure out this Epcot thing without Walt, the boys were stumped.

They had no clue how to create a functioning futuristic city that would also work as a tourist attraction.

Ultimately, the working city had to be retooled. That's a kind way of saying it was scrapped in favor of a more traditional theme park. Ultimately Epcot would be anything but traditional, to its credit and, to some, its detriment. Walt was known for saying he wanted to entertain audiences first and hope something educational snuck through. To critics, EPCOT Center, as it was called until the mid-nineties, felt a little heavy-handed with the educating part. I first visited EPCOT Center in 1984 and I was there recently, and I've seen and loved every variant in between. If you're a guy like me, you love history shows, vegging out in front of science and engineering shows for hours on end, watching how things we take for granted came to be. Epcot was and is a living 4-Dimensional version of those specials, infused with entertainment and excitement.

To stay on top of changes in technology and culture, Epcot has to continually grow and adapt to meet audience desires. Sadly, some of Epcot's greatest attractions are already long gone—or have been unforgivably *monkeyed* with . . . *cough* . . . *Journey into Imagination*!

You will hear many hardcore Epcot fans lamenting the loss of the great attraction, *Horizons*. An Omnimover ride, *Horizons* depicted visions of what the future of mankind might look like. Scenes using Audio-Animatronics depicted the American family living in space, colonizing the desert, and building cities under the sea. It was an optimistic and often funny vision of a hopeful future. But how long can a ride about the future built in the early eighties stay relevant?

All real men loved *World of Motion*. Similar to *Horizons*, this attraction, sponsored by GM, depicted the history of transportation, from the invention of the wheel all the way to and beyond what could be next. After the ride, you could see GM concept cars up close. Alas, *World of Motion* is gone as well. However, if you're a gear head or just love horsepower, you will love what they put in her place.

But I'm getting ahead of myself!

Spaceship Earth

If I'm going to do it right, we need to take this tour in proper order. The first attraction you encounter through the gates is the icon of the park, *Spaceship Earth*. You probably know the one I'm talking about, even if you don't realize it. At 18 stories tall and 180 feet in diameter, *Spaceship Earth* is one of the most impressive pieces of architecture standing on its namesake planet. Known by a myriad of nicknames from "the globe" to the "giant metal golf ball," *Spaceship Earth* is the first geodesic sphere of its kind. Passing under the gigantic silver "Spaceship" with its triangular panels, it's almost hard to believe it's real. As a bit of manly trivia for you, some pretty smart guys figured out those triangular panels would help deflect and reroute the Florida rain so it doesn't come pouring down on the guests queuing up for the ride.

That's right, the big shiny ball isn't just there in case you get lost and need your (big, shiny ball) bearings. It's a ride as well! Not the great attraction it once was (see previous statement about *monkeying* with attractions), but still worth riding out of respect for history, literally. From hieroglyphics to the printing press to the telephone, television, and eventually the Internet, *Spaceship Earth* takes guests on a ride through the history of communications. I realize the idea of slowly rolling through scenes of history portrayed by life-like robots doesn't exactly sound riveting. You just have to see it. The first two-thirds are still really fascinating and beautifully done. For a first-timer at Epcot, it's a nice introduction to the idea of the park.

 The official Ears of Steel recommendation: A nice way to ease into Epcot, it gets a thumbs up out of respect; but let's hope one day they return the finale to its former glory!

Test Track

Maybe you're not a History Channel guy. Maybe a slow ride through robotland isn't going to hook you. Maybe you're partial to roaring engines, exhaust fumes, wind-whipped hair, and speed. Sweet, sweet, dirty speed! Hang a left from Spaceship Earth and get ready to burn serious rubber. Remember earlier I told you about an old attraction called *World of Motion*? An original EPCOT Center attraction, it was funny, historical, and somewhat educational, like watching one of those old "Car of Tomorrow" cartoons. That is, if you consider sea monsters and flying carpets historical. While the attraction covered the past and present (of the 1980s), it also imagined the future of transportation. By the mid-nineties, that future was really dated. Sponsor General Motors decided they wanted an update to the attraction and thus was born *Test Track*.

Test Track is the definition of a modern real-man's ride! Remember that old series of seat belt PSAs featuring talking crash dummies? Ever wanted to be one? On *Test Track*, you get your wish! And within the protective confines of a computer testing program so you're never in any real danger—or are you? In 2012, Disney Imagineering gave *Test Track* a super-cyber-charged upgrade.

The queue is clean and sleek, featuring real concept models from Chevy, as well as video of designers describing the creative and engineering process. It leads you into a glowing room with rows of touch screens where each group of guests gets to design their own concept vehicle. You are given the option of a car or a truck and you can customize the shape, color, wheels, engine, even detailing. As a real man, of course, I went for the truck. To be honest, when I first saw video of this process I didn't think I'd really care about it. It looked too much like a video game. But within seconds I was completely sucked in, designing a badass suburban assault vehicle fit for Stallone in his next ridiculous sci-fi action flick.

Your design is saved on a card that you scan in as you board your car. As soon as a CM confirms everybody's seat belt is fastened, you are off transitioning from the real world to the cyber world, tires squealing on a high-speed cyber adventure. You are put through a battery of tests, including traction, handling different terrain, how she corners (like she's on rails), and even temperature tolerance, and of course the anti-lock braking system! Since you've been zapped into a computer testing program, the terrain and obstacles are all "digital" with lots of neon and black light. Sure, maybe it earns the fan-made moniker "Tron Track" but that said, it looks really cool! It does feel a bit like being zapped into that sci-fi cyber world from the movie, and what guy who saw the original *Tron* as a kid didn't want to do just that?

Test Track lets you experience a car the way you've always wanted, but would find yourself calling for bail if you did. Since it's Disney, you can experience it all without worrying about any real damage to your beloved Bessie, or Mabel, or whatever you secretly call your chariot in the garage. You don't even have to steer. Plus, when it comes to *Test Track*, I've saved the best for last.

As they say on the interwebs . . . **SPOILER ALERT**. No, not *spoiler* as in the thing mounted on a race car! I am about to reveal the big finale of the ride. If you'd rather be surprised, skip down a couple paragraphs. Seriously . . . last warning! No angry letters later. Save your crayons!

You are suddenly made aware of the final test scheduled for your vehicle—the **collision** test! You find yourself facing down a wall and you're still buckled in. The engine roars and the tires scream and suddenly you are barreling toward that wall like a bat out of a Meatloaf concert! At the last second, the "wall" opens up and you are spit back out of the computer and into glorious Florida sunshine as you rocket onto an elevated track strategically built around the ride building.

The car tops out at 65 mph as you fly around the circular track high above the ground below. Imagine for a second driving in a convertible on an open highway, no other cars for miles, nor any state troopers or County Mounties in radar range. You can just put the hammer down. Trust me, Andretti, *Test Track* is one of the most exhilarating rushes you will ever feel. Especially inside a car. Unless, of course, you really are one of the Andrettis, in which case . . . never mind.

It's worth mentioning when you come off the ride—when Security has to forcibly remove you, telling you to wait in line again like everyone else—you exit into an aftershow where there are more concept cars, virtual displays, interactive games and exhibits, even digital photo ops where you can take your picture next to the vehicle you created! You can also see, touch, even sit in the latest real-live GM models. Sure, it's a thinly veiled sales pitch, but why not?

What other opportunity will you have to check out new cars without some greasy salesman crawling up your butt?

 The official Ears of Steel recommendation: Gentlemen, start your engines! *Test Track* was the first thrill ride at Epcot and it is still thrilling 'em!

Mission: SPACE

Stepping off *Test Track*, you'll be completely amped up from your joy ride. Want to chase that adrenaline dragon? Hang a Roscoe toward the weird *Star Trek*-ish facade with a space shuttle zipping around gigantic marbles. Think blasting off in a race car got your heart pumping? Take some deep breaths, chug a bottle of water, and make sure your life insurance is paid up. I'm not kidding. Next up is *Mission: SPACE!*

On the intensity scale, *Mission: SPACE* dials it up to 11 . . . if that scale is from 1 to 5! It's not an attraction for the faint of heart, and I'm not trying to be clichéd. Seriously, we men enjoy our red meat and beer. If you know you have any kind of heart *situation*, it doesn't make you a pantywaist to pass. I'm not joking when I say people have died on this ride. However, for a man in relatively good cardiovascular health, that warning should only get your blood pumping faster.

Like everything else at Walt Disney World, *Mission: SPACE* follows a storyline. You've joined a shuttle crew on a galactic mission to harvest rare space minerals or Martian eggs or deliver a pair of humpback whales or something. Okay, honestly the plot, thin as it is, doesn't even matter! The thing you will remember—the part that will make you question reality—is the launch!

After passing through a queue resembling a cross between the Smithsonian Air and Space Museum and a *Star Trek* prop house, you board your spacecraft. Be warned, the ride vehicles are tight. You will feel like you're being stuffed (along with three other humans) into a tuna can. If you are claustrophobic, you might want to go grab some ice cream instead. When the cockpit closes, you'll find a monitor right in front of your nose and a panel of controls.

While incredibly creepy, it adds to the illusion as you quickly forget where in the world you are. You could very well be in some kind of spacecraft. In reality, you're attached to a giant centrifuge about to throw you into a *Spin Cycle!*

You may be saying: "Whoa! Wait a minute! I can deal with roller coasters and speed and all, but I'm not into spinning!"

I'm with you, brother. I won't even ride the Teacups! I'm only telling you how the trick works because once it begins, you'll have no idea. The "window" in front of your eyes reveals a crystal blue sky. You hear the countdown from Control. The thrusters rumble beneath you. The only motion you'll feel is your craft *rising*. The clouds grow closer and this incredible pressure begins to squeeze your chest (hence the whole heart thing). You'll feel like there's a gorilla squatting on your harness. The speed of takeoff increases and your face begins to peel back off your skull. Then you break atmosphere and baby, you *are* in space!

It is possibly the most surreal, intense feeling I've ever experienced. You will actually feel weightless! Imagineering used something called a *VIS screen*, which creates the curve and depth of peering into space. The graphics are so crisp and so real your mind will never doubt the view for a second. Sadly, shortly after takeoff, the ride becomes more like a . . . well, a theme park ride. It loses some of the technological wonder in exchange for thrills. But that takeoff is beyond anything you'll ever experience.

 The official Ears of Steel recommendation: *Mission: SPACE* may not be one you'll hit multiple times—don't tempt fate and all— but it's definitely got the Right Stuff!

Ellen's Energy Adventure

When you leave *Mission: SPACE,* you might look over to the right and notice another attraction building covered in solar panels. That is the Universe of Energy. At least the building—or pavilion as they say at Epcot—is still the Universe of Energy. The attraction inside is now called *Ellen's Energy Adventure.* Let's cut to the chase here.

There was a time I would have said, "If you want to see some pretty cool life-size dinosaurs, here's your chance—but beware the boring movie at the end." Even adding star power by inserting comedian Ellen DeGeneres in the attraction—they literally installed an animatronic Ellen in the ride—couldn't breathe new life into this nearly extinct attraction. Besides, these days if you want amazing lifelike dinos, just head over to Animal Kingdom. But we'll get there.

 The official Ears of Steel recommendation: You'll be pretty pumped up with vacation energy. So you can skip this pavilion!

Soarin'

Once you've ridden *Test Track* and *Mission: SPACE*, you've done all the really *manly* stuff Future World has to offer. But, you're not finished. Being a real man hasn't always been about fire, metal, and grease. The original "real men" survived off the land and quickly learned to respect it. This country was built on agriculture by hard-handed farming men. So head back to the other side of Spaceship Earth and keep going. You'll come to a strangely shaped building at the top of an incline called The Land.

The Land was to be a showcase of biotechnology, featuring how science and nature can work symbiotically to nurture man. Unfortunately, it often became the butt of "Epcot is boring" jokes. Admittedly, alternative growing techniques weren't exactly thrilling attractions. For a time you could have walked through the rotunda and wondered "Is this pavilion closed?" Aside from *Kitchen Kabaret*, an Audio-Animatronics show featuring singing food (which by the way was awesome), The Land's most popular feature was its food court!

Then, in 2005, Disney conceptualized a way to breathe new life into Walt Disney World that would especially help the limping Land. During 2005's *The Happiest Celebration on Earth*, which marked the fiftieth anniversary of Disneyland, they picked a handful of popular attractions from other Disney parks around the world and cloned them in Florida. The Land pavilion became home to arguably the most popular ride at Disney California Adventure park in Anaheim.

Veer to the left when you enter The Land (you can't go straight, un-less you can fly), take the escalator down, and look for the huge crowd of guests. That's not the entrance to an attraction. It's just the FASTPASS kiosks! FASTPASS tickets are almost always essential if you plan on taking flight on *Soarin'*!

Known as *Soarin' Over California* in its home park, *Soarin'* is a whole different breed of flight simulator. The engineering behind it may be just as innovative as that for *Mission: SPACE*, but with slightly less worry over heart palpitations. *Soarin'* is a virtual hang glider flight, cruising low over the state of California. While *Mission: SPACE* utilized NASA-engineered technology and simulation programs, *Soarin'* was inspired by a dusty old Erector set. Imagineer Mark Sum-ner was wracking his brain to figure out how to make an indoor hang gliding experience a reality, especially with limited space. While tool-ing around his attic over Thanksgiving, he pulled out his childhood Erector set and, as they say, the flash of genius struck. Within a few hours, he had built a crude model with gears, pulleys, and strings—not too different from the ride system you'll find yourself boarding.

Be prepared. Even with FASTPASS, it's a long walk before you reach the actual attraction theater. When they enter, guests are assigned to one of three rows of hanging seats facing a floor-to-ceiling screen. Once buckled in, all three rows rise into the air on a mechanical arm as the film begins. Within a split second you are flying over the Golden State. You actually feel wind on your face and smell aspen trees and orange groves. The only thing missing is water splashing at your feet as you fly low over the rolling surf.

You break the clouds, passing over San Francisco's Golden Gate Bridge, and zigzag down the state, over snowy mountains and down along the coast. You cruise back inland over Palm Springs (watch out for that wild tee shot!) and ultimately end in Anaheim over Disney-land just in time for fireworks. *Soarin'* is a total immersion experi-ence. You may actually experience momentary confusion when you find yourself back outside in central Florida.

Here's one of those fancy travel guide tips: when they line you up outside the doors, get in the first row! I don't care what you have to do. When the seats rise, the front row heads all the way to the top. I wouldn't say there's a **bad** seat on *Soarin'*, but I really don't dig the bottom row! Flip-flops and sneakers hanging in my line of sight take me out of the moment. As in life, when you're on top the view is always clearer!

 The official Ears of Steel recommendation: Spread your wings! You'll want to take this flight over and over!

Living With The Land

There are few occupations that require the strong back of a real man as much as farming. Farmers made this country. If you want a glimpse at the future of farming, check out the attraction next to *Soarin'*, *Living With the Land*.

Living with the Land is an O.G. Attraction (that's *original gardening*) dating back to the opening of EPCOT Center. It's a relaxing little boat cruise through the greenhouses of the six-acre pavilion. It showcases working alternative methods of growing food as we continue to deplete our resources. Hey, *pay attention!* I saw your head bobbing. It's okay to think about these things once a decade. Somewhere John Mellencamp and Neil Young are singing a song about it! Besides, you may have to help a kid come up with a science project one day.

I admit, as a kid, I found it just slightly more tedious than visiting a nursing home. As an adult male, I now find it fascinating and encouraging. If nothing else, the first couple of scenes—cruising through the rainforest, the desert, and finally an early American farm—are cool. Plus, you'll be cooling off on a ride along an indoor lazy river. Tell the kids to shut up and learn something while you doze off.

The Seas with Nemo & Friends

When you exit The Land pavilion, be prepared for major gridlock. The Land houses one of the parks most popular attractions yet has only one set of escalators. It can feel like a mosh pit. Once you make it outside, you'll hear the sound of water splashing against the rocks.

You may notice a strange and enticing structure calling you like your life, your lover, your lady, the sea. Her facade curls around like an inviting wave, beckoning you to enter. Resist her siren song.

At one time this pavilion was called The Living Seas, and it boasted the largest indoor aquarium in the world. Deep-sea elevators called hydrolators whooshed guests down to the ocean floor in a matter of moments. All right, so in truth you only dropped a matter of a few feet, but with bubbles and sound effects it really felt like you were diving many fathoms below. You stepped off the hydrolator and found yourself aboard Sea Base Alpha, a futuristic deep-sea laboratory. At each enormous Plexiglas window you watched all manner of sea life swim through blue water, peering back at you. The illusion was so real that you forgot you were at an amusement park. Well, until Mickey Mouse swam by in his yellow scuba suit. Whatever scientific merit the attraction once had has since gone down . . . well, down the drain. Sea Base Alpha is no more, and the pavilion has been renamed The Seas with Nemo & Friends.

Lest you be confused, that's not a nod to the infamous Captain or his steampunk submarine, evading the clutches of a giant squid and squaring off with a chisel-jawed Kirk Douglas! This pavilion is all about Nemo, the little orange clownfish who didn't listen to his father. I've got no beef with the fish (wait, what?). Neptune knows, he's been through enough, poor kid. The problem is the major attraction of this building, which could have been a homerun, is the lackluster *The Seas with Nemo & Friends* dark ride.

On this ride, not dissimilar from the Magic Kingdom dark rides Disney has become famous for, you board slow-moving shells called "clam mobiles." Once aboard, you dive into the ocean, where you'll come across Nemo and other characters, impressively projected onto the glass so it appears the cartoon fish are swimming among real live ones. It's a cool carnival trick. That and the sets are real colorful. Otherwise, I got to say, this underwater adventure is a little *dry*. Fans (there are a few) will chastise me that it wasn't made for adults. Kids will want to ride it. That's right. They will, and they'll be bored too.

 The official Ears of Steel recommendation: The clownfish ain't funny enough to save a weak ride. Just keep swimming.

Coral Reef Restaurant

However, agreeing to take a slow boat to Sydney, where the Nemo story is set, may have its benefits. There is one attraction in The Seas pavilion a man like you will enjoy. Some men like to watch fish. Real men like to eat 'em! It's not a ride, but the *Coral Reef Restaurant* is definitely an attraction! The food is great and you can't beat the ambiance. The Coral Reef is situated right alongside the aquarium, so from any seat in the house you can watch exotic fish, rays, even sharks swim by. I won't get into the psychology of watching fish while eating them. If it really bothers anyone, they also grill up a nice New York Strip and I'm pretty sure you won't see any swimming cows.

Between the decor, funky lighting, and that rippling glow of the aquarium, it's an awesome dining experience. There's no guarantee of a table next to the glass, but it never hurts to ask. Your odds improve the earlier you make your ADR. (Or slip the host a twenty!) Take your family and you may actually earn *Father of the Year*. Lock the raptors in the room, take your wife for a romantic dinner, and . . . well, you might earn *something else!*

Once you've stuffed yourself silly at Coral Reef, chug a cup of coffee and get out quickly, lest ye be lulled into a food coma watching the pretty fishies. Follow the path straight until you come upon a building that resembles a series of giant prisms. This is *Imagination!*

Journey Into Imagination with Figment

Inside this pavilion waits the polarizing attraction *Journey Into Imagination with Figment*. It's been a subject of much controversy among rabid Disney fans. The original ride featured a jovial bearded fellow called The Dreamfinder and his little purple dragon, Figment. As a kid, this was one of my favorite rides. After all, real men are creative men and creativity springs from imagination. Nothing to be ashamed of there. If you can't be silly once in a while, you're just asking for a big *gripper*.

Back in the nineties, ignoring the spirit of "if it ain't broke, don't fix it," Epcot overhauled the ride, turning it into some strange, sterile, *characterless* experience. Many fingers pointed to Michael Eisner and an alleged hatred for the little purple guy. Whatever the inexplicable reasoning, public backlash came hard and fast. Disney quickly *re*-refurbished *Imagination* returning the iconic little reptile Figment. Sadly, Dreamfinder remains in exile, retired to an imaginary seniors' community in Boca.

Now I realize you probably haven't seen little purple dragons that sing or paint rainbows since college (and the next morning swore you'd never do it again). Once again, *Imagination* is one you should ride, even if just for your kids. It's harmless fun. Well, mostly harmless. When you find yourself facing a giant slot machine, take a deep breath and hold it. You'll understand when the reels come up Triple Skunks! Disney and their smell effects! The ride's not as fun as it used to be, of course, but you'll get a chuckle.

 The official Ears of Steel recommendation: It's goofy, but still an Ears of Steel favorite!

Captain EO

Don't be afraid to step inside the Imagination! pavilion. Just make sure you walk through the main entrance. Go in the wrong door, you'll find yourself in a darkened theater experiencing a real man's nightmare. A 10-foot-tall Michael Jackson "*hee-hee'ing*" and pelvic thrusting in your face!

Back in the eighties, Disney partnered up with two giants of the movie industry, George Lucas and Francis Ford Coppola. These were the men behind *Star Wars* and *The Godfather*! I'm not a huge *Star Wars* guy (as you'll hear later). I've seen them all and thought a few of them were pretty cool. As for *The Godfather*, I mean, come on! If you're a real man, you love *The Godfather* and *Godfather 2*. That's just how it is. Most of us will even sit through *Godfather 3* on a Sunday afternoon, assuming it's not football season. Sadly, what they would create for Epcot was about as far from the Dark Side and the Corleone saga as Sicily from the Dagobah System (geek check!). Even as science fiction, it makes Jar Jar Binks look like the

Terminator. I'm talking of course about the original 3-D Michael Jackson space adventure, *Captain EO.*

At the time, they spent something in the neighborhood of $30 million for this space oddity about a ragtag crew of rejected Muppets led by Jackson's non-threatening, rainbow-T-shirted Captain EO. Their mission: deliver a gift to a nasty alien dominatrix. It was an immediate hit for Epcot (remember, it was the eighties). I'll put it right on Front Street—I'm not a Michael Jackson fan. (I'm not from Eastern Europe or Japan.) That aside, if it were good (or at least watchable) I would say so. It's not.

The effects are laughably dated. The plot is just laughable. And watching Michael Jackson dance around with puppets in a costume stolen from Elton John and blast multicolored light beams out of his chest is just disturbing. Don't waste 20 minutes of your vacation (or your life). There's nothing manly about *Captain EO.* Other than avoiding it!

 The official Ears of Steel at the Movies review: God-awful!

CHAPTER FOUR

Epcot:
World Showcase

A REAL MAN IS A MAN OF THE WORLD

pcot was Walt's last big dream. After he passed, there was confusion, fear, and debate about the future of the company in general, let alone continuing Walt's "Florida project." There were two ideas on the table and neither side would concede. One idea was a theme park celebrating technology and innovation. A tribute to Walt's original future city, it would become what is now called Future World. The other concept was a Disneyfied World's Fair, celebrating international culture and diversity. The legend goes that scale models were mocked up of each concept. The management team was torn over which should move forward. Finally, the Imagineers, led by Marty Sklar, the genius who spearheaded Walt Disney World with Walt's brother Roy, got the idea to shove the two models together. As always, a real man of action solves the problem, ending the debate. Both concepts in one park separated only by a lagoon—they had their Epcot.

As you pass through the last few attractions and gift shops of Future World and approach the World Showcase Lagoon, you will recognize strangely familiar architectural icons across the water. The Eiffel Tower, a Japanese pagoda, an Aztec temple, and right in the middle of it all, a building complete with white columns and a cupola straight out of our Colonial history. Choose either path around the lake and find yourself traveling through nearly a dozen different countries (11.5 if you count what represents Africa) without even walking a mile. This is World Showcase.

Don't let anyone accuse you of being an uncultured lout. I challenge you to take on World Showcase with gusto. Each international pavilion showcases its people, its history, culture, artistry, and most importantly its cuisine! The Cast Members at each stop are recruited from their native land to work the pavilion and interact with guests. It's your opportunity to school them about us as well, and assure them we're not all "ugly Americans." Still haven't sold you on World Showcase? How about this? Every country sells a regional cocktail and beer! *Aha!* Suddenly you're a U.N. Dignitary!

I'll make you a deal, get through this chapter (I promise to keep it as concise as possible) and I will reveal the best part of World Showcase. It's a little game we like to call *Drinking Around The World!*

World Showcase is laid out along the crescent curve of World Showcase Lagoon. There really is no right or wrong side to start. I gravitate to the left and the ancient Aztec temple rising above the trees. The shadows on these steps don't signal the end of the world. For me, it's always the beginning. Especially when I'm hungry. *Bienvenido!*

Mexico

Inside the giant temple of the Mexico pavilion you'll find yourself in an old plaza right out of *Zorro* (or *The Three Amigos*). There are banners and piñatas and señoritas in festive dresses. It's a fiesta atmosphere. No matter what time you enter the pavilion, inside it's always a beautiful Mexican night. Even the ceiling reveals a starry tropical sky. Like the real Cancun or Riviera Maya, I could stay in this pavilion for days. Especially with the recent addition of **La Cava del Tequila**. The name means the "tequila cave" though something tells me *tequila* translates easily, even if your eighth grade *español* is *un poco* rusty!

La Cava is a cozy, dimly lit bar hidden away inside the Mexico pavilion. It's the kind of place where you'd gather in the corner with a group of banditos, drinking, laughing, and swapping sordid stories all night. The problem is after dos margaritas, you'd likely be all out of pesos. La Cava boasts some tasty and unique margaritas, but they also boast a price tag of $13 *apiece*! You read that right. $13 for UNO margarita! *Con permiso?!?*

Man's Journal

I walked in to La Cava del Tequila like Bogey sauntering into the cantina looking for a score in *Sierra Madre*. I knew immediately this was my kind of place. The sort of cantina where an expatriate could disappear inside a bottle of tequila for a few days. I'd been told this was the right watering hole in Epcot for fans of the agave plant. The Blood Orange Margarita came particularly recommended. Unfortunately, they didn't tell me you need a line of credit to order one. Paying 13 bucks for one drink was not really in my *plans*, but I'd come for a reason. This was research. A fact-finding mission. I needed to gather info for my readers. I had no choice. I'd pay the grossly inflated fee to faithfully report on what they were serving.

The bartender set down a regular-looking plastic cup with an orangeish-red beverage inside, topped with pinkish foam. Strange ruby sugar crystals encrusted the rim. They quickly began to melt, sending sticky red syrup oozing down the sides.

"I like my steaks bloody," I told the barkeep, "not my drinks! Savvy?"

I will say this, the drink tasted damn good! If I were sitting outside on a summer evening, I could happily put away a half-dozen of these. And yes, it was premium liquor. Triple Sec, premium silver tequila, hibiscus syrup, pureed blood oranges (from the last tree in Eden no doubt), the tear of a Mayan virgin . . . I don't care! That's too expensive for one drink! If it came in one of those fishbowl-sized schooners you get at the average Chi-Chi's cantina

and grill, I might understand. But much as I'd like (and I really
would like), I doubt I'll be spending a lot of time in La Cava again.
Not unless I write a best seller one day . . . *ahem!*

The main draw of Mexico is **San Angel Inn**, the "outdoor" restaurant situated right on the river in the shadow of the volcano. If
you're looking for a simple taco platter or the newest 99-cent *Fiesta
Con Queso Snack Wrap* you get at home, this may not be for you. In
fact, I can't tell you where the nearest Taco Hell to Walt Disney World
is, but if you want delicious, authentic Mexican food make an ADR.
Some of the items will probably seem foreign (no pun intended) but
don't worry. I'm going to tell you what you want. You're a man, you
love steak, and you love Mexican food. Order the *Carne Asada*!

Grilled New York strip steak served with peppers and onions,
along with a cheese enchilada, (holy) guacamole, refried black
beans, and rice. It's the best of both sides of the border—a perfectly
cooked piece of meat and the traditional flavors of Mexico. You
won't stop eating until your teeth hit the table. You might even eat
the plate, or at least lick it clean.

I have eaten here multiple times and the food has always been excellent. The authentic Mexican atmosphere is like a vacation within
a vacation. I've only ever had one complaint at San Angel Inn, but
oddly enough the issue repeated itself on separate trips. The service
in the Mexico pavilion is *no muy bueno!* That exemplary guest service Disney is famous for apparently gets lost in translation on those
temple steps. The employees have never shown any urgency to help
or serve in any capacity any time I've visited. This is one place on
property I don't buy into the CM title—clearly they don't either.

In fact, the last two times I was in the Mexico pavilion I had the
same bad experience, three years apart! The first instance was stepping up to the check-in podium for San Angel Inn. The next time
would be waiting to board the **Gran Fiesta Tour Starring The Three
Caballeros**, a river ride, also inside Mexico. In both instances, just
as I stepped up to the podium, two strangers bulldozed past me and
the employee let out an excited squeal, ran from their post to hug

them and proceeded to chatter excitedly in Spanish. Meanwhile I (and the growing line behind me) stood dumbfounded. Vacation crippling offenses? Maybe not, but still irritating and off-putting, especially at the restaurant when we were all tired and hungry! Oh yeah, and *paying to be there!* What bothered me most was when each offending employee eventually returned, I smiled and pretended it hadn't happened yet got a reaction of "What's your problem, gringo?" I forgive it because I like the food and the setting, and because I'm on vacation. What's the hurry, right? I just wish the employees didn't have the same attitude.

Speaking of the *Gran Fiesta Tour*, while it could qualify as a "kiddie ride," I think it's a nice little cruise through dimly lit air-conditioned set pieces featuring the Three Caballeros—Donald Duck, Jose Carioca (who is actually a Brazilian parrot, but let's not argue semantics), and a pistol-packing rooster aptly named Panchito Pistoles. They sing, they dance, and after a few margaritas you probably will too! Even if you don't get into the party spirit of the ride, it's another great way to keep the family entertained while you lean back, let dinner settle, and catch a little *siesta.* Either way, it's a good time!

 The official Ears of Steel recommendation: Oye! Take the cruise!

The Mexico pavilion can get a little crowded, especially in busier months. Don't want to deal with elbow-to-elbow tourists? (What man does?) You can always slip outside to Cantina de San Angel. An outdoor counter service location on the water's edge, the Cantina is where you can grab that plate of tacos (sorry, still no *Cheesy Crunchy Gordito Con Pantolones*) and a cerveza! This spot used to be a great place to grab a table an hour or two before the nightly fireworks extravaganza and guard it like a churro-chomping hawk until show time. It's not as ideal as it once was due to the repositioning of the courtyard, but if you're close to the water, you'll still have a pretty good view.

After you've spent some time wastin' away in the lower latitudes, thinking of señoritas and Jimmy Buffett tunes, you might want to pull a parka over that Aloha shirt, *mi hermano.* 'Cause once you leave the Mexico pavilion you'll find yourself suddenly transported to a climate far less hospitable to flip-flops and a good farmer's tan. Old World Scandinavian buildings replace Mayan ruins in this seaside village. *Velcome to Nor'vay!*

Norway

Vikings, trolls, and polar bears! Sound like another family holiday? Norway is not the biggest pavilion, but real men know size doesn't matter. On a "manly" scale of 1 to 10 Norway conquers its way to 11, oozing testosterone like a yak! You'll shred your tank top and cargo shorts for the skin of a wild beast and a horned helmet! Of course, some snotty know-it-all might tell you Vikings didn't really wear horns. At which point clonk them with your hammer, son of Asgard! This is a place where a man feels a kinship with his barbaric roots! You can sample a nice cream puff too!

As soon as you enter Norway make straight for the back of the courtyard where you'll find the main attraction of this pavilion, **Maelstrom**.

Maelstrom is the final, and possibly most popular, of the Epcot boat rides. With a name that means "grinding current" you might expect a churning, twisting, adrenaline-pumping water coaster that soaks you to the core. You'd be disappointed then. It is fun though, and certainly not like the leisurely Epcot cruises you'll have grown accustomed to by now. *Maelstrom* may not be *Splash Mountain*, but it ramps up the excitement level a couple of notches. It's certainly the most thrilling attraction on this side of Epcot.

Man's Journal

I entered the queue area for *Maelstrom*, surprised to find such a long line on this side of Epcot. You'd think they were handing out free tankards of mead. After trudging along, checking out the mural featuring contemporary Norsemen doing manly jobs like fishing and working the oil rigs with their locks braided like the Swiss Miss, a mini-Viking ship pulled ashore (the loading platform) and I took my place at the stern. I assured the other passengers I'm descended from seafaring men and could handily steer the vessel to safety should things go awry. By that I meant I've spent many an afternoon on a pontoon boat, snoozing with a can cozy between my knees and a line bobbing in the lake. They didn't speak English anyway.

In a moment, I found myself whisked upstream, and I mean **up!** I was certain I hadn't drunk the bottle of peppermint schnapps I'd seen in the gift shop, but suddenly there was the face of Odin, All-Father, Cyclopean Norse god and father of Thor—and this was built long before Disney bought Marvel comics! Ol' *Odin One-Eye* began to mumble something in a slurred accent, making me wonder if he'd also dipped into the Aquavit! It was a warning, preparing us travelers for the journey. We were sailing back to the early days of those Norwegian seafarers, the Vikings.

Our ship leveled off and we gently floated past an old Norwegian village where hirsute men traded skins and furs. These were the days when true Vikings reigned (not those purple-clad imposters in Minnesota). My crew and I sailed on from the peaceful village into the darkness of the forest. It quickly became apparent we'd taken a wrong turn at Oslo! Our tiny vessel had strayed into Troll territory. Bulbous yellow eyes appeared from the trees and plants. A three-headed beastie rose up before our boat and growled—we were indeed on the wrong side of the glacier. This creepy *unwelcome* wagon was less accommodating than a hostess at the Mexico pavilion.

Before we could apologize and row our way back out, some jackass troll cast a curse over our ship and sent us plummeting back, *back* over the falls! We survived the plunge, narrowly avoiding the rocks below. Didn't actually see any rocks, but I'm certain they were there. If not for my steady hands on the wheel, our vessel, sturdy as she was, might have been dashed to pieces.

Somehow gliding down the waterfall carried us back through the wormhole. We found ourselves floating into modern-day Norway again (where *Maelstrom* tends to lose people, including me). We sailed the open sea, past a tiny . . . sorry, distant oil derrick. Polar bears on a glacier waved as we sailed by. Soon we were back at the dock. It was a bit of a lackluster ending to the voyage. I suppose there's not much more they can do to increase the excitement, aside from having the polar bears in the water actually attack the boats. Still, I sensed the adventure made real men of us all. Even the women!

 The official Ears of Steel recommendation: *Maelstrom* may not rival *Splash Mountain* or *Pirates of the Caribbean*, but it's a fun, manly voyage!

When you disembark, you must pass through a theater to exit. Be grateful you *can* pass through. There was a time when there was no exit. Not until the boring Norwegian tourism filmstrip ended anyway. Like many of the pavilion films, it was ten minutes of tortuous boredom. Mercifully at some point management wised up, allowing guests the option to watch or pass through. Because I wanted to be sure this book steers you right, I did something I hadn't in 20 years. I sat down and watched the movie. It wasn't quite as bad as I remembered, but just the same, I recommend you get the *Valhalla* outta there!

You might miss your local donut shop while on vacation, so I suggest you hit Norway's **Kringla Bakeri Og Kafe** (or simply *the bakery*, for anyone not Hagar the Horrible). They're baking cookies, cream puffs, and some other rich-looking pastry selections. There's also a restaurant called **Akershus Royal Banquet Hall**. It's a buffet, which is always a plus for us men. Unfortunately it is a "character buffet," and specifically it is a *Princess* buffet! I find that ironic and a little insulting as a *man of stature*. Clearly none of those royal ladies has spent a lot of time around a buffet. Secondly, while the food may be an interesting mix of American and Scandinavian favorites (pickled herring, anyone?), this isn't the celestial beer-hall of Viking lore where warriors drink, dine, and fight until the end of the Universe. In other words, it's no place for a real man to eat! Unless, of course, you have daughters, in which case you may have to suck it up and put on your tiara, buttercup!

China

After Norway comes China. At least on Epcot's globe. What can I tell you about the China pavilion? It's red and gold, and if you're in the mood for sweet and sour chicken there's a nice little restaurant called **Nine Dragons**. Otherwise, skip it. You'd have more fun watching the Norway movie.

The Outpost

As you journey on from China, you will walk over a bridge and on the other end you will approach a tent, a few drums, and a curio stand. In the early eighties, Walt Disney Imagineering had a grand pavilion planned for Africa. There was going to be a savannah, a watering hole and animals, tribal presentations, even some kind of safari experience. A network television special, aired before Epcot opened, had author Alex Haley present the planned Africa pavilion to the world.

It never came to be. It was clear from concept art that the Africa pavilion was to come at a considerable expense even for a large corporation like Disney. Which African region would be represented and which government would kick in the funds to build, staff, and maintain such an exhibit? Epcot's loss would eventually become Animal Kingdom's gain, as there is an incredible representation of Africa—beyond any simple pavilion—in that park's *Harambe*. But that's for another chapter.

Stop in to see the wood carvings, bang on the tribal drums (I mean that *is* pretty manly) and then tighten up your *lederhosen!* You're but a short hop from a manly Bavarian pavilion full of sausage and beer. *Willkommen* to Germany!

Germany

This is where World Showcase separates the men from the frauleins! There is a wine shop and a shop with an impressive selection of German beer steins. You can even pick up one of those weird pickle ornaments for your Christmas tree. Plus all the usual German culture, yadda, yadda, yadda. Let's cut the schnitzel! What you want to know about is the Bavarian beer hall, **Biergarten Restaurant**.

In here, it's always Oktoberfest! Pull up a bench, raise a beer so heavy it hurts your forearm, and sway to the *Oom-pah-pah*! Oh, and as you might have guessed, there's food too. The buffet at Biergarten wins high praise! A festival of sausages, schnitzel, sauerkraut, and spaetzle capped off by strudels and cakes. It's a great way to kill time between giant beers! Although, good as it is, there's an argument to be made for skipping the German buffet and just grabbing a pretzel and a beer (or three) out front.

It's a question of appetite. Are you a fan of boiled meats and cabbage, or more of a pasta kind of guy? On the World Showcase skyline just past Germany, you'll see what might be a familiar bell tower. For a second, you might be confused as to whether you're in Florida, Europe, or Las Vegas. Just ahead waits an incredible re-creation of several Venetian landmarks grouped around an area Disney calls the *Plaza del Teatro*. The only thing missing is the pigeons. You'll really want to save room for this pavilion. Some say pasta and pizza are Italian clichés. If cliché means "freakin' delicious over here" then those jerkoffs would be correct. *Benvenuto* to Italy!

Italy

The Italy pavilion takes its inspiration mostly from Venice, right down to the gondolas in the water. No, there are no canals, but there are gondolas. Use your imagination, *Topolino*! Behold the mighty statue of Neptune. Toss a penny into Rome's Trevi Fountain and make a wish that the Cubs finally get to a World Series—it's a legitimate wish! Then prepare to *mangia*! If the way to a real man's heart is his stomach, the Italy pavilion really has the hots for us! There are two amazing restaurants to choose from. For classic Italian cuisine in an upscale atmosphere there's **Tutto Italia**. If oven-roasted pizza makes you drool on your *Space Mountain* T-shirt, **Via Napoli** is your destination. Dilemmas like this are the reason God made Park Hopper tickets. You're going to want to eat at Epcot many nights.

The jury is split on Tutto Italia. I've heard some fans say it's simply "meh." I've also had trusted sources tell me it's fantastic! Hey, the proof is in the Sunday gravy! I will say while I'm not Italian, the menu at Tutto Italia has a more rustic flare. The menu features roast pork, fish, and chicken, along with hearty lasagna and other pastas. The atmosphere in the dining room is just as classic, with hand-painted frescos on the walls and plush red carpeting. I will make one recommendation, but it's not something from the menu. Make your reservation late. By the time you're sipping your espresso, you'll be lucky if you can get back to the front gate without a wheelchair, or maybe a forklift. You certainly won't feel like walking much more, even though you probably should!

Let's say you're not in the mood for a full three-course Italian meal like fresh antipasti and hand-rolled gnocchi, topped off with tiramisu and fresh cannoli. Let's say, you happen to be in Epcot on the night your family normally considers "pizza night!" No need to call for delivery. All roads lead back to the Italy pavilion.

I'm from Chicago. Pizza is a sensitive subject for me. It's almost a religion. My city makes the greatest pizza in the world. That's right, I said it! I know denizens of a certain city to the East like to claim that title. They're also insane. They're so ashamed of their pizza they fold it over to eat it. They even call it "utility pizza." My washer and dryer are utilities. I wouldn't eat those, either.

Chicago didn't invent pizza, we perfected it. Real men live deep. If you're a real man who loves pizza, you love deep *dish*! However, I once worked for an Italian restaurant from Boston that made gourmet brick-oven pizza. I wouldn't say they were better than my Chicago-style pies, but they were incredible in their own right. Fresh vegetables, cured meats, and artisanal cheeses roasted on a smoky, flavorful crust with a sweet, robust tomato sauce. It was the first place I ever had Italian staples like prosciutto and caponata, let alone on a pizza. Best job I ever had and I learned the art of wood-fired pizza!

Why the extraneous personal pizza lesson, you ask? In 2010, Epcot's Italy pavilion got a culinary shot in the arm with the opening of Via Napoli. Baking wood-fired artisanal pizzas, Via Napoli elevated the concept of theme park pizza miles above anything other resorts could hope to achieve. This is the food of the gods, literally.

The faces of the ovens represent three Italian gods. You may also notice that these stone visages share the names of famous Italian volcanoes; Mount *Stromboli*, Mount *Calzone*, and uh . . . Mount *Boyardee*. Just testing. They are actually Vesuvius, Etna, and yes, actually Mount Stromboli. Just like the guy in *Pinocchio*, I swear! Ask your server, when you're done stuffing your face with pizza, calamari fritti, and freshly topped bruschetta.

Fall off your chair and have the family roll you out of the Italy pavilion. Try not to throw up on the costumed street performers. They're just trying earn a living. As you waddle your way out of Italy, you'll be halfway through World Showcase, a.k.a. the International Tour of Gluttony!

The next pavilion should need little explanation. Colonial architecture. The sounds of fife and drum floating on the breeze. Old Glory flying high over sticky-faced kids eating funnel cakes. You're in the good ol' U. S. of A., son!

The American Adventure

The America pavilion is the only pavilion other than Mexico that is completely indoors. This may be an unpopular opinion, but there's not much to see around the building itself. Artwork that looks vaguely like a U.S. history textbook. A choral group performing period music in the rotunda. So I'm told anyway. I've never actually experienced it. I did say *choral group*. But do not skip past America thinking you gave at the office, so to speak. Inside is a show that should be required viewing for every citizen.

The American Adventure show does more to make American history come alive than any Social Studies class I ever took. I know in these troubled times we've got a lot to worry about in this country, but we've still got so much more of which we should be proud. *The American Adventure* will remind you of that in spades. For visitors reading this from other lands, this show might help you understand us a bit more, even our little idiosyncrasies. In other words if we seem a bit nuts, you might learn why. We've had a lot of ground to cover in a just a couple hundred years. Most of you had a millennium or more.

Of course, the show takes some entertaining liberties with history. Your hosts through highlights of the last 200-plus years are Audio-Animatronics twins of Ben Franklin and Mark Twain. Don't bother with the math. No, they didn't live in the same era. They were separated by a good century. But thanks to that old Disney magic, it just works. The robotic doppelgangers for our historic forefathers are so scarily lifelike it's easy to get emotional about the whole thing. Plus, it's really entertaining.

It would be easy to draw comparisons to *The Hall of Presidents* in the Magic Kingdom, but for my money I'll take *American Adventure* any day. You get an overall picture of the story of *US* with more laughs and excitement. To be honest, I can't even tell you who was President the last time I was forced to sit through *The Hall*.

But *American Adventure* is a rare instance where it's worth making your kids learn something on vacation. Heck, their grades might even improve. And yes, when the show is over hang a hard left to grab a hot funnel cake. You deserve it!

 The official Ears of Steel recommendation: You're a red-blooded American man. Check it out.

Japan

Now as you lick ice cream and powdered sugar from your fingers, you'll find yourself approaching an enormous black pagoda. This is Japan. I know I've been kind of a shill for World Showcase, but to prove I'm not on the Disney take, *keep walking*.

It's a nice, well-designed pavilion. Even has a hibachi restaurant if you're still hungry. But honestly not much to keep the interest of a real man. In the shops as well as outside on street vendor carts you can purchase imported Japanese snacks and treats. Some of them don't look so bad. There's quite a selection of candy and gummy items. The prices are high, I assume because of the import fees. I picked up a package of candy made to look like sushi which I thought was a cool little novelty item. Threw that particular candy fish back when I saw it cost the better part of a Hamilton.

You can get real sushi here too, but no thanks. There are only a few fish I'll eat when cooked, so raw fish, wrapped in seaweed with a pile of its own eggs, makes my stomach do a ninja kick.

Although if you're thirsty and adventurous, they do sell sake and, I'm told, a killer plum wine made on the premises. I've had sake once before, served warm. Warmed booze equals rancid in my book—and therefore literally in my book! The experience didn't live up to the stories my Granddad used to tell about sake-drenched nights on the shores of Okinawa after WWII! Okay, he never shared such tales with me, but it sounds more exciting, right?

If it's exotic adventure you seek, head straight to the next pavilion. The sand-colored walls and the sounds and smells emanating from that direction will call out to your spirit of adventure. The sense of exotic locales and intrigue will excite the kid inside you that always wanted to be Indiana Jones. Or if you're like me, Rick "Play it again, Sam" Blaine. Welcome to Morocco.

Morocco

This one might be a tough sell. I have heard people say this pavilion is boring. That there isn't enough to see or do inside its walls. The unfamiliar culture holds no appeal, especially to a real man. First of all, those people should be spat on by a camel. It's true, Morocco is a country many of us know nothing about. Beyond what we learned from *Casablanca* anyway (and really what more do you need to know?). Yet ignorant as I am, I love this pavilion. The mysteriousness is part of what makes Morocco one of my favorite World Showcase pavilions. Don't just pass this one by. Step in. Take your kids. Spend some time getting lost in the authentic architecture and artwork. Wind through its tight corridors and hidden rooms and shops. Your children will like discovering the little parlor area where an ancient book is on display, sitting open, featuring a familiar magic carpet pilot.

I spent some time exploring this pavilion recently and it is so immersive and authentic that I nearly forgot I was at Walt Disney World. I was a traveler in Marrakesh. Until I saw Aladdin posing for pictures with guests. The addition of a Disney character aside, everything about this pavilion is incredibly authentic. It should be, considering the King of Morocco (the real one) sent his personal architect to oversee construction and make sure the pavilion met the royal standard. Unfortunately there's no boat ride (we all know from *Casablanca* there are no waters). As for a ride, Aladdin's flying carpets are over at the Magic Kingdom. But the lack of rides does not equate with "nothing to do." Just bring your adventurous side with you.

There is the Moroccan restaurant, **Restaurant Marrakesh**, with an exotic and actually delicious menu. Be just a little bit daring. You can get chicken fingers or sliders at home anytime. They're not serving chilled monkey brains! I've been called a picky eater (my gut would beg to differ) and I've loved everything I've eaten here. Even if you're not crazy about trying a new cuisine, there's another reason to make an ADR at Marrakesh. Something equally as thrilling as any roller coaster—*belly dancers*!

If the smell from the kitchen doesn't get your mouth watering, these attractive performers dancing the Seven Veils just might. Just don't get caught ogling too long. Your wife might exile you to the couch, and that's if you're in a deluxe resort. Otherwise you're sleeping on a lounge chair by the pool! Although, it is Florida. Hey! Snap out of it! Don't get caught eyeing the bellies, if you catch my midriff . . . er, *drift!*

All right, if I can't excite you with Middle Eastern architecture or exciting new cuisine, and you're the "lead me not into temptation" type, I understand, Flanders. You don't have to wander too deep to taste the best of Morocco. There's a beverage stand right outside the pavilion. I've mentioned I don't normally go for colorful drinks, least of all bright orange ones. Nor do I drink frozen cocktails. When I do indulge in the occasional margarita (or seven) it's always on the rocks. That said, Morocco's tangerine daiquiri has on more than one occasion almost changed my philosophy on blended beverages. I won't delve too deeply into description because, well . . . it's a daiquiri that tastes like tangerine. Apparently the Clever Names Team was off that day. It is sweet without being thick and syrupy. For a nice treat in the middle of a hot day, I'd certainly take one of these over a Popsicle.

The star of that drink cart for a real man, however, is definitely Morocco's home brew, **Casa Beer**. Apparently one of North Africa's best-kept fermented secrets, it's a nice, crisp lager with earthy, citrusy notes and a perfect balance of sweet and bitter. Seems somewhat appropriate for a desert environment. I've never seen it sold in my part of the world and I'm actually glad. As a beer drinker, it's one of a thousand little details about Walt Disney World I look forward to as each new trip approaches.

Man's Journal

I found myself roaming the antechambers of the Morocco pavilion. I decided to take a little breather. A live band called Mo'Rockin was playing this wild blend of rock meets traditional Arabic meets electronica. I found a bench in the courtyard and sat taking in the pavilion and watching tourists all around. Aromas of grilled meats and vegetables from the Tangierine Café across from me filled my nose. I sipped my cold Casa Beer and sighed, happier to be here than almost any place in the world.

A handful of guests from Morocco, the real place, friends or family of one of the Cast Members, wandered about. I watched as the manager appeared to greet them. On his way, he stopped a few feet from me to bend down and pick up a piece of trash. Again, that Disney difference. Not even a second thought, regardless of his position. The park is everyone's responsibility.

I watched as he was introduced to this new group and everyone smiled warmly and hugged and kissed each other. There was this genuine friendliness and affection among them all. Maybe I've seen *Casablanca* too many times, but it made me think again that Morocco is a country I must visit before I kick off. If it was good enough for Bogey, it's good enough for me.

For me there is nothing better than the few minutes I steal for myself, to get my beer and relax in the Moroccan courtyard. It's then I really appreciate being on vacation. Especially since Epcot is almost always my first-day destination. I'll sit in that intricately tiled courtyard, hearing music, smelling good food, hearing laughter, and inevitably look at my watch and think, "Any other day, I'd be at work right now."

There is a Moroccan proverb that hangs almost hidden inside the pavilion: "The first thing one should own is a home; and it is the last thing one should sell. For a home is one's castle this side of Heaven."

The moments I spend in Morocco are always a little sample of the *other* side.

When you leave Morocco you quickly come face to face with a very familiar icon. As if to continue the *Casablanca* theme, the proximity of Morocco to the next pavilion seems fitting as you'll be staring at the Eiffel Tower. *Zut alors!*

France

France is also one of those pavilions that looks *très magnifique* but once again, keep walking. Now before I get accused of being an Ugly American, I am not anti-French. Look, I love the French! I actually dig their attitude, their culture, and their *joie de vivre*. When I watch *Casablanca* I get this strange swell of patriotism when the French expats sing over the Nazi officers. I feel some, dare I say, French connection. I'd call it that *je ne sais quoi*, but I don't know what that is. (That last sentence is actually funny—Google it. I'll wait).

There's just nothing really man-centric about the France pavilion. The restaurants look nice and I'm told the food is quite good. I'm just not really looking for snails (okay, so I may not be an *ugly* American, just a "slightly unsettling to look at" one).

I am a sucker for French wines and cheeses (and warm summer breezes). There is also a great bakery. Sorry, *la patisserie c'est bonne!* You'll want to pace your empty calories though, as there are some great gut-busters coming up.

As you pass France you'll find yourself curving back toward Future World. You'll also see a gate in and out of the park. This is the same exit through which my buddy and I fled the giant chipmunks! It is the **International Gateway**. Exit here and you can board a boat to Disney's

Boardwalk, Beach Club, and Yacht Club Resorts and the WDW Swan and Dolphin hotels. If you've got the time and patience (any seven-year-old, YMCA-trained swimmer can out dog-paddle these skiffs) you can even ride all the way to Disney's Hollywood Studios.

At this point you'll find you have to cross another bridge. Look down at the water below. There's a fantastic cruise you can book from the Beach Club dock that circles around the lake before cruising in and dropping anchor at this spot. Why, you ask? It is a primo location for watching the nightly fireworks and flame extravaganza, *IllumiNations*. We'll talk about the show later. I've done this cruise and while it is an extra expense, the view you get is unrivaled anywhere else in the park. You're so close you might lose some eyebrow. Sure beats camping out for a spot along the lake an hour before the show. Not to mention you can have refreshments right on board. When it's over, you cruise back to the Beach Club and avoid the exiting masses.

United Kingdom

Crossing the bridge is like a light-speed ride through the Chunnel. You start in France but when you reach the other end you're in *Merrie Olde England!*

Actually you may think you've wandered onto the set of an Austin Powers prequel. This is another of my favorite areas to wander around. Take your wife for a romantic walk through the English garden complete with a hedge maze. Let her browse through the tea shop and even pick up a ceramic plate with an image of the Queen. OK, is that over? Good, you've scored yourself some **man time!** Take a walk across the street to the real reason I led you here. Your spider senses will be tingling long before you see the sign above the door. It's not a mirage; it's a real live English pub! Welcome to the **Rose & Crown!**

The Rose & Crown Pub is where ale doth flow. Bass Ale and Guinness are available on tap and you don't even have to go inside. You can, of course. Inside the pub, it's just as you'd expect. Crossing the threshold is like a special effect straight out of *Doctor Who*. You'll believe you've been beamed to a London pub. It's not the biggest room, however, and can get packed quickly. My advice—poke your head in and say *'ello!* Then grab a half-yard of Bass and pull up a bench along the water. I'm told they serve food here, but I can neither confirm nor deny. When I get the munchies in the UK pavilion, I pop over to the Yorkshire County Fish Shop for a quick fish and chips.

If you have a hankering for bangers and mash, the Rose & Crown offers outdoor seating in a gated-off patio over the lagoon. It's a nice spot, but it also fills up quickly around dinner time. While most tend to wolf down their meals at Walt Disney World to get back to the fun, on the Rose & Crown patio you'll see some of the slowest, most prolonged masticating in the history of the species. The reason being this area is perfect for watching *IllumiNations*, but it's reserved for dining customers only. Don't think you'll be able to saunter up at 8:45 and grab a spot for great pictures. They don't even guarantee those tables for those with reservations. If you happen to have a dinner ADR and they happen to have availability outside and it happens to be within an hour or so before show time, well, go buy a lottery ticket because it's clearly your lucky day.

The UK pavilion is mostly a photo op, but it's also a great place for a pint! Not exactly the manliest spot in Epcot, but oh, buddy! Get ready for your next stop, *eh!*

Canada

Our tour of the globe is nearly at an end, and we're winding up close to home! The final stop is our friendly neighbor to the north, Canada. Breathe easy. They're a big and burly forest-dwelling, hockey-playing people but also possibly the kindest, most gentle people on Earth. Most of them even speak English. They speak it weird. But if you can master their butchery of words ending with the letters o-u-t, and realize not every sentence is a question (it just sounds like one), you'll do just fine!

From Inuit totem poles to miniature Rockies to the Canadian Parliament building, Canada is a beautiful and rustic place to spend a little time. It's about as manly as cuddling with a moose or a grizzly!

Talk about getting in touch with your inner-woodsman! Even the gift shop is a cross between a fur trader's outpost and a hockey rink pro shop. Pick up a Leafs jersey or a new flannel or a bottle of maple syrup or a beaver hat! Hell, a real man would buy all four!

There's such a friendly, barrel-chested optimism to the people and their pavilion. You'll see what I'm talking *aboot . . .* er, about! Give me a frosty Labatt's and a full-figured woman and there's nothing I can't do, *eh?* O, Canada, indeed!

Speaking of, one attraction you might want to see in the Canada pavilion is their new(ish) Circle 360 film, ***O Canada!*** Aside from some seriously breathtaking footage of the vast and beautiful, mostly untouched country, the movie is hosted by Canadian treasure, Martin "I'm going completely mental, I must say" Short! I'm always amazed by the wealth of comedic talents imported from the land of the maple leaf. Even the Blues Brothers were 50% Canuck!

The other "attraction" of this pavilion and truly a star of the entire Walt Disney World culinary scene is **Le Cellier Steakhouse**. I've claimed this book isn't really a touring guide, but that said there are two tips you should know about eating at WDW. The first is you can book a restaurant ADR as far as 180 days in advance. The other thing you should know is, unless you've got embarrassing photos of Bob Iger in your safe deposit box, you can never ever make reservations at Le Cellier. It's nigh on impossible. Try it. I dare you. 181 days before your trip, set your alarm for 11:59 p.m. Grab your laptop or your cell, dial (407) WDW-DINE, and try making a Le Cellier ADR. I guarantee you 100 people will have dialed or typed faster and there will be zero availability! Offer to eat dinner at 9 a.m. They'll be booked solid. Even so, you must try. The food at Le Cellier is legendary.

At least that's what I hear from those who sold their souls to Lucifer and their firstborn to gypsies for a table. Yes, Le Cellier is famous for steaks seasoned by angels' tears and flipped on the grill by Gretzky's first stick. However, they also brew up beer cheddar soup and with fresh baked pretzel bread that would bring tears to a Sasquatch's eyes. One hope for those wishing to sample the delicacies of the north is Epcot's International Food & Wine Festival. Canada has a booth outside its pavilion where they ladle out the golden elixir without the need for a reservation.

Before we leave Canada, this book wouldn't be worth a Loonie or Tim-Bit if I didn't stop to mention the live entertainment provided by a group of insanely talented fellows. **Off Kilter** is a band of real men (even if they do wear skirts) that delivers a blend of Scottish and Canadian folk music blended with rock 'n' roll! Think Rush with bagpipes! These guys are great, as you will see by the crowds assembled around the stage between sets. They've been taking the stage between Canada and the UK for years and are a fan favorite. Hopefully they'll be there for years to come. Off Kilter is the kind of free entertainment Disney offers that you'd actually be willing to pay for. They're awesome! And their rendition of "Loch Lomond" would have even Scrooge McDuck stage-diving off a pile of money! Grab a brew and give the lads a listen when you're passing through.

So there you have it my friend! We've toured all of World Showcase. Around the world in 80 minutes, give or take! Don't you feel so continental now? If you travel this multicultural wonderland by day, you'll have crisp and clear memories, not to mention a head full of facts and new ideas to share with your own little world. That's all well and good, of course, but there's another way to really *drink in* World Showcase. I've alluded to it before. *Alluded?* I practically smacked you with a wet carp!

CHAPTER FIVE

Drinking Around the World!

few years back, Epcot created an interactive, role-playing experience called the Kim Possible World Showcase Adventure. The game was a high-tech scavenger hunt sending players throughout World Showcase with communicators that gave them clues to hidden surprises. Epcot has often had trouble engaging younger visitors especially on that side of the water. It's not uncommon to see tweens carried off by medics after spraining their eyes from rolling them too much at their parents. Kim Possible breathed new life into World Showcase for the teen and preteen demo. More than a few adults enjoyed it, too. In 2012, the game got a massive overhaul, in line with a very popular television series for kids (and certain grown-up authors) *Phineas and Ferb*! The new experience, **Agent P's World Showcase Adventure**, features Perry, the secret agent platypus and his arch-nemesis, Dr. Doofenshmirtz. Don't act like you don't watch it!

That's great and all, but the reality is there's been an interactive World Showcase game being played for years, at least by the over-21 crowd. While not officially sanctioned by Disney, like a number of unofficial traditions and events at WDW, if you're spending money and not bothering other guests, they're not gonna discourage it! When in Epcot and that big orange ball slips from the sky, there's no better way to enjoy yourself then with a game beloved by those in the know—***Drinking Around the World!***

It's the easiest game you'll ever play, although there are those who would argue that it's not only a sport but a true test of physical prowess. It's certainly a test of your constitution, and I don't mean that famous document at The American Adventure pavilion.

> **The objective:** It's simple. Make your way around World Showcase sampling a cocktail or beer (or wine, *if you must*) in every nation. The word "sample" is tricky, once you see the rules.
>
> **The rules:** Finish said drink in each nation. Never let it be said Americans are wasteful.
>
> **The winner:** That's the best part! If you're at Walt Disney World imbibing numerous delicious beverages and you don't have to operate any heavy machinery the next day, you've already won!

Now I in no way represent Walt Disney World or the Disney Company. I'm certainly not endorsing or condoning public drunkenness—though I've certainly enjoyed it! There's no reason *not* to catch a nice buzz on vacation. If Disney didn't agree, they wouldn't serve alcohol. Hell, Walt was no teetotaler! But I'm sure park management would agree with me when I say the philosophy is simple—***handle your high!***

Remember, there are kids around. You're not at Mardi Gras! If you find the ale, sangria, wine, and tequila catching up with you, hold it together! Sit down with a bottle of water. Don't act like a cigar-smoking jackass on *Pleasure Island*! I mean the movie one! Have fun. Enjoy the moment—even if you may not remember it! Just behave yourself!

Oh, and if you plan on playing the game (or just having a few casually) in World Showcase, lock your credit cards in your room's safe.

The last time my wife and I went to Walt Disney World prior to breeding, we found ourselves getting a little misty as we sat on a bench outside the Rose & Crown watching happy families stroll by with balloon-clutching kids. As I gulped down a half-yard of lager, she said to me "You know, the next time we come we better have kids with us."

I nodded, knowing this would be our last grown-up trip and we'd better enjoy it. We made our way across World Showcase sampling aplenty and having the most fun, romantic night since our honeymoon. At one point, somewhere around Germany, I had to visit the little Bürgermeister's room. I told my wife to wait near a glassware stand. As best I remember, it was but a few minutes later that we were on the shuttle back to Coronado Springs.

Roughly a week later, I came home from work to find a large box sitting at our doorstep, postmarked Florida. Inside were eight etched character glasses and one large stein with Mickey Mouse on one side and my name etched into the other. Neither of us had any recollection of selecting them, nor telling the fraulein Cast Member my name, nor paying the price listed on the invoice. And trust me, in a clearer state of mind I'd have remembered signing *that* credit card slip!

All the glasses have since broken. They were nice but very thin. The stein however lives and is my favorite vessel for barley and hops. Still, *caveat emptor*—drinker beware! Even so, get down to Epcot and take the tour. No matter what you drink, drink mightily and drink globally.

Salute! *Sláinte*! Cheers!

CHAPTER SIX

Illuminations: Reflections of Earth

I t would be highly irresponsible to tell you the best thing to do at Epcot after dark is to drink a lot. I still say it, of course, but it is highly irresponsible. Admitting is the first step. There is one more experience that happens after dark that's a fitting and perhaps more family-friendly ending to any night at Epcot. Plus, it's flammable!

But first, let's talk fireworks. Under any non-Disney circumstances, highlight the next sentence and show your wife. **Men don't care about fireworks!** When we were kids our parents would pile us into the Family Truckster on July Fourth and haul us out to some field for the annual fireworks display. Accompanied by John Philip Sousa on the local radio station, it was kind of cool. *Kind of.* However, in the years you've been shuffling around this rock, have fireworks really changed? Of course not. The Chinese more or less cracked the code on that one. You got your loud booms then colored lights parachuting through the night sky followed by robotic "*oohs*" and "*aahs*" from the crowd.

At Walt Disney World, Magic Kingdom has always traditionally been the place for fireworks. It is unique seeing an otherwise traditional nighttime display exploding over the majestic blue-turreted castle. Certainly beats sitting on grass behind a church. Still, as a man you might quickly find it just another (extremely loud) snooze fest. Fireworks are fireworks. You've seen one pyrotechnics display, you've seen 'em all. Not here. You'll want to stick around Epcot at night. Their nighttime pyro-production is a spin on fireworks you have not seen before.

IllumiNations: Reflections of Earth is amazing! In fact, to call it simply a fireworks show would be dishonest. First off, there's fire—real, white-hot fire. Plus video, lights, and lasers, set to a score on a par with any epic blockbuster you've ever seen! Oh, there are also fireworks.

IllumiNations has gone through a couple of tweaks since its inception but it has been the nightly entertainment at Epcot for over a decade now, which is saying something. Prior to this show, that lagoon saw numerous short-lived spectacles. In the eighties, there was a daytime show featuring a witch, speed boats dressed up as sea monsters, and even fireworks in the daylight (which always works).

Reflections of Earth is about storytelling and how all cultures are tied together as children of one planet. Not bad, right? I just made that up. Seriously though, from the moment the show begins and all World Showcase goes dark, you're all in! The use of fire is especially impressive. Again, it harkens back to some primal instinct—from our hairiest ancestors (well, yours perhaps) gathered around a communal fire, to the first time we melted a toy soldier with the electric barbeque starter, to when we were handed our first stainless steel spatula and told "Son, you man the grill tonight." We men love fire.

The centerpiece of the show is a giant steel globe. Floated out to the lagoon's center stage it illuminates with images from around the world, or *reflections of Earth*. See what they did there? I've heard it referred to as the first spherical television set. If your wife complains about you watching television on vacation, here's where you point and say "*See?!?*" There are explosions, synchronized water jets, and pyrotechnics all set to a story and music. *IllumiNations* harkens back to the earliest days of civilization when communities listened to an elder spin the tale of his people. It's a great moment to gather your family to watch together. You're not rushing to the next ride or arguing over which park to hit next. And again, get close enough and you could make s'mores from the heat blazing off the water!

In the interest of full disclosure, exiting Epcot after *IllumiNations* is usually a *nightmare*! Another term for it begins with the word *cluster*! When the show is over, the park is closed (unless it's Extra Magic Hours). That means everyone stampedes toward the front gates. Grab your bags and belongings. If you can't grab your kids, pray you've raised them strong and swift. Hail Mary and charge boldly into that sunscreened, bug-sprayed, sweaty mosh pit and run like it's Pamplona and you're wearing a red beret.

Worst of all, once out of the park, you still have to get on the bus back to your hotel. Take a deep breath and hope you've got water and snacks because you're going to be in that bus shelter awhile. No matter which resort you've to chosen as home base, when you find the proper bus stop, it will appear that every guest at Epcot (and possibly some who snuck over from SeaWorld) is staying there too. And they're all in front of you. This almost always feels like the worst time and place to be waiting for a bus, rivaled closely by Magic Kingdom after its own fireworks show, *Wishes*.

All I can say is remember you are on vacation. I know by this point your legs probably hurt. Forget about your feet, you probably won't even feel them anymore. Worst of all, your buzz is probably fading as you've sweated out most of the alcohol. We all know how cranky that makes us.

Take a deep breath and repeat this mantra: "I'm on vacation. I'm on vacation."

There's no hurry. The hotel will still be there. Let your family see you as the personification of *cool under pressure*. It's a good example to the kids and it will turn your wife on. (You did get the kids a separate room, right?) You'll be on a shuttle sooner than you know.

Believe it or not, there's something relaxing about the hum of those cramped buses at night. I'm not kidding. When the driver kills the lights, you'll doze off faster than you do in front of the news sitting in your recliner. Once you get to the room, while your wife washes her face before bed (whatever that means), you'll hit the pillow like it owes you money and be happily dreaming of scantily clad pixies faster than she can say "aren't you at least going to wash your hands?"

Again, *what* my *what???*

It's worth the little extra aggravation to see *IllumiNations* in its entirety at least once in your life. The spectacle is damn cool, even for fireworks.

CHAPTER SEVEN

Jnternational ffood & Wine ffestival

FEEDING (AND WINE-ING) FRENZY!

When I originally mapped out this book, I wasn't going to include any special or seasonal events at Walt Disney World. What am I gonna do? Tell you about the Flower and Garden Show? I'm not a chick! Besides, why should I bother writing about something that only happens during a specific window of time? If you're not there during that time, it won't concern you. When I booked my "research trip" for this book, I didn't even realize I was landing right in the middle of the **Epcot International Food & Wine Festival**.

Man, am I glad I did!

Now, having experienced it, it is my duty as your brother to report on this event and advise that you plan your trip during that specific window! Smash through that window if need be! You don't want to miss this!

Food & Wine takes place from late September through mid-November. Don't let the word *Wine* fool you. It's not some snooty, pinky in the air, spitting in buckets kind of affair. I hit at least a third of all the kiosks set up for the event, and I only had wine once (allegedly). This event is not just for fancy people who vacation in

Napa, wherever that is. It is *any* food lover's fantasy. By the end of the first night I felt like the fat rat in *Charlotte's Web*, stuffing my snout and singing the praises of gluttony!

Like a World's Fair of Food, Epcot erects kiosks all around World Showcase, each representing a new country, in addition to the nations already present year-round. We aren't just talking tents or booths. The Greece structure, for example, reflected the classic white architecture you immediately equate with the Greek isles. Each country offers tasting portions of national dishes. Still, using Greece as an example, they were serving Chicken Souvlaki with *Tzatziki* (God bless you! Never gets old!) as well as grilled Greek cheese with pistachios and honey. There was salad, too (damn lawyers again). To drink, you could choose from a few different Greek wines.

None of it is free, mind you. Prices at the different stations varied between $3.00 all the way to almost $10, depending on the item. If you're using the Disney Dining Plan—and you should be, especially when it's often a free add-on during these slower times of the year—you can use snack credits for many of these entrée samples. That certainly helps on the more expensive items. With the cheaper options, I suggest holding on to your credits and paying cash.

Sorry, I know I said there'd be no math in this book!

Man's Journal

I told myself I'd lap World Showcase first, checking out every booth before trying anything. Seemed like the prudent thing to do. Get a feel for what I absolutely had to try before dropping any cash. That plan went out the window pretty quickly. Against tradition, I started to the right and came upon the Ireland booth near the Rose & Crown Pub. They were serving something called Lobster and Scallop Fisherman's Pie. Sounded good, but a heavy creamy dish in the 80-degree-plus Florida sun?

Then I saw one. It looked like a delicious little cloud of goodness. Creamy whipped potatoes covered in melted cheese. That alone could easily undo me. Imagining chunks of lobster and scallops swimming in a delicious sea of sauce underneath, it was more than I could resist. And thank Guinness! It only took one steaming bite to know it was the right choice to start my eating adventure. Right off the bat I got a huge hunk of lobster, mixed with whipped potato and sauce. I felt connected to my Irish ancestors and to the sea gods themselves. This was comfort food from an ancient home. It was going to be hard for anything to live up to this first sample.

Being new to Food & Wine, it somehow didn't occur to me that I should have ordered a drink. Ireland was pouring Guinness naturally, but also *Bunratty Meade*—honey wine. I've had Guinness a few (thousand) times before so I opted for the mead. I'd heard about mead in *Robin Hood* and *Game of Thrones*, but never had the opportunity to raise a goblet. Not what I expected, but very addictive. It was sweet, slightly syrupy, with a distinct flavor of honey. I could see sipping on that all evening, slinging blarney with old family and friends like Irishmen of yore. Although I can also imagine the rockin' hangover something that sweet can produce.

I moved on, looking for a dish that might top my first. Straight through France without slowing down. Not interested in snails. I'm open to trying new things, but . . . snails? What, am I on *Fear Factor*?

Morocco had a special booth for Food & Wine. I wasn't going to eat, but hopped in line because they were serving my favorite Casa Beer, and it was actually a little cheaper than in the pavilion. While waiting, I thought of how often I'd considered trying Moroccan food. This seemed like a good way to dip a toe in the water without committing to a full meal. I ordered a *Kefta* pocket. Seasoned ground beef in a pita. How bad could it be, right?

Turned out not bad at all! It was like a thicker burger flavored with foreign and delicious seasonings served in a pita along with a kind of Moroccan cole slaw. When eaten all together, it was one of the best things I've ever put in my mouth. And I have had some things in my mouth! (*What?!?*)

Trying to be conservative with my cash and my snack credits, I didn't want to just fill up on everything I came across. I wanted to hold out for the foods that just called out "eat me!" (All right, take it easy!) As I was thinking this, I nearly walked right past a small sign that read Singapore. I know Singapore's most famous beverage, but one thing I didn't know was what they ate with it. I read over the menu and the words "coconut braised beef" caught my eyes. My mouth began watering.

Normally, you say "coconut braised" anything, I grab my fork. Coconut braise a flip-flop and I'll be licking my chops. Actually, that's a lie. I'm actually wondering if the coconut braised Beef Rendang was formerly footwear. I voraciously shoveled the first steamy mouthful into my mouth, and was immediately overwhelmed by this strange, un-beef-like flavor. It almost tasted like plastic or melted crayon. I would have been better off eating the fork. To make matters worse, while it lacked any enjoyable flavor, it over-compensated with spices. The heat wave started rippling over my tongue and across the roof of my mouth like it was practicing parkour.

The hot mess on a plate was also actually hot! The jasmine rice served alongside was hard and crunchy, like it had been sitting out too long. I still ate it, of course, along with a Tiger Beer, the regional brew. It was bitter and flowery and had hints of *I'll-never-drink-one-again!* I tried not to think as I used the beer to wash down the sweet and sour sewer rat. But even though I hated the taste, like Stockholm syndrome, I started to accept the heat and in some masochistic way enjoy it. More than anything, I finished my plate simply because I had paid for it. I hate wasting money—and food! Throwing it away would be a double insult. Appropriately, I ate it hunched over a garbage can.

Thankfully, culinary salvation was just a few feet away! At The American Adventure pavilion stood a sizable structure reppin' the U.S. I'd read on the map they were featuring something called *Linda Bean's Perfect Maine Lobster Roll*. I had no idea who Linda Bean was, but I do love me some lobster, sir. However, I'd always heard of this New England staple as a hotdog roll loaded with a jar of mayonnaise and flake or two of lobster meat. I caught sight of another guy's sandwich and I was stunned. I saw hunks of lobster meat bigger than a baby's foot. What I didn't see was mayo splooshing down his chin. I decided it was time to introduce my palate to this New England favorite.

I was also stunned by this perfect roll's cost—$7.25. The lobster roll was literally half a hotdog bun. Still, I had to try it and snack credits were accepted. Having taken advantage of Free Dining from Disney, I got my seven-dollar snack for free. One bite in, I would have gladly handed over a twenty. I know that seems unlikely, but trust me. The first bite made my eyes roll back into my head like a shark with a fat seal. Fresh, thick lobster meat, just a touch of mayo, oil and light spices and herbs. I had to sit down. This was possibly the greatest sandwich I'd ever tasted.

Admittedly, being from the Midwest, I had no basis for comparison. Lobsters haven't quite crawled their way to the Great Lakes. They billed this as the "Perfect Lobster Roll" and I couldn't possibly argue.

I would have paid them 14 bucks for a full-sized roll. The last bite brought a tear of loss to my eye. Seafood separation anxiety!

Also, it turns out this Linda Bean character is the granddaughter of L.L. Bean, the outdoorsy clothing magnate. I might actually buy some flannels in honor of that Lobster Roll. That sandwich alone is reason enough to book a trip to Walt Disney World between October and November. Seriously.

The only negative thing I can say is that it stripped away any desire I had to try anything else. What could possibly compete? Instead, I decided it was time to shift my focus. I'd had a nice travelling lunch. It was mid-afternoon in Florida, but it had to be five o'clock somewhere. Time for happy hour(s).

I passed Italy and Poland. The usual, pasta and pirogies. Meh. In the distance I saw Germany had also erected a miniature beer garden. A heavy pilsner seemed like too much right after the lobster roll. But this garden also grew wine! They weren't pouring my favorite Gewürztraminer. Couldn't afford holding up the line with an unpronounceable wine! I ordered the special Selbach J&H Riesling Classic. No part of that name meant anything to me, nor did I care. I just wanted something light and cold. It happened to be really tasty, too! A very crisp, refreshing, slightly fruity wine for a hot afternoon. Yeah, yeah, I know! Enough wine talk, Frasier!

You'll be happy to know they were also pouring German beers big enough to snap your radius bone. As they should!

By the time I left Germany it occurred to me I had gone from grains to grapes . . . and back to grains. I was trying to remember the little nursery rhyme that predicts which combination will have you praying to the porcelain god. Unfortunately between multiple alcoholic samplings and the hot sun, I could barely slur, "Beer before liquor . . . good for your ticker?"

However it went, I decided it was time for a break. A little more food seemed a good idea after all, to soak up the spirits. I had the option to get in line for the free Pointer Sisters concert, but decided to pass when I remembered it wasn't 1983 and, again, I'm not a chick!

An additional feature of Food & Wine is the series of nightly concerts called **Eat to the Beat**. I haven't mentioned it because the majority of acts rival the worst of county fairs and rib fests. On any given night you can catch acts like Night Ranger, Taylor Dayne, and the aforementioned Pointer Sisters. The two nights before I arrived, they had those nineties one-hit wonder moppets, Hanson. Apparently one of them has finally sprouted facial hair, a plus considering when their song *MMMBop* hit the radio, nobody knew if they were boys or girls—even after seeing the video! I felt no overwhelming urge to fly in a day early. Occasionally, they do book some cool acts like 38 Special in 2013. I believe they even had two original members, the bass player and a roadie. What're you gonna do?

Man's Journal

I worked my way around World Showcase passing a number of booths. South Africa, Korea, Scandinavia (pickled herring, no thanks!). I found myself back at the ancient temple of Mexico. The special festival offering was a choice between grilled shrimp or rib eye tacos. I have never been one to pass up a good taco. Actually, I've never passed up a taco, *period.* Along with food they were serving a strawberry lime margarita.

The line moved fast and with my grilled rib eye taco and margarita in hand, I glanced around for someplace to eat. That's one major challenge of Food & Wine. Far less table space than people. If you're with a group, that could cause an issue. Fortunately, I was alone. I'm also not proud. As I said, I ate the spicy sewer rat from Singapore over a trash can. A kindly, middle-aged man and his wife stopped me and asked how the margarita tasted. I hadn't even tried it yet, so I obliged them by taking a sip. My immediate reaction spilled out of my mouth: **strong!** Seemed I hit the tequila pocket on my first attempt. The strawberry and subtle mint caught up shortly after the initial alcoholic mushroom cloud passed and it was quite tasty.

The gentleman chuckled and said "that's just how I like 'em!" I laughed and carried on in search of a little out of the way spot to eat my taco. Incidentally, that's how I like 'em too!

I found space near the condiment counter of the San Angel Inn, across from the main Mexico pavilion. Back in the day, what stood in its place was little more than a glorified churro stand with margaritas. That and it used to be one of the best spots in Epcot to watch *IllumiNations.* I wasn't stopping to watch fireworks. I had a prime beef taco to eat.

I should have just gotten a plate of tacos from San Angel. The grilled rib eye taco was a real disappointment. It was a few strips of lightly marinated (as in barely at all) beef with chipotle pepper sauce and scallions wrapped in a flour tortilla. It was dry and nearly flavorless. Even a little lettuce would have helped this sad little taco. When I was in line, I thought if it was good, I'd go through again and order the grilled shrimp taco. Then I could say I'd tried everything Mexico was offering at Food & Wine. After this limp excuse that didn't even measure up to the 99-cent selections at Taco Bell, I decided not to bother.

It was getting late, and I felt I'd sampled some of the best and worst of the International Food & Wine Festival. My size-13 dogs were starting to bark. I was shuffling back toward the front gate and the shuttle waiting to take me back to my nice value-tiered hotel bed when I noticed it. Out of the corner of my eye, the Hawaii hut appeared. They were serving a pulled pork slider. Normally three melodic words that would have made it my first stop. However, there was something that just hadn't sounded quite so appetizing when I'd read the description on the map. What the hell, I figured? Let's burn one more snack credit! Who needs another Mickey Mouse ice cream bar anyway, right? Well, this guy right here does, obviously, but just go with me!

There was no line. Most guests were crowding around the lagoon for *IllumiNations*. I ordered my Kalua Pork Slider with Sweet and Sour Dole Pineapple Chutney and Spicy Mayonnaise. That's what had initially thrown me, the name *Kalua!* I thought they were talking about that syrupy liqueur people pour in coffee (and mudslides!). That didn't sound like something I'd enjoy on a sandwich. In a kiddie pool with a straw, sure, but never on my pig!

Fortunately, this Kalua had a few less H's. Even more fortuitous (it's a word), this Kalua slider was simply AMAZING!!! An explosion of flavor rocked my mouth! The pork was tender. The sweet and sour pineapple relish had a zing.

And that spicy mayo perfectly balanced it out and added a kickin' flavor without just being hot! It was definitely unlike any pulled pork I've ever tasted. I would paddle a longboat all the way to Honolulu to taste it again! I've been to Hawaii. Why the hell aren't they handing these babies out when you step off the plane? Screw those silly flower necklaces! Oh right, it's because fat *Haoles* like me would never leave, and that would not look good on a tourism brochure! My look hasn't been considered *hot* in Polynesia since before Kamehameha!

That Hawaiian pork slider was the perfect exclamation point to my Food & Wine experience. Early fall has always been my favorite time to head down to Walt Disney World. But between the Fisherman's Pie, the Lobster Roll, and that Kalua slider, I've got at least three solid reasons to start pushing my trips back a month or so! Seriously, this is even worth altering your travel plans for!

Plus like everything at Walt Disney World, the International Food & Wine Festival is always changing. It can be a different experience every time you go, whether that means yearly or a couple times in one week. There's only one really negative thing I can say about Food & Wine. Not the beef in Singapore or the bland taco in Mexico. They sucked, but at least they were interesting. The real problem with Food & Wine is you're too damn full to eat in any of the amazing restaurants already planted throughout World Showcase. Be smart, buy the Park Hoppers! That way you can come back a couple times during your trip.

CHAPTER EIGHT

Disney's
Hollywood Studios

REAL MEN KNOW MOVIES ARE THE PERFECT DATE . . .
WE DON'T HAVE TO TALK! OR LISTEN!

et me throw a few names at you—John Wayne. Humphrey Bogart. Clint Eastwood. Burt (do I really need to say Reynolds?). Sylvester Stallone. Arnold Schwarzenegger. I say again Arnold-*freakin'*-Schwarzenegger!

If you're a real man, some of your biggest heroes, the guys who taught you what real swagger is, came out of the movies. These were the kind of guys who would light their cigar with a machine gun while taking down an alien menace. They took their whiskey straight and would have punched any bartender who dared stick an umbrella in it! And they always, *always* got the girl.

Real men love movies! That is why Walt Disney World built an entire theme park dedicated to the movies and all things Hollywood. And I'm telling you, make sure you schedule a whole day for it. Not only is this park an ode to entertainment and the Tinsel Town of myth and legend, it's also home to two of the most intense thrill-rides in all of Walt Disney World!

Disney's Hollywood Studios (originally called Disney-MGM Studios) opened in the spring of 1989. Some say Disney rushed to build a movie-themed park after being sucker-punched by Universal

Studios staking out land farther up the Interstate. Believe what you want, but Disney had their movie park on the drawing board first. Universal leapt to catch up, as usual. The story goes Imagineering was planning a new Epcot pavilion all about movies. Apparently, Michael Eisner was considering a third park for Walt Disney World, and he dug the concept of the movie pavilion so much he upgraded the idea to an entire new theme park. It probably didn't hurt that prior to joining Disney, Eisner had run Paramount Studios. Under his leadership, they released a couple of small flicks you may have caught, like *Raiders of the Lost Ark* and *Beverly Hills Cop*. Seriously, if you call yourself a man but can't quote at least three Axel Foley lines, turn in your man card and go wait in the minivan!

Eisner described the new park as "the Hollywood that never was and always will be." Walk through the gates and you get it instantly! The park transports visitors back to the days when movies were still referred to as "pictures." The architecture, the billboards, the costumes in the windows, it all makes perfect sense. There's even a shiny new filling station near the gate, where you expect a team of attendants to appear at any moment to fill you up, top you off, and clean your whitewalls—and you're not even in a car! Hollywood Studios was built right around the time Disney was producing great "Old Hollywood" era flicks like *Dick Tracy*, *The Rocketeer*, and *Who Framed Roger Rabbit?* You feel like you're stepping into that Hollywood.

Who am I kidding? Nostalgia is great, but as soon as you pass through the gates, haul ass down Sunset Boulevard to get a FAST-PASS for *The Twilight Zone Tower of Terror* then get in line for *Rock 'n' Roller Coaster Starring Aerosmith*. (Yes, fool, I said *AERO-SMITH*!!!) Or maybe it's a FASTPASS for *Rock 'n' Roller Coaster* and go ride *Tower of Terror*! Either way!

Then again, if you've got kids, cut around the Brown Derby restaurant to get to Pixar Place and ride *Toy Story Midway Mania!* But then you're taking your chances with standby lines for the aforementioned thrillers, and I haven't even mentioned *Star Tours*! This is where you'll need to use your judgment.

Hollywood Studios is basically laid out like the other parks—a central hub and spokes (assuming the wheel is shaped like a kidney bean). Unlike Magic Kingdom, I can't recommend picking one road and working your way around the park. The rides you're look-ing for—the hardcore, white-knuckle, gut-twisting thrillers—are randomly spread all over the park. And they're all popular! What to do first really depends on the day and what you're in the mood for. You may have to do a little work here. Look at the park map in your room. Plot out what you absolutely want to do. Check the wait times on the Guest Information Board when you get to the park. (Or if you're a high-tech type, there's an app for that.) How are the lines looking? Is the *Toy Story* wait short? Hit it right away. No line for *Tower*? Head to your right. You've always dreamed of audition-ing for *American Idol*? . . . close this book, you weirdo . . . but there is *The American Idol Experience*. You want to visit galaxies far, far away on *Star Tours*? Well, my first question would be how long ago did you eat breakfast? Seriously!

I know how I like to tackle Hollywood Studios and it works pretty damn well.

Man's Journal

Pop Century. Woke up so early the sun wasn't even up. Thought this was the sunshine state! Splashed white rum in my eyes. Hopped in the shower and dressed quickly, specifically choosing a Blackhawks T since the boys were in town. Noticed a strange spot, like grease of some kind. Shrugged it off because, well, I'm a guy. The shirt is black, and anybody looking that close needs a smack. Decided to eat breakfast at the food court before catching a bus. The day's destination was Hollywood Studios. The bus wasn't that full, which I hoped was a good sign as DHS is home to some rides with notoriously long wait times. And I hate crowds.

At the park, I sat waiting for rope drop. The sky was gray and a cold wind started to whip down Hollywood Boulevard. The CMs were bundled up in jackets and ponchos, like they knew some-thing. I wondered if this day might be cut short. Began crafting plan B in my head. I'd hit the essentials I came for right away and get back to base camp for lunch and a beer.

I noticed some strangely dressed younger guests. Kids wearing brown robes, sporting plastic cylinders at their sides. I knew student wizards hung out at the park across town, so this could only mean one thing—*Star Wars* nerds. All right, they were just kids having fun. As for the adults dressed the same way . . .

Star Tours—The Adventures Continue

I'm no sci-fi geek, but I admit I enjoy a few flicks from the genre. If I have a geeky guilty pleasure, it's super hero and comic book movies. If the choice is Star *anything* or Batman, Batman wins every time. Obviously. Sci-fi is fiction, Batman is real. Duh! Plus this is a Man's guide and most super heroes have *Man* right in their name. BatMAN! SuperMAN! AquaMAN! Okay, Aquaman forfeits. No movie—plus talking to fish is a lame superpower! Disney even owns Iron Man.

That said, I recognize if you're a man born any time after the mid-sixties, you were very likely affected by George Lucas's groundbreaking sci-fi epic, *Star Wars*.

In the early nineties, before Lucas decided to murder his own franchise, he and Disney teamed up to take his creation to the next level. They created an interactive cinematic thrill ride called *Star Tours*. Thanks to flight simulator technology, cinematic special effects, and a little Disney magic, guests could fly right into the *Star Wars* universe.

That was the eighties. Just like the flicks, the technology got dated, and then outdated. The ride was rough and the visuals grainy. So in 2010 they shut her down and went to work on a massive overhaul. New technologies and a host of new worlds from the *Star Wars* prequel films gave Imagineering and Lucas a new toy box to open up. The result: *Star Tours—The Adventures Continue*.

Say what you will about those prequels, the visual effects and imagery were about as amazing as it gets—pre-*Avatar* anyway! If the trench shot from the first (which is somehow the fourth) *Star Wars* made for a fun attraction, imagine a handful of sequences from the new films in mind-blowing 3-D. That's just what Disney did! Not only did they replicate one amazing simulation, they created a bunch! Every ride on *Star Tours 2.0* takes guests on a hyperspace ride to three different planets from the *Star Wars* universe. Each is randomly selected, each time the ride begins. That means there are endless combinations. (Okay, so there are actually like 50 or something. What am I, *M.I.T.*?!?) You can ride multiple times in a row and always have a different exciting experience. Not only do you visit exotic locations and have action-packed adventures, you'll even be visited by icons from *Lucasland*.

Some trips encounter Princess Leia, while others find themselves boarded by the deep space dark knight, Darth Vader. And of course, if you're really lucky, you might find yourself face-to-pointy-earred-face with the green galactic Gandhi himself, Yoda. The visuals are amazingly crisp. It literally looks like peering through a windshield at an army of Stormtroopers drawing down on your ship. Darth Vader *was* right outside our ship threatening to destroy us all. Not a filmed version. The *real* guy!

I mean, um . . . that is . . . of course, I know there's not really a . . . Whatever! You get what I'm saying!

Whatever your feelings toward the movies, you're going to be a fan of the ride. In fact, where for some the ride is a fun reminder of the film series, guys like us might be more tolerant of the flicks just to reminisce a little about the attraction.

One word of caution—I was serious when I cautioned against riding after a particularly big breakfast platter.

 The official Ears of Steel recommendation: *Star Tours* rules harder than the Emperor!

Man's Journal

Our shuttle prepared for takeoff and we were immediately surrounded by Stormtroopers. Always something! Then his royal *badassness*, Darth Vader, appeared in front of our ship, holding us from taking off with his magical kung-fu grip. Our shuttle began to sway from side to side trying to break free. That's when my bacon and eggs asked, *"What's this?"*

We broke free from his telekinetic grasp and light sped our asses out of Planet Dodge. Our first destination turned out to be the home planet of everyone's favorite space Sasquatch, Chewbacca. *Kashyyyk* (bless you) was a densely covered forest planet, very much like the one the dancing teddy bears lived on in the third, uh, sixth movie, *Return of the Jedi*. We were cutting through the forest, dodging trees, pulling evasive maneuvers against Stormtroopers on flying *crotch rockets!* I found myself focusing more on the motion-sickness bag in the seatback in front of me than on the action on screen. The ship lunged upward and the contents of my stomach started to breakdance! I had a dreadful vision of creating my own work on the screen, *Revenge of the Scrambled Eggs* or *The French Toast Menace*.

We zoomed toward a planet with the silent but deadly (heh, heh) infamous bounty hunter, Boba Fett on our six. To make our escape, we flew directly through an asteroid belt. Great maneuver for an already questionable stomach status. Up, down, blast giant space rock, fly right through blasted space rock (made perfect sense), and get knocked around by pieces of meteor. Thankfully we stopped blowing apart rocks before I blew chunks and we warped to safety. C-3PO landed our ship in some rebel base and I took a few deep breaths to squelch my own stomach's rebellion.

Lesson learned. Don't eat a big meal before hopping on *Star Tours* (or any other intense motion ride). The *Star Tours* janitorial staff and the riders in front of you appreciate your cooperation!

After saving the Universe (as usual) while riding *Star Tours*, true fans hoping to pass the light saber to their own heirs should check out **Jedi Training Academy**. In this interactive stage show, a handful of lucky younglings are given practice light sabers and taught to use the Force before a live audience. Their newfound skills are quickly put to the test when training is interrupted by Stormtroopers and

Darth Vader himself. (What's up with park security—this happens every day?!) The partial-man in black appears to recruit young talent for his evil army. Each young "Padwan" gets the opportunity to go toe-to-cyborg-toe with Vader. It's possibly the cutest nerdy thing you'll ever see. Just know if your kid really wants to be part of it (or you really want them to) get to the park early.

Remember those costumed kids I mentioned seeing before the park even opened? They were there to get on the list because that's how early they start taking names. It's a popular event, so don't sleep in. Or else risk waking up to a light saber at your throat!

After all that *Star Wars* talk, excuse me while I give myself a wedgie and stuff myself into a locker.

MuppetVision 3D

Since Hollywood Studios is somewhat maze-like, for lack of better directions make a left and cut around *MuppetVision 3D*. It's the big brick building with the Miss Piggy fountain and the yellow Kermit the Frog balloon on the roof. I grew up with the Muppets and this attraction is a nice piece of nostalgia. The 1980s 3-D is really dated and the picture is grainy, but it's still good for a few chuckles. I've watched it a couple of times and that's good enough. At least with the recent Muppet resurgence and a new movie out, your kids won't just stare at you wondering what's up with these weird puppets. There are also a number of hidden gags throughout the theater as you're waiting, so keep your eyes peeled.

 The official Ears of Steel recommendation: I won't say *MuppetVision* is an Ears of Steel absolutely do not miss, but check it out in the afternoon if the line is short.

Once you cross through the Streets of America backlot area (keep moving—nothing to see here till Christmas!), you will see a distant amphitheater and a sign that reads *Lights, Motors, Action!* Make a note; we are definitely coming back to it. Yes, I know. I said *motors!* Be patient. I want you to hit the high-traffic attractions first, no pun intended (all right, maybe a little). There's all day for the car show. First, you need to head back to the hotel. Not your hotel. The Hollywood Tower Hotel.

The Twilight Zone Tower of Terror

As you entered the park, hell when you were driving up, you no doubt saw that ominous monolithic tower on the horizon. That is the Hollywood Tower Hotel, home to our next destination, *The Twilight Zone Tower of Terror*. At first glance you might think, "One of those "droppy rides." You go up. You come down. Real scary. When I was *ten!* You've never been on a *droppy ride* like this! *Tower of Terror* is one of Disney's best examples of combining exciting rides with a thoughtful story and just enough terror to keep you wondering.

As you wind through the garden and approach the hotel, you find yourself slowly walking back in time. Surrounded by thick overgrown foliage, an old path leads through the garden as scratchy jazz floats along the air from some unseen gramophone. Suddenly you're not just a tourist, you're checking in as a hotel guest. Once inside the hotel lobby, it's eerily clear that something has gone awry. The hotel appears long abandoned, but it must have emptied quite suddenly. A mahjong game, still in progress, waits eternally for the next move. Tea cups, long cool, sit collecting dust on tables, their contents evaporated over decades. Cobwebs cover everything. Yet the music is still playing. A bellman appears and bids you follow him to the library. You know, if something weird is going down, it always seems to start in the library.

ꟿan's Journal

I followed the creepy bellboy to the library. Ironically, just as I was about to suggest he maybe get some sun (and eat a sandwich) everything went dark. An old television suddenly switched on. I was shocked. Black and white—in this day and age! There on the

screen appeared the master of suspense, mystery, and the macabre, Rod Serling. I assumed it was a TV Land marathon, but Rod
was speaking directly to us. Back in the twenties, the Hollywood
Tower Hotel was *the* place to stay in Los Angeles. One night lightning struck the building and four guests and a bellman were mys-
teriously zapped into the electrical system of the hotel. Now the
five of them haunt the tower, and this particular night I was invited
to enter an old service elevator, the only one still operational, and
take a ride into *the Twilight Zone.*

Do-do-do-doo, do-do-do-doo . . . !

Apparently there was no box for "Regrets" on Rod's invitation,
since we were ushered through a secret door. The other guests
and I were seated (this crazy hotel had seats in the elevators—only
in California) and strapped in. The bellman poked his head back
in to make sure we were all comfy and secure. How many floors
did this joint have, I wondered? The doors slid shut and we began
our ascent into madness. The elevator stopped on a random floor
and the doors opened. Things seemed normal albeit dimly lit.
Suddenly nothing seemed normal at all. The creepy voice of Rod
Serling returned telling us, in so many words, we were screwed!

The spirits of the departed guests from nearly a century ago
materialized at the end of the hall, beckoning us to join them.
The doors shut violently and up through the darkness we flew. It
was extremely disorienting. I had no clue how high we climbed.
We just kept going and going. The doors opened again and some
strange force pulled us forward into a much stranger part of the
hotel. This room was bathed in black light and looked like some
unfinished floor of the hotel. More important (and creepy) we
were surrounded by the shimmering silhouettes of those past unlucky visitors, looking much more ethereal. Eerie music played all
around as we were pulled forward, deeper into the unknown. All
at once, we stopped and things went dark. Very dark.

We were hurled upwards at unexpected speed before coming
to an abrupt stop, almost falling forward. The darkness opened up
and sunlight flooded the elevator. It took a second for my eyes to
adjust and see that we were high above the park. Down below,
little ant-like Hollywood Studios guests watched from the street,

pointing and grinning, waiting for the moment when the blood drained from our faces. And then that moment came.

While still processing the strange new view, the whole world fell away beneath my butt. Had we plummeted some distance before coming to a sharp halt once, it would've been heart-challenging. But the tower wasn't finished with us after just one drop. It toyed with us like a cat with a ball of yarn. We experienced momentary zero G's as we rocketed back up and then down again. Yet again we were staring out over the resort before dropping. Again and again. Up and down. Sometimes the fall was longer. Sometimes the rise. With each drop, I quietly prayed the ride was over. Unfortunately, by the time I reached the moment of religion, we were only halfway done. I began questioning the strength of the loose seatbelt. I looked around to see the other passengers' faces—so white they were practically transparent. Finally, the elevator slowed to a halt and retreated back into the bowels of the hotel. They could keep my deposit. I was checking out early!

Okay, so the plot of *Tower of Terror* may be a little thin, but it is Disney. They can only go so dark and scary. Still, there is something creepy about the entire attraction from the minute you enter the queue until you exit the building, like there are unseen Cast Members playing with a Ouija board in the break room.

 The official Ears of Steel recommendation: Man up and cross over to another dimension! This elevator's going down!

Rock 'n' Roller Coaster Starring Aerosmith

When *Tower* ends and you regain your wits, head back out to Sunset Boulevard and hang a right. You'll feel you've been catapulted from the golden age of Hollywood to modern-day L.A. and rock clubs like The Whiskey and The Viper Room! Cock your head to the right and you'll see a giant electric guitar. You'll hear a familiar soundtrack. Could be "Walk this Way" or "The Other Side" or "Dude Looks Like A Lady." There is no mistaking the shredding guitar of Joe Perry and those screeching vocals of Steven Tyler! Aerosmith is one of hardest rocking, hit making, *kicking life straight in the nuts* bands of the last four decades! Don't agree? Close this book and turn in your man card.

Steven Tyler qualifies for the seniors' discount at Denny's, yet he's the only man alive who can wear leopard print spandex and a feather boa and still leave the club with your girlfriend. There's no questioning his manhood—figuratively, and in some of those outfits *literally*! The only thing that might beat the excitement and energy of an Aerosmith concert is riding *Rock 'n' Roller Coaster Starring Aerosmith*!

R 'n' R is an indoor coaster, but also a hybrid, incorporating elements of a classic Disney dark ride and good old-fashioned rock 'n' roll! Not to mention that Magic Kingdom's *Space Mountain*, while really fun, is essentially just a wild mouse coaster. *Rock 'n' Roller Coaster* is a rocket-launched, upside down, twisting, turning, turbo-charged, hard-rocking experience!

ﬔan's Journal

I followed the signs for *Rock 'n' Roller Coaster* and somehow found myself walking the halls of **G Force Records**! Posters lined the walls featuring great classic rock bands. Of course, there were some teeny bopper artists I'd never heard of (on the Disney Channel . . . countless times . . . and downloaded to my iPod . . . *allegedly*). The walls thumped from some invisible baseline I was certain sounded like "Walk This Way." I was ushered into an observation room with some tour group and found myself staring into a pretty swanky recording studio. Oriental rugs covered the floor and lava lamps provided cool, dim mood lighting.

A group of guys were huddled across the room in the production booth. I peered to see better, thinking I was having one of those weird hallucinations they warned me might happen years down the road. No, it was Aerosmith! They were listening to the playback with an engineer. Why were they recording a song they'd already recorded 35 years prior? Hey, it was not for me to question rock 'n' roll deities like Tyler and Perry! As opposed to my daily questioning about the mysterious career of Tyler Perry!

Actually what you see across through those windows isn't the real live Aerosmith. In fact, those aren't windows at all. They're video screens making it appear that the band is a mere 30 feet from you. Pretty convincing too! They've been rehearsing before a big gig in downtown Los Angeles. The band's manager appears to usher them into their car and get them to the venue. But Steven and Joe and the boys won't leave until she makes arrangements for their devoted fans, us, to check out the show with V.I.P. access! She makes a quick call and arranges for a special car to be waiting in the alley. A stretch limousine in fact—a really big stretch!

Remember, here at Walt Disney World, it's all about story. You wind your way into the "alley" behind the building. Within a few minutes (ideally) your ride vehicle, designed to look like an old Cadillac limo, will arrive. Get in and stow your gear in the compartment in front of you, especially your Goofy hat and sunglasses. This one goes all the way around! I don't care what the circumference of your noggin is. Any headgear will be long gone by the time the ride ends.

Man's Journal

I boarded the craziest convertible I'd ever seen and we drove around the corner to the entrance to a tunnel. A DJ's voice came out of the headrest speakers saying Aerosmith was about to take the stage! This driver better hit the gas, I thought to myself. I don't like missing the opening number! Music began, the crowd erupted, and a countdown ticked away overhead. Countdown to what, I wondered? We were just sitting there. Suddenly a traffic light turned green. With little warning, the engine roared and we rocketed forward like a jet flung off an aircraft carrier. Steven Tyler's voice erupted in my ear. Normally I might belt out the lyrics along with him, but I'd left my voice at the tunnel entrance!

We blasted through a day-glo cartoon fantasy version of Hollywood, passing over, under, around, and through brightly colored icons of Los Angeles. All to a medley of live Aerosmith jams. I began to think I might have died on *Tower of Terror* and this could be Rock 'n' Roll Heaven!

Not surprisingly . . .

 The official Ears of Steel recommendation: Walk This Way to *Rock 'n' Roller Coaster* immediately, lest you want to be a Dude Who Looks Like A Lady!

Walt Disney: One Man's Dream

If you follow my lead, by this point you'll have hit the three biggest thrillers at Hollywood Studios. They could make even the most iron-willed daredevil squeal. If you've managed to conquer all three before lunch, you are definitely all man. The best part is now you can take your time and just enjoy the rest of the park. Hollywood Studios has a lot more leisurely paced fun to experience—even for a real man like you.

Being a real man isn't just about taking on dangerous, high-speed, sensory overloading rides and attractions. Real men respect history. We admire men of vision, determination, and courage. They are the men who made this country the great land it is. So you have to respect the man who made everything around you possible. Take the time during your visit to the Studios to check out *Walt Disney: One Man's Dream.*

A walk-through attraction, *One Man's Dream* is part museum exhibit, part tribute, showcasing the life and accomplishments of Walt Disney. You can do it as quickly or as methodically as you wish. It's not guided. It's not timed. I highly recommend it. You'll appreciate where you are even more.

Walt didn't live to see Walt Disney World, but it's because of every innovation he had the balls to conceive, even when told he couldn't or shouldn't, that the parks exist today. I won't get weird on you, but there is something about being in there. There's a little bit of magic seeing his actual school desk from 1912; seeing his real office reassembled and preserved like a shrine; knowing what dreams were conceived in that chair. Every man wishes that one day his desk or workbench will be just as revered.

You'll thank me for suggesting this exhibit. This time, don't skip the film at the end. I confess I only recently took my own advice. After seeing the archival footage and hearing the voice of Walt himself, I walked out of that theater feeling motivated to do something big, or at least something different. There is a Disney difference. If you're a man of bold vision, you'll get it. It took a real man to create all this. All right, I'll get off my soapbox. I got in your head, that's what matters. You'll just have to trust me.

Listen, I'm normally the last guy to suggest sitting for a show in a theme park. Not when there are roller coasters, thrill rides, and gigantic barbecued turkey legs nearby. What's that? Oh, I'm sorry. Did I not already mention the sweet, smoky, tender turkey legs as big as your forearm sold throughout the parks? Then it must be time for a . . .

Turkey Leg Tangent!!!

Lately I've noticed every carnival and fair sells turkey legs. But the first place I ever enjoyed one was at Walt Disney World. I tried one at our local County Fair once. I spit out the first bite and pitched the rest to the raccoons. It was heinous. A criminal offense to my taste buds. I was so pissed I tied the vendor to the Tilt-a-Whirl and punched a prize-winning sheep on my way out.

However, the barbecued turkey legs at Walt Disney World are amazing! I don't know that anyone would ever plan a trip just for these babies, but they're almost reason enough! They've become something of a staple snack at every Disney park, but I tasted my first one in the Studios. Theme park food is often hit or miss, but these ginormous drumsticks are a definite hit! Perfectly smoked, with a nice pinkish color, they taste more like pork than poultry. Drop one (or let's be honest, two) of these babies on my Thanksgiving plate and I'm a happy Neanderthal.

There was a time when a turkey leg constituted a "snack" and you could buy one with a snack credit from the Disney Dining Plan. Apparently someone in management wised up because that option has been removed. At nearly $10 bucks a leg, they may be the most expensive snack on property. Fortunately, it's a snack that eats like a meal. And let's be real, if you drove down the center of the park on a Harley, wearing a Viking helmet, smoking a cigar, with two Hooters waitresses on the back of the bike, you wouldn't look as manly as when your canines are ripping bird from bone, as nature intended! You'll feel like Henry the Eighth! Plus, no table required. You don't even need a plate. The bone is nature's handle. You can keep on walking while you eat; guaranteeing you won't miss out on any fun! If only more food came with a built-in utensil!

Now that I've got you salivating, back to Hollywood Studios! I mentioned this park has a less predictable layout than the others. In fact, it's a little screwy. If that's a "hub and spoke" layout the architect had in mind, he must have been nearsighted, farsighted, or drunk. I imagine it had more to do with the land itself, but it's far more fun to blame booze—I do it all the time! At Hollywood Studios the navigational rule is simple—when in doubt look for the big blue Sorcerer hat. That's the center from which you can find anything.

For some reason, the giant hat erected in the center of the park has a lot of haters. I've actually heard (firsthand) from an Imagineer that some of them even hate it, the complaint being the big wizard's cap doesn't fit the old Hollywood theme. It eclipses the replica Chinese Theater. Personally, I'd like my life to be so simple I could think about a giant hat that much! Like it or not, the hat has become the icon for the park. Look off to the distant horizon and you might notice a little water tower similar to those on old movie sets, but with Mickey ears. Called the Earful Tower, it was the original park icon back in the MGM-Studios days.

It's weak sauce. I'll take the big hat. I will admit it doesn't exactly jibe with the old Hollywood vibe. Still, it is from a movie made in 1940. At least the hat fits the pattern of Disney park icons—it's big, bright, and visible from space (or Google Earth). That puny water tower is hardly visible from a few feet away. The poor thing has icon envy! Either way, fans of the hat shouldn't worry. I was also told the foundations can't be so easily ripped up without major demolition and chaos, so the hat will probably be around a while. Haters can go climb the water tower, Gilbert Grape-style. (Ten points if you get that obscure movie reference!)

Toy Story Midway Mania!

After you've done the *Tower / Rock 'n' Roller Coaster* corridor on Sunset, head back toward the hat. You will see an archway that reads Animation Courtyard. Most people head straight for that arch. My advice: keep walking a few more feet until you see a set of unobtrusive stairs. They lead down to Mickey Avenue, but more importantly an overhang that reads PIXAR.

This is Pixar Place, home to the most recent addition to Disney's Hollywood Studios, *Toy Story Midway Mania!* Opened in 2008, *Midway Mania!* combines a little of every element that makes a great Disney attraction. It's a dark ride, sort of. It utilizes the latest interactive technology. It is entertaining for every member of the family. And it includes a state-of-the-art AA character.

This particular character is that sardonic spud, Mr. Potato Head! Portrayed in the *Toy Story* movies by Mr. Warmth himself, Don Rickles, this one is an incredible real life facsimile, right down to the attitude! The animatronic figure talks directly to guests, sings, whistles, even removes his parts. Potato Head is the sideshow barker of *Toy Story Midway Mania!*, greeting guests waiting in line! Well, greeting might not be the right word. It's an appropriate introduction to an attraction where guests play virtual carnival games, while whipping and whirling around in their ride vehicle! All, of course, themed to the *Toy Story* movies!

Guests wind through a giant replica of Andy's room straight out of the movies before boarding double-sided ride vehicles. Each rider puts on a pair of 3-D glasses and slides behind a cannon mounted on the dash. In olden days of carnivals past, cannons like this would have fired baseballs at plates. It's the same idea on *Midway Mania!* except the balls and plates are digital.

Your vehicle spins its way inside the attraction before quickly coming to a stop at the first game screen. Sheriff Woody appears and your job is simple—yank the cord on the cannon to blast away! After a few seconds, that game ends and off you spin in another direction to the next task. In total, the ride consists of six games. Mercifully, that first one is a practice round called the *Pie Throw Practice Booth.* Yank back on that cord and—you might have guessed it—virtual cream pies blast out at targets onscreen! Other games include *Rex & Trixie's Dino Darts,* in which your cannon fires darts at balloons, and the *Green Army Men Shoot,* which fires baseballs at plates, shattering them into digital oblivion. For every balloon burst or plate shattered you amass points. At the end you're even awarded a virtual prize for your effort. Sadly, you can't take 'em with you. They're not *that* three-dimensional.

Midway Mania! is one of the wildest, fastest-paced, entertaining attractions on property. It is also one of the most popular. Even though it's not new, it is still a ride you should make a beeline for early. As soon as the ride's over, go straight to the kiosks and get FASTPASSes to come back later. You will want to ride it again. Come afternoon, if you try to casually stroll up and hop on, good luck Space Ranger. You'll be in line for infinity and beyond! This is an attraction where I've seen FASTPASSes run out.

One reason *Toy Story Midway Mania!* has a strong re-rideability factor is that the set pieces are all digital. The attraction was barely three years old when Imagineering figured out that they could remove and replace games virtually overnight. *Rex & Trixie's Dino Darts* didn't exist until the summer of 2010, around the same time *Toy Story 3* hit theaters. With this new technology, an attraction refurb no longer means weeks or months of closures. A complete overlay can be accomplished in a matter of days and, someday, very possibly in hours.

 The official Ears of Steel recommendation: Be a Midway Maniac! It's a blast!

Some Dining Tips

So far, we've gone through four attractions on our virtual tour of Disney's Hollywood Studios. I hope you've still got room after your turkey leg because it's surely getting close to lunch time! DHS has a bunch of restaurants, and more than a couple would be acceptable picks for a hungry man like you. There's great fried chicken at fifties-themed Prime Time Café and you can pull up a buffet at Hollywood and Vine. But the coolest restaurant in the park and the best spot for a guy to grab some grub is **Sci-Fi Dine-In Theater Restaurant**.

Again with the long-winded literal names! The food is good, but you eat at Sci-Fi for the experience! Once inside, you'll find yourself *outside*. Numerous booths disguised as old cars are parked under a night sky and face a large drive-in movie screen. The feature is a montage of old black-and-white B-movie trailers. It's a great place to grab a milkshake, burger and rings, or even Sci-Fi's famous cola ribs. Hey, while you're there, why not have a cocktail or four? You may be in a car, but you're not driving anywhere!

Since you're reading the book I wrote, you obviously know I fancy myself a writer. I'm also something of a coffee fiend, as are many of us guys. It's the fuel that kickstarts our internal engines every morning (and in some cases afternoon and evening as well). So I'd be remiss if I didn't mention a little spot just next door to Sci-Fi. In fact, it's attached! It's a tiny little coffee shop and bookstore called **The Writer's Stop**.

Florida or not, sometimes you need a steamy pick-me-up! You can grab a little dessert, too, if you need something to tide you over till your next feeding. If you pop in at a quieter moment, there are comfortable easy chairs where you can sip a little Joe, browse through a book, wolf down a cookie or pastry, and just mentally regroup. It's not a ride or a show, but I wouldn't write a book about Walt Disney World without giving it a paragraph. Who knows, maybe one day you'll see my name on the shelves in there. Right, who am I kidding?!?

Okay, back to the attractions.

The Legend of Captain Jack Sparrow

With the humongous success of the *Pirates* movies and Jack Sparrow's seven-seas-spanning mojo, it had to be hard to contain Pirate fever to one land in one park! So in late 2012, somewhat out of the blue, Disney opened a new attraction featuring a familiar face, eyeliner and all—*The Legend of Captain Jack Sparrow*!

Initially, the web was abuzz, billing it as simply another boring "walk-through" attraction featuring props from the movies. This prediction wasn't completely off base since in the past, in the same location, walk-through attractions based on the Narnia movies had been opened then quickly forgotten. Even I, a diehard *Pirates* fan, brother of the sea and aficionado of rum, found the prospect of this being an exciting attraction dubious.

Listen up, ye scurvy dogs! I was wrong and I admit it. I really liked *The Legend of Captain Jack Sparrow*! The adventure begins when your group approaches the doors to Jack Sparrow's secret cavern hideout. This uncharted trove is where he stashes the spoils from his life of shivering timbers and buckling swashes (or is it swashing buckles?). First, however, you must get through the heavy doors outside, over which hangs an ominous skull and crossbones. Some phantom electricity dances across the doorframe and suddenly illuminates the skull, which, since I'm not aware of any official name, I'll just call Roger . . . as in *Jolly*? I'll wait.

Before you can enter Jack's cave, you'll have to swear an oath before Roger. Once he's satisfied you won't be giving away the location to the Royal Navy, the doors open and in you file. Fans of the movies will certainly see the similarities to Ship Wreck Cove, featured in the third installment. It's a cave, but along with treasure and relics, there are random pieces of ships surrounding you. Including the bow of Jack's own vessel anchored before you. Yes, in the cave. One side apparently opens to the sea. Listen, if you're going to over-think it we'll just stop. Have another swig of rum and let's move on. Once you're all in and the doors are sealed, who should reappear, this time floating in the sky before you, but old Roger. He informs you that you'll be put through a battery of tests to see if you're worthy to join Captain Jack's crew. Based on some of the crew members we've seen, I wasn't too nervous about said tests. That is until the skeleton pirates started appearing all around us, crawling up over the rocks, appearing like shadows out of the walls, even on the ceiling (though I'm still not sure that's intentional). We were surrounded. Fear not, matey! With the help of a magic key—quietly handed off to one lucky child in the audience before the show—and a rousing chant of "send those bones to Davey Jones," the boney buccaneers are banished back to the netherworld from whence they came!

Hope you've got a piratical nerve because you barely have a moment to catch your breath before ol' Captain Sushi-face, Davey Jones, appears . . . well, his ship does and we hear the cursed calamari summon his gargantuan cephalopod, the Kraken! Steel your nerve as those wormy, squirmy tentacles rise before your very eyes as if they might wrap around the entire cave and rip us all out of the earth and into the sea! Actually, it turns out this beastie's not as hard to put down as you might think. Its mucus is far worse than its bite. All we have to do is roar right back at the Kraken and it shrivels and oozes back into the sea. Captain Jack might have appreciated that information in a previous adventure. With the Kraken gone, we're left to face one more test, another from the sea, but far more attractive. A pale angelic mermaid appears and tries to ensnare us with her siren song. Soon more of her sisters begin swimming all around us. On the rocks and walls . . . but let's not overthink it. Once again, the solution is simple. Like stamping out slugs on a rainy afternoon, all one needs to do to survive a mermaid ambush is stomp your feet hard. Probably more effective if you're not wearing flip-flops.

The tests are over but the danger is far from gone. Davey Jones returns, and this time Roger decides we, being a bit green as pirate crews go, might need a bit more experienced leadership. He summons the master of the ship, the clown prince of plundering, the heat-stroked, hedonistic pirate himself, Captain Jack Sparrow. Before our very eyes, Captain Jack appears on the deck of the ship. And this is no imposter from Adventureland, nor is it Penelope Cruz—although that would've been nice! This is the real deal—that pirate straight from Jump Street himself, Johnny Depp. And I'm not talking about recycled dialogue or scrapped footage from the movies. This is original Jack Sparrow material. I won't give away any more of the adventure, but as usual, Jack saves the day in his own eccentric, almost accidental way.

Honestly, I loved this attraction. Is it up there in my Top 10? No. It's a little silly and the initial projection effects of the skeletons and mermaids are a bit sketchy. It doesn't help when the Kraken's tentacles stretch higher than the walls and disappear against the soundstage ceiling. Still, I found myself having a blast! You're surrounded by pirate-ness! If they'd handed out tankards of rum punch on the way in, I'd probably never leave! More importantly, let me tell you here and now, when Johnny Depp appears in full Captain Jack regalia just a few feet above you, it's mind-blowing. I know it's just a really amazing projection, but that's the point—it's amazing! Any minor issues earlier in the experience are rendered irrelevant. You might really step up to join the crew. Not to mention, he's so dreamy!

Wait, . . . what? I didn't type that, right? Anyway, I know there was trepidation among hardcore fans when this attraction opened. It was all for naught. *The Legend of Captain Jack Sparrow* is a good time. The only caveat I'll place here is that the audience has a great deal of influence over the experience. Since it is so interactive, you get what you give. Allow yourself to have fun. Resolve to get loud and rowdy before you pass under that floating skull. You will have a blast as will everyone around you. On one visit, I got stuck with a group comprised mostly of Brazilian tourists who had no idea what was happening and they stared ahead quietly like they were picking out wallpaper. Still, being a boisterous, and some might say boorish, loudmouth from Chicago, I whooped and hollered like I was selling sausages at Wrigley Field!

 The official Ears of Steel recommendation: Ye come to Walt Disney World seeking adventure and salty ol' pirates . . . so don't pass up this one!

Lights, Motors, Action! Extreme Stunt Show

Live theater can be a controversial subject among guys. It should come as no surprise that Disney's Hollywood Studios features a number of live shows. Generally, live productions in amusement parks are not for me. Even at Disney I tend to avoid them. If there's anything I have less interest in than a theme park stage production, it's a theme park stunt show. However, this *is* Disney and they make every experience better than the norm. As Walt would say, they *plus it*!

There are two shows here I can recommend without feeling like I just said "I've got orchestra seats to the ballet!" The first is almost a no-brainer. The title alone secures its place as a real man's show. It's a large-scale automotive stunt spectacular called *Lights, Motors, Action! Extreme Stunt Show!*

Remember those cool three-dimensional, die-cast car play sets you had as a kid? If you've got a son, you probably have more advanced, highly detailed versions in your living room right now. Imagine if someone built a scale action set for playing with real cars! That's what *Lights, Motors, Action* looks like! Located in the northeast corner of the Studios is an enormous amphitheater. It is recommended that you get there a good 30 minutes before the show as it's bleacher seating. In slower months like September through early November, there should be no problem getting a good spot closer to the start time. Not to mention it's a huge set. There aren't that many bad seats. In fact, this is a theater where you may not want the front row. High up in the center provides a full panoramic view, and there's a lot to see in this show!

The backdrop is a seaside Mediterranean plaza straight out of an Ian Fleming novel. Whoops, sorry. A James Bond film! Better? Although with all these compact cars bombing through the cobblestone streets, it reminds me more of the awesome underrated De Niro flick, *Ronin*. The attraction begins with a video montage of great car chases and crashes from the movies. Not surprisingly, more than a few have the name Michael Bay attached. Shortly after, a truck rigged with cameras and film equipment appears on set with our Director. He quickly explains we are on the set of a new action movie taking place in the south of France.

That's about all the story set-up you need. It's easy to get caught up in this premise, especially if you realize that when it opened, the park was a working Disney studio. The plot of this particular blockbuster is irrelevant. Especially once the motors start revving and the show bursts into a cavalcade of cars—speeding, squealing, jumping, nearly crashing, guns shooting, stuntmen falling, motor bikes zooming all over the joint! It's an automotive adrenaline booster for any car junkie!

While we don't know who the star of this epic is, there is a celebrity appearance by Mr. Speed himself, Lightning McQueen, of the *Cars* movies! A life-sized Lightning McQueen cruises around the set, preening for the crowd until his buddy Tow Mater appears onscreen to warn of an evil European spy car (a Gremlin—the worst kind) spotted in the vicinity. With the help of Special Agent Mater and the shouts of the audience, McQueen thwarts the dubious hatchback and saves the day.

All the action, noise, and impressive stunts are incredibly fun and will entertain any guy! Plus the drivers actually pull back the curtain ... er, garage door, and reveal how each stunt is accomplished. They even open up some of the stunt cars to show you the special mechanics and fabrications that create the real movie magic. Basic Hollywood tricks were revealed that I'd never known. *Lights, Motors, Action!* might change the way you watch that next summer blockbuster. You can garble through a mouthful of popcorn that you "know how they did that!" I'm sure your wife will be super impressed.

If *LMA* sounds cool to you, get your butt to Walt Disney World soon! While there's been no official announcement, rumors are swirling that the Mediterranean village has a date with the wrecking ball! The scuttlebutt is that Cars Land, which was an instant hit at Disneyland will be cloned at Hollywood Studios. The area where the *LMA* amphitheater sits will likely be a prime spot for *Radiator Springs*! Of course, Cars Land is an entire themed land tailor-made for guys (come on, it has Car in the title), but it will be a slight bummer to lose this show.

I've also read a number of Internet fan boys and heard geeky podcasters verbally tear *Lights* to shreds. They say it's boring watching cars do stunts and learning about how stunt vehicles work. To them I can only say, I'm sorry. Sorry it's about something that's actually cool—***cars***! Sorry they didn't build an attraction where you can play World of Warcraft, eating hot pockets, and posting snarky comments about attractions real men dig! If that's what you want, just stay in your mother's basement!

 The official Ears of Steel recommendation: This is top gear entertainment!

Indiana Jones Stunt Spectacular!

Past the other end of Streets of America, near *Star Tours*, there is another, smaller amphitheater that looks a little older and more exotic, not unlike the shelter for *Jungle Cruise* at Magic Kingdom. This is the *Indiana Jones Stunt Spectacular!* I'm not going to say Dr. Jones *isn't* a good excuse to get off your feet in the afternoon. It's a fun way to relive some of those classic scenes featuring everyone's favorite butt-kicking archaeologist. There's even some pretty suspenseful use of an airplane, complete with working propellers. It's certainly a show designed for dudes based on a movie for dudes. It's another Ears of Steel: "If there's time or your feet hurt, see it."

Just know, while you're losing half an hour or more watching Indy, I'm getting on another ride. Once again, it comes down to preference.

Fantasmic!

Before you end your day at Disney's Hollywood Studios, there is one more live theatrical experience that receives a great deal of praise and is undeniably popular. If I didn't at least present it in this book, I'd probably receive an Everest-sized pile of hate mail. The show in question is called *Fantasmic!*

Fantasmic! is a nighttime spectacular presented in its own custom-built outdoor amphitheater cleverly hidden in an obscure part of DHS property. You won't see it from the park, and yet it's pretty humongous. In fact the set looks like a sharp, craggy mountain not unlike *Big Thunder Mountain* at Magic Kingdom. It's surrounded by a wide moat that completely circles the stage. I like to think that as well as being used during the show, this river helps keep would-be spelunkers from exploring the set. When the sun goes down and the show begins it is a cavalcade of characters. For that alone it is a favorite of families whose little ones can see all their favorites appearing together in this theatrical extravaganza. The basic storyline is simple: Mickey Mouse falls asleep and awakens in a dream world where he has to battle some of the baddest Disney villains. Or perhaps in this case, villainesses.

Some scenes might freak out the short humans in your pack. There's a giant day-glo python that slithers in and out of the mountain intent on devouring our favorite mouse. Of course, the set is pretty far from the audience, but that sight could still be the stuff of toddler nightmares. Not to mention a fire-spewing dragon trying to fry little Mick to a crisp. Come to think of it, the things I'd caution those of you with kids about are probably the manliest features of the show! We don't often see the main mouse in such peril.

Of course, in the end . . . **SPOILER ALERT** . . . the Mouse triumphs and evil is once again vanquished, at least until the next show. The big finale is a water pageant . . . sorry, water parade (real men don't watch pageants) where some of the biggest (and even a few obscure) Disney characters float by on decorative barges to a medley of Disney tunes, while classic animated feature scenes are projected on screens formed by walls of water. *Fantasmic!* is a very popular way to end a day at the parks. In fact, I dare say it rivals the nightly fireworks at Magic Kingdom, which at this point have become an institution.

As a man, I'm torn on *Fastasmic!* As I said, there are some cool, man-centric elements that you'll really like. But it gets a little long and, at the risk of stepping on some fans' Crocs-wearing toes, *Fantasmic!* is primarily for kids. It is fun once, for the most part, but there's not much reason to see it over and over. Shh. Did you hear that? It was the sound of a thousand fairies falling to Earth.

Show aside, getting in and out of that theater can be a nightmare. *Fantasmic!* only runs a few nights a week, giving many guests a sense of urgency that they better see it. The trick works, as it's often packed and you're herded like cattle, shoulder to sweaty shoulder, into the amphitheater and out again after. It can be slow going and frustrating, especially if you're claustrophobic (or just don't like other humans).

Plus, the theater is mostly first-come-first-sit bleacher seating. But as I said, the show is extremely popular. Ninety minutes before show time, people are waiting to storm the gates. Thankfully, I will mention one solution to this problem that will make *Fantasmic!* a more enjoyable experience. There are *Fantasmic!* Dining Packages where you get to dine in one of a couple restaurants in Disney's Hollywood Studios, including The Hollywood Brown Derby and 50's Prime Time Café. After the meal, you are entitled to sit in a special reserved section of the theater. Knowing I won't have to wage a battle of my own to get a seat for the show puts me in a much more pleasant frame of mind. Certainly it will let me enjoy the production considerably more!

 The official Ears of Steel recommendation: See *Fantasmic!* at least once, but definitely book the dinner package for the reserved seating first!

So there you have the best attractions for a real man at Disney's Hollywood Studios! When I first visited DHS way back when, I wasn't sure there was enough to warrant a whole day. I thought it was all Dorothy and the Tin Man stuff. Don't get me wrong, that's all there too. Yet I soon found it was closing time and I was still having a blast. Follow my lead and you can avoid the road of yellow bricks (yet easily find it too—hey, I won't tell!). Many guests say the Studios is their *second* favorite park. It may not rank that high on the Ears of Steel list, but it's definitely a great place to spend a day!

Like the Muppets said, life's like a movie. Let your vacation be like one too!

CHAPTER NINE

Disney's Animal Kingdom

REAL MEN GET IT ANIMAL STYLE!

ow many times have you had to blow a day off schlepping your kids around the local zoo? Don't get me wrong, I love animals. Many zoos do a great job caring for and presenting exotic animals. But how many times can you watch a polar bear tossing around an empty beer keg in a concrete moat? At least have the decency to give him a full one—and a big straw!

Courageous men crave the adventure of the jungle. Real men are drawn to creatures that exude strength and power and sharp pointy things! Especially more exotic predators like lions, tigers, and crocs!

Walt Disney loved animals. He practically invented the modern-day animal documentary with his *True Life* series. Walt had a passion for making their strange and fascinating lives accessible to Americans. When designing Disneyland, Walt wanted an attraction that incorporated wild animals, where guests could have real up-close encounters. As is often the case, the logistics were daunting, especially given the unpredictability of living creatures. How could park staff make sure animals would always be visible and active? It was decided to rely on that invention that would become synonymous with Disney attractions, Audio-Animatronics. Robotic animals took the place of live beasts, guaranteeing guests would always walk away entertained and satisfied (and uneaten). Today, *Jungle Cruise* with its mechanical wildlife is a popular attraction both in Anaheim and Orlando. But Disney never abandoned the dream of incorporating living animals into a theme park.

It wasn't until the late nineties that Walt's dream was finally realized, in a way even he could not have imagined! In 1998, the gates to a fourth theme park were opened at the Walt Disney World Resort, Disney's Animal Kingdom, or DAK for short.

Not simply a zoo and not just another theme park, Animal Kingdom took the best of both, pushing the envelopes of technology, entertainment, and even eco-tourism beyond anything they'd achieved before. Nature is the theme, and it shows (and grows) over everything. Animal Kingdom is the most organic, natural-feeling park in all of Walt Disney World despite how technologically advanced it is. Even where a giant steel roller coaster stands, so much lush greenery and natural landscape (real and created) surrounds it, you would believe the tracks themselves sprouted from the earth.

Clearly, I'm a huge fan of this park. Not because I hear The Kink's "Apeman" running through my head every time I'm there. Okay, not *only* because of that. I love animals, and, yes, I love thrill rides. This park has both. But there's something intangible, even, if I may use a 30-point Scrabble word, *ethereal* about it. This park is my Eden. My Shangri-La. I can't really explain but, since you paid for the book, I'll try. The true theme of this theme park is nature and our place within it. Yes, I know. I'm drifting into tree-hugging, Birkenstock-wearing, granola-munching territory here. But a real man knows that the preservation of our way of life includes the preservation of our environment and all that play a part therein. As we take, we should be giving back or else we're screwed. Or something. So where do warthogs, gorillas, and roller coasters play into that message? Honestly, I'm not entirely sure but it sounded pretty good, didn't it?

Animal Kingdom has been branded by some nerds in their parents' basements (i.e. bloggers and podcasters) with the nasty moniker of "*half-day park.*" In other words, a park you hit in the morning before the sun's really blazing, see and do the best parts, and get back to the hotel for an after-lunch swim. I call *bullshit* on this thinking. Or lack of. Anyone who calls Animal Kingdom a half-day is a half-wit. Disney's created another world inside those gates. There is so much to see, do, and experience that I could (and have) spent entire days in this park. I'm never ready to leave when they shut off the lights. I dare say DAK is the perfect vacation experience. There is the high-adventure, kinetic-attractions aspect of it with amazing thrill rides. At the same time, there's the quiet, Zen-like spirit of the park. For instance, you can just sit and watch a family of gorillas interacting in as close to their natural environment as most of us will ever get to see.

Watch tigers at play and see how close to you they really are. No bars. No chatty guides (unless you ask). I literally once spent an hour just watching four tigers lounging around the simulated ruins inside the *Maharaja Jungle Trek*. It was mesmerizing. I think my blood pressure went down 20 points. After a while, it became unclear who was observing who. They almost grew a playful grin as they stared back. All the while, I understood that a simple foot of concrete, give or take, is the difference between which of us is the dominant species. It was beautiful, humbling, and I dare say spiritual.

Disney's Animal Kingdom is laid out along the lines of Magic Kingdom, just with a helluva lot more trees! When viewed from above, there's a central hub from which a series of themed lands branch out like spokes on a wheel. However, in this case that hub, Discovery Island, is surrounded by manmade rivers that look as though they've flowed for eons. Discovery Island is reached by bridge from the main gate and is connected to multiple bridges leading guests into the different worlds. Another major difference you might notice on park maps is the vast size. All three other Disney parks could just about fit inside Animal Kingdom. Animal Kingdom is a beast in its own right. It has to be. It houses a functional savannah, which hosts running safari tours. That requires a lot of land, not only to give the animals space to exercise, but for management to exercise enough control that guests never see lions picking gazelle out of their teeth.

As opposed to a castle or some other obvious manmade structure, Animal Kingdom needed a strong central icon that represented the natural world. A giant animal statue was problematic as the question becomes *what animal?* The park is home to wildlife from Africa, India, and Asia, as well as North America. What they came up with instead is an astounding work of art and an engineering marvel now as recognizable as Cinderella Castle (or the giant Epcot golf ball!)—*The Tree of Life*, a 14-story, 50-foot-wide tree, its trunk and branches adorned with hundreds of animal species from all over the world. The tree is so gargantuan its base is actually the framework of a deep-sea oil rig. Being fitted to withstand the pressures of the ocean made it perfect for standing up to tropical winds and hurricanes in Florida.

There is no way to describe the *Tree* in words. It's just straight-up impressive—another perfect example of how Disney combines engineering and craftsmanship to create something amazing. You could spend hours slowly circling the tree trying to spot every different critter intricately carved into the bark. Even then I'd bet you wouldn't see them all. Of course, as you circled, you'd also be constantly bumping into other park guests because the path around *The Tree of Life* is also the queue for an attraction hidden *inside* its root system.

It's Tough to be a Bug!

Disney shares the philosophy of most real men that if you've got empty space, you've got wasted space! Top brass realized that inside that oil rig framing was a big empty space just ripe for one more attraction to draw people in. Anything they built inside the tree had to feel organic, had to fit the story. What lives within the roots of a tree? Bugs! Around that time, Disney was prepping the release of their second collaboration with a little computer animation studio called Pixar. Serendipitously, that was *A Bug's Life*!

Thus was born the "4-Dimensional" film experience, *It's Tough to be a Bug!* I know you're probably wondering how a cartoon about bugs is a manly attraction. Okay, on its face it wouldn't seem like it. But the 3-D animation is top notch and the humor is completely guy level! The audience has been shrunk down to bug size to see a live show hosted by Flick, the ant star of *A Bug's Life*. It is a showcase of super heroes of the insect world, showing off their highly evolved methods of defense. It's way more entertaining than a *National Geographic* special. There's a termite that spews acid out of its snoot, and be careful because you might catch splatter! A mighty stink bug lives up to its name, ripping a nasty fart over the audience. (Disney Imagineers just *looove* their smell effects!)

Speaking of backdoor blasting, watch out for the tarantula shooting spikes out of her derrière. She does a little target practice over the audience, and you will feel it! Of course, it's not all fun and flatulence. Not all bugs are fans of humans. Hopper, the evil ant-squashing grasshopper makes an appearance in the form of a fully articulated life-size animatronic. If you've got small cubs, this is where things can get a little dicey. Hopper hates people and makes it known. His tirade is loud and menacing, but when he sics his spider army and hornet minions on the audience, pull the little ones onto your lap. I've seen parents have to scramble out with completely freaked-out tots on many occasions. In fact, you might want to scoot onto the edge of the bench yourself. You see the spider attack coming from above. You don't see the hornets. You feel them. If you're prone to a bad back (from a lot of manly heavy lifting, of course), sit closer to the lip. You've been warned. That said, check this one out!

 The official Ears of Steel recommendation: Minor scares aside, the animation is cool and vivid and, more importantly, you'll laugh your spike-shootin' butt off!

Flame Tree Barbecue

The Tree and *It's Tough to be a Bug!* are the obvious "big draws" of Discovery Island, but there's a third reason to linger around the area. I dare say it's an attraction in its own right! Especially if you're hungry. Scratch that! Even if you're not hungry when you get there, you will be the minute that smoky aroma soothes its way into your nostrils. I'm sure some brainiac could point out the irony of a visiting a park dedicated to conservation and ripping into a rack of ribs. And I'd smack him in the jaw. There's some primal connection between the lush green jungle atmosphere and the smell of animal flesh roasting over glowing embers. Welcome to Flame Tree Barbecue!

Look who just perked up! That's right, I said B-A-R-B-E-C-U-E! Right inside Disney's Animal Kingdom—and it's good, too! So good in fact that there have been times when I've found myself in another park, realized I was hungry, and left what I was doing to catch the shuttle to Animal Kingdom just for a half-slab and a cold beer. Oh yeah, they have their own beer too!

Flame Tree sits on the edge of Discovery Island just before the DinoLand U.S.A. bridge. You can spot it by the coral-colored sign with the brightly painted animal carvings. But a blind man could find the place with only his olfactory senses to guide him. Flame Tree is a counter service dining option. The pink, teal, and I'm guessing burnt umber (thank you, Crayola super set) building up front is where you order and pick up your grub (probably a bad choice of words after *It's Tough to be a Bug!*). There are three dining areas around the corner, both outdoors but with plenty of covered tables should a 10-minute monsoon roll in. Be warned, both sides are teeming with avian moochers! Ducks and birds of various plumages wander freely around your ankles waiting for a fry to fall. You're not supposed to feed them. Not intentionally anyway. I've seen diners firmly rebuked for slipping scraps to a long-beaked beggar. Not to mention, birds are dumb. They can't tell where French fry ends and finger begins. I've seen (and sadly sat with) people who've gotten nipped. Plus, if you order chicken and try feeding it to a bird, that's weird and wrong.

The menu is simple. When the food is good why complicate things? You can get a half-slab of ribs, half a smoked chicken, a smoked pork sandwich, or a smoked turkey sandwich (for dieters I guess). If you're like me, you're thinking, "Why no full slab? Me hungry!" Trust a fellow big eater, the half slab is plenty. Especially on the Disney Dining Plan. The entrees come with Flame Tree's bbq baked beans and a corn muffin (which is great for dipping in the beans and a little sauce). And, like all counter service meals on the plan, you get a dessert. I get the chocolate mousse parfait (yes, real men eat mousse on occasion . . . and moose, on occasion too). I'm usually so full I can barely finish it. I do finish it, of course, but I actually have to breathe between spoonfuls. The sole negative against Flame Tree is that fries and onion rings are a la carte. But even though they're an extra expense, one basket is enough for two people to split—as long the other person understands the *king* gets the lion's share! The rings at Flame Tree are excellent. Thick cut onion with delicious golden brown beer batter, not those crumbly breaded fast food onion rings. They're the right amount of greasy— won't upset your stomach, just give you a healthy, shiny coat! I finished off a basket by myself along with my ribs and beans. And you wonder why I had a little trouble with dessert?

Forget all the poultry options. The star of the show is the ribs. I admit, even at Disney it is surprising to find good ribs in a theme park—tender juicy pink meat with smoky bark that just peels off the bone. They serve them with minimal barbecue sauce (preferred among these modern urban yuppie barbecue fans). Personally, if ribs don't dreadlock my beard with barbecue sauce, I'm not interested. Fortunately, the condiment station has plenty of extra sauce (and napkins . . . whatever those are). Just don't choose a white shirt the day you visit Animal Kingdom. It may lead to the unplanned purchase of a new souvenir T-shirt! I speak from experience. An acceptable sacrifice to the barbecue gods. After you've sucked the last bone clean of any sauce or sinew, wash it down with DAK's own Safari Amber. Even the beer is jungle-themed!

Brewed for Disney by Anheuser-Busch (pay no attention to that other animal-themed park with Busch in the name), Safari Amber can be found on tap at multiple locations around the park. It's a beautiful amber brew with a sweet, malty, caramel flavor. I'm no beer snob but I definitely place this on the high end of theme park refreshments. Every Safari Amber I've ever ordered (and I've ordered a few) has been ice cold! That is a definite plus on a Florida afternoon. In fact it should be a law!

However, I have one major beef—mmm, beef—with Flame Tree Barbecue. Shortly after the park opens you can smell that sweet smoke on the air. But the brightly hued shutters of Flame Tree will stay cruelly shuttered until 11:00 a.m. I guess it could be considered a good thing. Gives you an excuse to hit some hardcore thrills and hang out with some serious meat-eaters before the lines get too long. That ought to work up a ravenous appetite.

Expedition Everest

If you're still with me, then we've established you're an adrenaline junkie with no fear of high speeds or extreme heights. How about travelling backwards, complete darkness, and hulking, hairy mythic monsters? Upon entering Animal Kingdom, you'll notice a strange sight. Rising high above the dense tropical greenery is an ominous, snow-capped mountain. If you think that's mysterious, you ain't seen nothin' yet. Follow the signs to Asia (or cut through DinoLand if the crowds are light and you're not easily distracted by shiny objects) and make your way to that mountain. Get ready to embark on *Expedition Everest*, a roller coaster like no other.

Erected in 2006, Disney's Forbidden Mountain stands over 200 feet tall. Visible from miles away, Everest eclipses the park's mighty tree. I was down at the World when *Expedition Everest* was just a steel skeleton. Even in its bare form, it was an impressive engineering marvel! It was obvious that riding this high-speed attraction would require a brass set. A high-speed roller coaster disguised as a Tibetan tea train runs up, down, across, and around the mountain. And I didn't even know then it would also go *backwards!* The design called for nothing short of an engineering miracle. Of course, that's what Disney Imagineering produces on a regular basis.

You may be wondering what a frozen mountain in Nepal has to do with wild animals. That is a good question. In lore, Everest is home to the guardian of the mountain, the Yeti. A legendary apelike creature, this abominable snow creature is believed by the Nepalese to reside in Everest's snowy peaks. The fact that the Yeti has not, to date, been proven to exist doesn't really matter. Animal Kingdom was built to pay tribute to all animal life, alive, extinct, and imagined. Imagined? Huh?

Turn the hands of time back to the 1990s, when Animal Kingdom was still being conceptualized. There were six proposed lands.

Five of them, Discovery Island, Asia, Africa, DinoLand U.S.A., and Rafiki's Planet Watch were indeed built and can be visited today. The sixth land, and what might have been the most exciting, was to be called Beastly Kingdom.

Beastly Kingdom was to be a tribute to that last genus—animals of myth, lore, and pure fantasy. Within the borders of Beastly Kingdom, guests would encounter magnificent creatures such as fairies, mermaids, dragons, unicorns, and such. The land itself was to be separated into two distinct themes—good and evil. On the good side, guests would enjoy the family-friendly attraction *Quest for the Unicorn*. A sort of maze/scavenger hunt type . . . whatever! This is a book for men. The good side doesn't sound like a place we'd want to hang around very long. Not by choice, anyway. I doubt they planned on serving Safari Amber on the "Good Side."

Looming over the evil side would be the roller coaster *Dragon Tower*. Whisking guests through the charred remains of a castle after a dragon attack, it would ultimately bring them face-to-face with the scaly invader. That sounds like a pretty kickass ride! Sadly, as you've gathered, it didn't happen. I only bring it up because a few years later, a particular theme park across town opened its own dragon coaster, reportedly designed by former Imagineers let go when Beastly Kingdom was scrapped. For the record, that ride kicks multiple levels of ass. Even the queue area was an attraction, winding through a castle sacked by dragons. Sound familiar?

That particular attraction still exists but it's been re-themed to fit a large magical movie franchise. Still, it's a sad reminder of what could have been at Disney. The proposed site for Beastly Kingdom is now called Camp Minnie-Mickey, a sub-land, if you can even call it that, geared toward younger children. There's not much there other than the wildly popular live show *Festival of the Lion King*.

There's a popular saying that "no good idea ever really dies" at Disney. So although Animal Kingdom's gates have been open for more than 15 years without Beastly Kingdom, there's always a glimmer of hope, false or not, that it may rise one day. Even now there are shadows of the mysterious land all over the park. Animal Kingdom's official logo features, among other species, a dragon. Over one set of gates at the park's entrance is a sculpted dragon's head. In some ways, another echo of Beastly Kingdom could be *Expedition Everest* and its brutish, hauntingly lifelike animatronic Yeti.

Or so we'd have thought. If the high cost of building such creatures in the modern theme park gives executives pause, imagine the bills to fix 'em! Throughout, *Everest* riders catch glimpses of and clues to the presence of something up there in those snowy peaks. Strange footprints. Haunting bellows from the caverns. Entire sections of track ripped and bent from the frozen rock, a feat requiring unimaginable brute strength. Then there's the moment a monstrous shadow appears on a rock wall before you, indicating someone or something is perched just above. The thing rips up more track with a ferocious roar then bounds off down the mountain.

The original finale for *Expedition Everest* was to bring you whizzing (not in your pants, necessarily) past the snarling, hairy, snotty, musty Yeti as he swung his oak-like arms at your train. To accomplish this, Disney Imagineers built the most complex (translate that to expensive) AA character to date. The problem is, when you build what we imagine is a life-size abominable snowman out of steel, hydraulics, foam, carpets of dreadlocked hair, a built-in slobber machine (I made that last one up), you're creating a lot of weight and putting untold stress on the foundation. To make it work, the Yeti had to be built on his own concrete foundation reaching all the way to the ground, with the mountain built around him—another amazing marvel of Disney engineering.

As is often the case with monsters, things went awry. While Disney hasn't exactly been forthcoming with details, the Yeti quickly went from a living, breathing predator heightening the danger and thrills to a very expensive piece of furniture. The Internet is loaded with rumors of what went wrong. Most agree the weight of the swinging Yeti cracked his own foundation and his arm function was shut off to prevent further damage to the attraction. Whatever the problem, it's apparently too expensive and time-consuming to fix. For the last several years, he's just stood there staring at passing trains. To salvage some intensity, a strobe light was strategically installed to give the Yeti some illusion of movement. Sadly, what it accomplished was gaining the creature the nickname, *Disco Yeti!* There are websites, podcasts, and even T-shirts dedicated to Disco

Yeti. It would almost be funny except for the fact that it's a major blemish on an otherwise amazing attraction.

The truth is you fly by so fast, you barely see him anyway. Still, as a fan, it would be nice to see the old boy doing what he was built to do. If you're a roller coaster nut like me, or you're not but want to hold on to your man card, you absolutely have to ride *Expedition Everest*. This ride is so insane it can induce heart palpitations. Don't worry, it will slow down again in a few minutes. Sit down and drink some water. You'll see *Everest* is a home-run attraction even with its star player injured.

 The official Ears of Steel recommendation: Your foundations are cracked if you don't ride and love *Expedition Everest!*

DINOSAUR

So you've faced the challenge of *Expedition Everest*, escaped the guardian of the mountain, and made it to base camp in one piece. Feel like taking your ticker for another fire drill? Follow the signs leading to *Finding Nemo—The Musical*. No, that's not where I'm leading you. It's just a shortcut back to DinoLand U.S.A. If the Yeti is disturbing, it's time to meet some creatures that are downright terrifying. Time to cowboy up and get on the ride simply called *DINOSAUR*.

Originally titled *Countdown to Extinction*, *DINOSAUR* might be the most intense attraction in all of Walt Disney World. You board a vehicle called a Time Rover, a Jeep on steroids, and *DINOSAUR* zaps you back into the prehistoric past. If the average Disney dark ride is a three or a four on the intensity level, *DINOSAUR* takes you to thirteen and a half! Using special effects, sensory-depriving darkness, and a blasting soundtrack in your ears, including narration by your "guide" back at The Dino Institute, *DINOSAUR* completely disorients you. All those high-tech tricks aside, this movable feast is all about the dinos!

The Disney Company has been blowing audiences away with their realistic Audio-Animatronics characters since Walt was still overseeing the designs himself. Legend has it that his animatronic

Abraham Lincoln, introduced at the 1964 World's Fair, was so life-like and bore such a resemblance to old Abe that audiences were convinced it was an actor in makeup. Their minds couldn't grasp that it was, in fact, a machine. I tell that story because, no matter how smart you are, no matter how certain you are that dinosaurs absolutely do not exist, when you ride *DINOSAUR*, your brain won't be able to grasp that the monster chasing you is just a giant hydraulic puppet.

The entrance to The Dino Institute leads guests into a large rotunda. Standing watch in the center is the skeleton of a super predator not too far removed from the familiar T-Rex. However, just to make it even creepier, nature gave this nasty fellow, called Carnotaurus, two thick devil horns protruding from his skull. If he couldn't lock his jaws down on his prey, this muscular hunter simply needed to get close enough to ram the side of his head into the target's side. A gaping horn gouge would certainly slow down any unlucky herbivore, making for an easy meal for Carnotaurus.

Imposing as this skeleton may be, it's a set of Lincoln Logs compared to what's waiting inside the attraction. You are no longer in a theme park. You're on a tour of The Dino Institute, a working laboratory built on the site of a major paleontological find. However, this Institute isn't relying on old bones any longer. Guests are led into a briefing room where plays a short introductory video with the Director of The Dino Institute (who, speaking of extinct creatures, looks like Dr. Huxtable's wife). She explains that The Dino Institute's greatest scientific minds have developed a new way to study dinosaurs. Real time. They travel back through time to observe them in their natural habitat. As if that's not crazy enough, today you, the guest, will embark on one of these primordial safaris!

That's when things get screwy. A junior paleontologist hacks into the feed to let you know you'll be committing some non-sanctioned, extra-curricular activities on your Jurassic jaunt. As is always the case, he's found a way to capitalize on this scientific breakthrough and wants you to help him snag a real life dinosaur. Oh, but don't worry, not the nasty bone-chomping variety like the menacing predator in the lobby. Your mission, should you choose to accept it (and not bolt through the chicken exit), is to track and capture an Iguanodon, a magnificent slowpoke leaf-eater. No problem since you're travelling in a tricked out SUV. So much trunk space, you could fit a dinosaur in there!

When the video ends, the doors open and you head down a corridor into a large loading bay. Pay special attention to some of the pipes running along overhead. You'll notice they're red and yellow and white with strange chemical codes. When this attraction originally opened, it was sponsored by McDonald's. Yes, those numbers and letters are indeed the chemical combinations for ketchup, mustard, and mayo. For the purpose of not ruining the continuity, we'll just say the white is petroleum, yellow is liquified plutonium necessary for time travel, and the red is, uh, liquid *flux-capacitorization!*

Man's Journal

When I reached the load gates, I was the first in my row to board. That meant I'd be stuck on the end of the row. Unlike a roller coaster, where the front or back tends to be most desired for thrills, on *DINOSAUR*, if you like having the bejeezus scared out of you, the ends are the spot! After all, when a hungry carnivore is looking to pick off a tourist, he attacks the middle and goes for the fool closest to the edge. Especially with such short arms.

But what was I worried about? That scientist, Dr. Grant Seeker (get it?) said we were perfectly safe. He showed us a video of the plant-eater we're after. The Iguanodon looked like Dino from *The Flintstones*. What could he do, lick me to death?

Our Time Rover pushed off from the platform and we rounded a corner into a giant convection oven. There were flashing lights and smoke, then stars and suddenly we were not in Kansas—or Orlando—anymore. We were surrounded by the dense jungle of the forest primeval. A voice crackled through our headrests. This really was impressive technology. I barely got cell service in Orlando! It was Dr. Seeker, assuring us again that everything was fine. Sure, a cataclysmic meteor storm was about to hit Earth, likely destroying every living thing (including a Time Rover full of time-traveling tourists), but we had two whole minutes before impact. No worries!

After just a few seconds of bumping along—these roads must be murder on the shocks—the computer alerted us to the presence of a dinosaur. We were treated to a close-up look at this scaly mutant Rhinoceros, which the computer identified as a Styracosaurus. Not too menacing, scratching his ass against a tree. We accelerated onward, knowing the clock was ticking, literally. No sooner did we move then we encountered our first carnivore. A smaller one called Alioramus. Don't let the description "smaller" fool you. It could tear any of us to shreds. Luckily, we caught him munching on some *McDino's Happy Meal!* I guess a fat lizard in the jaws is better than chasing a carload of tourists on the wheel.

Next, we were jerked around a corner and encountered the infamous Velociraptor! This one appeared to be a loner as he just hissed at us. Not so scary without the rest of his pack. I breathed a small sigh of relief. Perhaps things were going to be okay. Which was exactly when something happened that made me question Seeker's credentials. He announced the computer was picking up a large dinosaur, possibly the one we came for. The idiot locked our brakes and we lunged to a stop just as the fully fleshed, red, scaly, horned-rimmed Carnotaurus, that harmless skeleton in the rotunda, crashed through the trees!

Seeker hit the gas and we found enough traction to get the hell outta there before Big Red attacked. For the few seconds we had a good look at him, Carnotaurus was as nightmarish as you'd imagine! Dagger-like teeth lined his muzzle and his horns cast a demonic shadow on the vehicle! I thought again of those horns goring the side of an escaping herbivore and what they might do to the side of a Time Rover—or the unarmored passengers inside!

We were barely out of harm's way when the computer announced the appearance of another big dino. Turned out to be a plant-eater, but certainly a big one. The computer identified it as a sauropod. Specifically a Saltasaurus. Like a Brontosaurus, big body, long neck and tail. She's not going to eat us, but could easily stomp on us if she didn't want humans in her territory. Hell, a swipe of that tail could send us barrel-rolling!

We hightail it outta there just as we're informed the asteroid impact is a mere 90 seconds away. Super! Where was this stupid Iguanodon? I was snapped back to the danger at hand by a dive-bombing Pterodactyl. Have they never thought about putting roofs on these stupid Rovers? We veered out of the way before the leathery vulture snapped up one of the kids behind me. That's when we lurched sideways and discovered the Triassic Highway Department was really lousy 65 million years ago! We completely lost traction and got bogged down in the swamp. It occurred to me it would be a horrible time for that Carnotaurus to catch up to us.

Sure enough, the hungry monster came crashing out on our left. Dr. Seeker began screaming out directions like a girl! Our Time Rover took evasive maneuvers and we swerved left and right, barely gripping the mud enough to get out of the way! But we could still hear the monster stomping and breathing close behind. A panicking Dr. Seeker called out, "Abort mission!" as the Carnotaurus reappeared in front of us looking for lunch.

I could see sticky saliva running down his jaws as his serpentine eyes locked in on us. His red scales flared out as he roared and reared back to strike. I needed someone to remind me that none of this was real! Actually no, I wanted someone to remind him!

Finally, in a last ditch effort, our Rover lunged forward as the time-traveling tractor beam that hurled us here locked onto our coordinates. We felt the impact as asteroids slammed into the Earth's surface. In all the chaos, the crimson grimace of the Carno-taurus appeared out of the trees directly in front of our car, making one last effort to clamp his jaws around a panicked passenger! A hunter to the end. I almost saluted him. Just as I felt hot stinky lizard breath on my face (and that was just the hippie next to me), the car was pulled back into the flashy lights and smoke. We landed safely on concrete back at The Dino Institute in the dino-free twenty-first century.

In all the chaos of nearly dropping a rung on the food chain or being vaporized by flaming space rocks, I hadn't noticed any ad-ditional weight in the car. But as we rolled back into the loading bay, on the monitors I could see our two-ton hitchhiker making his escape down the hall!

I can't stress enough how intense and terrifying and friggin' awesome *DINOSAUR* is! I'm a man, I like being scared. Even now, I have to force myself to keep my eyes open through the ride. Those moments when the Carnotaurus is inches away, growling and eyeing you, all common sense abandons ship. Your knees start knocking and you just want to get the hell outta there before that beast lunges for your head. And since the last refurb, the Imagineers have actually ramped up the scare factor. The Carnotaurus appearances have increased. Including, of course, the finale when Rover plunges to safety as that monstrous muzzle comes down at you. That other theme park across town has a dinosaur ride based on a movie franchise with a similar finale, but it's nowhere near as exciting (or scream-inducing). Not to mention their dinosaurs look like giant rubber bath toys.

 The official Ears of Steel recommendation: *DINOSAUR* is a spiky, scaly, leathery-hide-kicking good time! It's as close as you'll get to staring a real dinosaur in its yellow eye—without a s___ load of amber and some frog DNA!

Maharajah Jungle Trek

Once you've ridden *Expedition Everest* and *DINOSAUR*, those *half-day* morons would say you're done with Animal Kingdom. Those people make me wish Carnotaurus would rip them out of their vehicle and shake them like a terrier with a sock monkey! Those are the two biggest thrill rides in the park (for now), but there's plenty left to do. You've seen the best in imitation animalia, now spend some time with the real deal. The only question is do you want to ride or walk? You have the option to do either.

You wouldn't guess it by my own gorilla-like physique, but I'm a fan of both walking tours at Animal Kingdom. Especially *Maha-*

rajah Jungle Trek in Asia. *Maharajah* might not be a favorite of the fairer sex, given it throws you right into the wild with a close encounter with about a hundred live bats. And not just little bats the size of a rubber Halloween toy. Some of these leathery night flyers are the size of cocker spaniels. These babies could give Bruce Wayne the shivers. While there is a Cast Member on hand to offer information and answer questions, you're pretty much on your own. The bats reside within a habitat that resembles a courtyard within some ancient ruins. They're fascinating creatures to watch, but I admit they're musky little critters. The scent gets a touch overpowering. Unless you've got teenagers, in which case you probably won't even notice.

Bats are dark and cool and turn into Dracula and all that, and you don't see them every day (if you do, clean your freakin' attic), but the real stars of this exhibition are just around the corner.

I've always known tigers were big, majestic cool cats. I've even seen some awesome tiger tattoos, but I'd never say I had a tiger obsession—until I found myself standing just a few yards away from a few of them. Not animatronic. These are the real, striped deal. Even just lounging or casually strolling the grounds of their habitat, tigers are mesmerizing to watch. Maybe there's something hypnotic about those stripes. You watch them move and you see every muscle firing, every sinew moving in time, doing its job, like a machine. A perfect evolutionary hunting machine, these cats seem ready to spring into pursuit at any moment if the opportunity arises.

It is embarrassingly clear that for all we consider ourselves the dominant species of this planet, one misstep into their territory and none of us would stand a chance. I'm a bigger guy, but I felt small in their proximity. Tigers command a sense of awe and an attitude of humility. And yet, there is something peaceful, something Zen-like in their presence.

Kilimanjaro Safaris

If you take the time and walk the *Maharajah Jungle Trek*, you've earned an opportunity to check out some more wild animals while sitting down. Get out the map, or simply follow the signs pointing toward Africa. You'll soon find yourself walking the streets of the African village of Harambe. The plaster buildings, the thatched rooftops, the faded advertisements, all feel authentic. It's easy to forget which hemisphere you're in. That is, of course, the point. Disney brought African thatchers to make those roofs. Imagineer Joe Rohde, the mad genius who spearheaded DAK, tells a great story about an African girl who came to work at Animal Kingdom and told him she was worried she'd be homesick. The story goes that once she walked down the streets of Harambe, she knew there was no chance of missing home because it felt as if she'd never left Africa. If you've traveled all this way, it's because you have a thirst for safari. It's time for you check out the signature attraction, *Kilimanjaro Safaris.*

DAK's man-made savannah covers 100 acres of land. Once it was Florida swampland, but now it is African savannah. It is a vast landscape that requires guests to ride in large safari trucks loaded up for a long stay in the bush. Extra fuel cans line the back, but the truth is these huge GMC trucks are electric to reduce pollution or harm to the animals. The savannah is stocked with hundreds of African animals such as giraffes, gazelles, lions, hippos, and rhinoceros. You'll also see more exotic creatures such as the okapi, God's funniest practical joke since the platypus. This poor creature has the head of a giraffe, the body of a horse, and the ass of a zebra. You're not likely to see one of these in your local zoo. And you won't see it or any other wildlife here in enclosures or cages.

All of DAK's African animals roam freely on the savannah during the day. As far as they know, anyway. Of course, the obvious question is wouldn't the lions be picking off gazelle like Christmas morning? Probably, if not for a couple of precautionary measures. Disney keeps them well fed. Lions are like men, we're not getting up for a sandwich if we know you'll bring us one.

Also, Disney Imagineers created invisible barriers within the various safari sets, enabling natural predators and prey to coexist without incident. If only they could help you with your mother-in-law! Camouflaged to the naked eye, some barriers look like rocks or shrubs. Others are a simple river or trench. On one safari, we rounded Pride Rock, home to the lions, and saw the lioness pacing excitedly on the backside of the rock. It was like watching myself at Dunkin' Donuts waiting for a fresh rack of Long Johns! Across the trail was a family of warthogs. Had we been on a real safari in Africa, the scene would likely have been very different. We'd have discovered a family of lions picking pork chop from their teeth.

Kilimanjaro Safaris is an amazing experience that you should definitely do once. In research for this book I recently embarked on the safari for the first time in years. It takes up a fair chunk of time, and for years followed a tired plot requiring your driver to deliver a memorized script, interacting with his boss over the radio (a prerecorded voice) and involving guests in a poacher-chasing adventure. Much like *Jungle Cruise* at Magic Kingdom and brain surgery, you really want a Cast Member who's still way into his job. My last driver came off like he'd been doing it for 10 years and was just regurgitating up his lines, while he plucked hairs from his nostrils (literally—I was watching).

I wanted to say, "Hey bro, if we're inconveniencing you, I'd be happy to let you go do my day job for the winter and I'll jockey the animal truck awhile!"

The occasional bad driver aside, you have the opportunity to see animals on this ride in a way you probably never will elsewhere. Even if you make it to the real Africa one day, you may end up like countless numbers of people who spend their savings for a real safari and end up seeing only a few gazelles and a ton of flesh-sucking, malaria-spewing, squirrel-sized mosquitoes!

There are also really good drivers who remain very tuned in to their role in the attraction. On one DAK safari, the driver slowed to a stop so a rhinoceros could walk right up to the truck and check us out. He was close enough to touch. I looked right into his black eyes. It was obvious he was observing the oddly dressed pink mammals just as they were him. That's the point of this place. Imagine your kids' expressions. Imagine your own. I don't care what a cool customer you fancy yourself—your jaw will hit the dusty truck floor during moments like that. Of course, there's that tiny voice in your head screaming, "Shake a can of pennies at him! He's gonna ram us!"

The official Ears of Steel recommendation: You have to do the sa-fari at least once. You get serious up-close access to some amaz-ing animals—without needing inoculations before you leave!

Wild Africa Trek

Of course, for a tough guy like you with no fear of fang or claw, maybe doing a drive-by in a truck just isn't exciting enough. For a few extra bucks, you can always opt to take the *Wild Africa Trek*! This is a walking tour like Armstrong walking on the moon was an evening stroll. This adventure requires vests, harnesses, and a waiver. With a guide, you can join a group of explorers and head into the bush, sans vehicle. Venture onto the game trail on foot, where you'll encounter hippos and climb past (maybe even dangle over) Nile crocodiles, all the while knowing you may end up the game. Of course, if you do survive, there's a nice picnic lunch on the savannah with an unparalleled view of giraffes and other wild-life. Jokes aside, every review of this trip is the same—unbelievable! Worth every extra penny. Bear in mind it's cruel to flaunt an appe-tizer in front of a hungry carnivore, so *Wild Africa Trek* is not suit-able for young ones (or wussies).

Pangani Forest Exploration Trail

Not up for spending the extra money—or providing next of kin in-formation? You can always take a walk down the *Pangani Forest Ex-ploration Trail*. The African cousin to the *Maharajah Jungle Trek*, this path brings you face-to-face with live gorillas. Well, there are a few feet between you and them, but it is still an impressive experi-ence. That said, if I want to look at big hairy primates sitting around chewing, I can do that at Thanksgiving.

These are the Ears of Steel highlights of Disney's Animal King-dom. Still far from all there is to do. Take your time. Take it all in. You'll get it. Remember vacations are for relaxing. Recreation means re-creating yourself. This, of all parks, is the place to do that.

All that plant life alone has to do something good for your blood pressure. Of course, restaurants like Flame Tree Barbecue and Yak & Yeti (yes, a strange name, but great pan-Asian food) might compensate with a few extra hits to your cholesterol, but what are you gonna do? Life is for living. Again, that's the point of this park. That everyone and every living thing gets the most out of life on Earth. The man who gets that is indeed a real man!

CHAPTER TEN

Magic Kingdom

HOW REAL MEN STORM A CASTLE!

egardless of where my publisher opts to stick this chapter in the book, I assure you it's the last chapter I wrote. The reason being it's the most daunting chapter for me as the writer. Magic Kingdom is the favorite of the four parks (at least as measured by the number of visitors) and the crown jewel of the WDW Resort. It is the very reason there is a Walt Disney World. That's why so many people say "Walt Disney World" when they're really referring to this one park. That's how major Magic Kingdom is to the Disney parks legacy.

Walt didn't survive to see it built, but he had tremendous input, directly and spiritually. It was to be his Disneyland of the East Coast, but also so much more. And it is! Prepare to be blown away! As legendary Disney Imagineer Tony Baxter famously said, "Disneyland is charming, and Walt Disney World is *spectacular!*"

The Magic Kingdom is probably the park you pictured the moment someone suggested a Disney vacation. You probably think it is all creepy singing dolls or fairies buzzing in your ears. Not a real man's spinning cup of tea. That is exactly the myth I'm writing this book to debunk—to show you that real grown men can and do vacation at Walt Disney World and have a blast! Though on its face it seems the park most designed for little ones, Magic Kingdom is no exception. You may enter the Magic Kingdom thinking it's just for kids but you'll exit with a stupid smile plastered on your mug, having put the tough guy inside you back in touch with his inner child. And they'll both be dying to go back!

The story of how Disney quietly snatched up acre after acre of Florida swampland for a song has been told many times. But I'll condense it into a few brief lines. Like trying to condense a keg into a shot glass, but what the hell!

Walt's biggest complaint about his beloved Disneyland was the lack of real estate. As soon as the park skyrocketed in popularity, opportunistic forces pounced. Seedy motels, ramshackle tourist traps, and curio shops popped up all over Harbor Boulevard, the main thoroughfare leading to Disneyland. Walt couldn't stand these eyesores being associated with his park.

When planning the "Florida project," a number of dummy companies were created to buy up cheap land, one small tract at a time. Like in a spy movie, Walt's business representatives would make multiple layovers when travelling back and forth, just to maintain the secrecy of the operation. When the news broke that these mystery developers were actually Disney, land prices in central Florida shot up over a thousand bucks an acre, overnight! Suddenly mosquitoes and mangroves had a lot more value.

Yes, construction is a manly subject, and the story of how they built this engineering marvel on top of all that swampland would fill an entire book, if not a series of them. In fact, it already has. I'm just going dive in and hit the highlights commando style. Heels up, head down, crowds beware or be damned. This is how a real man takes the Kingdom!

At the center of Magic Kingdom stands the majestic Cinderella Castle—the park icon and probably the first image that comes to anyone's mind when you say Walt Disney World. Even if you've never been there, you've surely seen the castle a thousand times through various media. She's as recognizable an architectural wonder as the Eiffel Tower or the Empire State Building, and as much a symbol of the Disney brand as Mickey Mouse. The castle marks the park's central hub, from which spokes radiate outward, providing a natural progression from land to land. Unfortunately, for the purposes of this book, throw that "natural progression" crap out the window. I want to maximize your fun and reduce time wasted on less-thrilling (i.e. lame, girly) attractions. Fortunately, there aren't as many of that last kind as you might think.

Main Street, U.S.A.

Once you enter the gates of Magic Kingdom and pass through the tunnels under the iconic train station, you will find yourself on the world famous *Main Street, U.S.A.*

It's a blast to the past. A simpler, more gentle America. It's the world Walt knew as a kid in Marceline, Missouri. The storefronts lead to numerous shops, including the main retail destination in town, **The Emporium.** There you can pick up every Walt Disney World T-shirt, stuffed animal, collectible pin, paperweight, oven mitt, and any other various and sundry items you can imagine. If it's not in The Emporium, they don't make it.

You may be thinking, "Real men don't shop!" There's nothing wrong with being a souvenir hound. I am a bit of one myself. Men have always collected trophies from their exploits. There's no shame in that game. I just suggest saving it till you're leaving the park. Nobody wants to be dragging bags around the park all day. Besides, let me tell you from personal experience, buying souvenirs too early can only lead to broken dreams, wasted money, and a pissed off spouse!

Man's Journal

It was morning in the Magic Kingdom. We were cutting through Liberty Square to hit *Big Thunder* and *Splash*. My wife spied a cart where an artist would create silhouette portraits as keepsakes. For a price, of course. She insisted we have one made of our son. The park was still pretty empty so I agreed. In fact I ran to grab my boy his first set of WDW mouse ears. An important rite of passage for a kid, ears must be chosen wisely. I found a shop on Main Street called The Chapeau, which I mistakenly thought was pronounced "Cheap-O." Perfect, I thought!

They had hundreds of designs to choose from, but I'm old school. I went traditional. Black hat, black ears, his name sewn into the back in gold thread; the classic! That's gangsta! When I returned to the cart, the silhouettes were done. Yes, as in plural. There was apparently a two-for-one deal going on. That's what she told me anyway. I wasn't thrilled about lugging around glass picture frames all morning, but they fit perfectly under the stroller, so no biggy, smalls. We spent the next few hours hitting a number of rides, eating lunch, even let the wife and offspring catch the parade while I ogled a pack of Brazilian tourist girls. (Wait . . . did I write that or think it?)

After lunch it was freakin' Tarzan hot. Clearly the boy needed a swim and a nap and his old man needed a swim and a cold beer (which would probably lead to a nap). We headed out the gates to our appointed bus stop. Each shuttle bus has a sign slapped on the side stating that the Florida D.O.T. requires all strollers to be collapsed prior to boarding. I'm not a jerk. I follow the laws, keep to the code. So I started to collapse the old stroller but for some reason I couldn't get it to click in place when folded. I hated this stroller. It never cooperated when I was in a hurry. My wife (and the rest of the bus) began to grow impatient with me. (What else is new?)

"Just bring it on as it is," she barked.

I pointed at the sign. "Rules," I said dutifully. "I've got it handled."

All men know whenever an inanimate (and sometimes, let's be honest animate) object isn't doing what you want, it just requires a bit more pressure. So I reared back and pushed like a gorilla on a tractor tire. Finally with enough brute force, I heard it click. I also heard another unfamiliar sound, also like a click but a bit more *violent*. But the stroller was folded and I got on the bus and took my seat.

As we rode on toward the hotel, I began to replay the day, starting with our delicious breakfast in the park, buying my son's ears while my wife got the . . . oh s**t! I suddenly had an idea why the stroller wouldn't fold.

Remember those silhouette portraits? The ones she got a great deal on? The ones we tucked in the bottom of the stroller and went about our fun? Yeah, they were still in the bottom of the stroller as I was body slamming it shut. I sat there a few moments debating how to handle this. Finally I just manned up and turned to my bride.

"Honey, I have a bad feeling when you open the pictures," I gulped, "it's not going to be pretty."

She reached down and lifted the plastic Magic Kingdom bag. As she did we heard the melodic tinkling of a million shards of glass. I figured at that point I'd be sleeping with the kid that night. Miraculously, when she unwrapped the first frame it was fine. But the second, the free one I rationalized, had pretty much shattered. The picture itself was fine, thank God. The glass hadn't punctured or harmed it.

"It's okay," my wife said, slipping it back into the bag. "That one was for your mother."

For first timers, the shops almost blend together in your peripheral vision. Main Street pulls you like a tractor beam toward the center of the park. Just before the castle is a little roundabout where stands a statue. The life-size bronze piece is a sculpture of Walt Disney holding the hand of his greatest creation (and only son), Mickey Mouse. They stand on a pedestal with wide smiles surveying all they've created together. Appropriately, the statue is called *Partners*. Without Walt, there'd be no Mickey Mouse. But if not for Mickey, the rest probably never would have happened. Show proper respect to a great man. And a great mouse.

Big Thunder Mountain Railroad

There's another reason I point out the Partners statue. For it is here you must make a crucial decision. I know, it's a vacation. You don't want to think. Rest easy, I'm steering the ship. All you actually have to do is follow directions. It seems many guests immediately make a right here, crossing the bridge to Tomorrowland. That, or they head straight through the castle into Fantasyland. When I was a kid, my family always made a hard left across the rope bridge into the wilds of Adventureland. It's the route I still follow, and it would seem the appropriate choice for a real man's Walt Disney World adventure.

However, I need to convince you straight away that the Magic Kingdom is a park fit for a man's man. You have to run before you can crawl, and you have to conquer a mountain (or two) before taking a leisurely boat cruise. This ain't Epcot. Veer to the left, wrapping your way around Partners and take the second path leading to Liberty Square. Pass quickly and you'll come to yet another body of water, where you will turn left. You'll soon find yourself moseying (at an aggressive pace, please) through Frontierland. At that point you will see two very distinct peaks on the skyline.

The first mountain you'll see has a waterfall running down it. For now, carry on toward the dry, rocky peaks just an armadillo's hair up the road. You're going to begin your adventure with a classic in search of a little fool's gold. Welcome to *Big Thunder Mountain Railroad.*

Walt Disney was a serious railroad enthusiast. His love of locomotives permeated much of his work. Walt even had a miniature railroad in his own backyard. On weekends employees would bring their kids over to ride Mr. Disney's train. No surprise then that trains feature prominently throughout Walt Disney World. But few measure up to this runaway locomotive!

Big Thunder Mountain Railroad premiered at Disneyland in 1979, a year before the Walt Disney World version opened, but its genesis dates back to the early seventies. It, along with a boat ride called *Western River Adventure*, was part of a planned land for the Florida park called Thunder Mesa. The water attraction was scrapped with most of Thunder Mesa due to rising construction costs (and because guests were clamoring for a *Pirates of the Caribbean* like in California). *Thunder Mountain* survived and rose out of the dusty terrain as the crown of Frontierland eight years after Magic Kingdom opened.

Thunder Mountain looks more like a cluster of rocky, craggy spires in some western outpost. Brave treasure hunters board a mine train in search of gold in them thar hills! Unfortunately, these mountains and their gold are protected by an ancient curse and greedy prospectors are not welcome. The moment your mine train pulls away and begins the climb out of the spooky cavern, it's clear things are about to go awry. There'll be no time for staking your own claim. You'll settle for surviving this wild ride on the out-of-control railroad.

Don't worry. The story plays up the danger, but *Big Thunder Mountain* is straight-up big fun! It's a wild ride, but still tame enough to be a great introductory coaster for kids. It's fast and furious, whizzing through seemingly dangerous mountain passes, up and down hills, around sharp corners, narrowly avoiding falling boulders and undetonated dynamite. It will always be one of my favorites and now it's my son's favorite. It certainly makes for a *helluva* introduction to the Magic Kingdom.

 The official Ears of Steel recommendation: *Thunder Mountain* is the wildest ride in the wilderness! It's a classic for a reason, so get on board!

Splash Mountain

As soon as you hop off *Thunder Mountain*, if the weather's right (and you're willing to walk the park in wet skivvies) head back to that other hill. The one we mentioned before with the waterfall— and the screaming tourists plummeting into a thorny briar patch. Get in touch with your redneck roots. If you like jug bands, monster truck rallies, singing varmints, and chicken fried anything, this is the right attraction! Welcome to *Splash Mountain*!

Walking through the queue into *Splash Mountain*, you'll think you are entering a real live cartoon. Interesting you should think that too, since it's inspired (loosely) by the Disney feature *Song of the South*. What's that you say? You've never seen it? Yeah, well, get in line. Long story, but suffice it to say, aside from controversies it stirred in more recent years, the flick introduced the world to those

hillbilly critters, Br'er Rabbit, Br'er Fox, and Br'er Bear. The attraction floats guests into their wilderness village built around the
mountain, Chick-A-Pin Hill. You reach the loading area and board
a hollowed-out log to ascend the mountain. You'll circle around the
peak, looking out over the park briefly. By the way, make a mental
note that, at night, this part of the ride provides an amazing view of
the park and the castle bathed in light. Trust me, you will want to
ride this one multiple times, so just make sure one of those times
comes after dark. During the fireworks, if you can!

After a few minor drops, just to wake you up a little, you'll suddenly descend into the mountain itself and find you're now fully
immersed in a cartoon land. Animatronic characters interact all
around you and play out the chase between Br'er Fox and Br'er
Bear and that wily old Br'er Rabbit. It's so fun and whimsical that it
is easy to forget all about that steep waterfall you saw on the way in.
Unrest assured, it hasn't forgotten about you. The ride floats guests
deeper and deeper into the mountain, lulling you into a sense that
you've actually escaped any peril. But as the story of Br'er Rabbit's
fate becomes imminently bleak, so does your own. Your log begins
to rise out of the gentle bayou as you're carried up and up on a con-
veyor belt. To add a little insult to injury, two vultures in undertaker
costumes stare down at you, discussing your fate. Then you see
sunlight. As you learned over at Disney's Hollywood Studios when
you rode *Tower of Terror*, what goes up at Walt Disney World is certainly going to come down. And so, my friend, must you.

For a brief moment you'll find yourself and your log-jammed
party suspended at the top of the mountain looking out at the park.
But only for a moment. Gravity and water quickly take over and
down you fall—five stories, seemingly straight down into the darkness of the briar patch just as a big surge of water rises overhead before falling back all over the log. If there's a secret as to where to sit
in order to get soaked or not, I don't know it. I've had the pleasure
of both experiences. I think a lot of it depends on the weight load
and distribution in each individual log. They seat up to eight riders in four rows of two. Strangely enough, I seem to have remained
the driest when sitting in the front left. On one recent excursion
down the mountain, I was by myself and a teenage girl was seated

next to me in the front of the log. By the end of the final drop, she was soaked to the core, and I was bone dry, save for the bit of water that ran off her onto our seat and under my butt. A damp ass beats a chafing crevice any day. Incidentally, she'd never ridden *Splash Mountain* and wasn't aware of the handful of teaser drops throughout the ride. Every time the bow began to dip she let out a scream that made my eyeballs bleed. So if you're going to ride with an anxious female, might I suggest keeping at least one ear plug on hand at all times.

Even after the big drop, the ride's not completely over. There's a big finale inside the mountain to complete Br'er Rabbit's tale. After all, as you probably know, being tossed into the briar patch was actually Br'er Rabbit's salvation and part of his escape plan all along. You can't miss the celebration when he returns home safe and sound.

Splash Mountain is not only one of the Magic Kingdom's most fun and most popular attractions, at just under 11 minutes it is also one of the longer thrill rides on property. Keep in mind, that also equates to some long wait times, which is why I had you head this way first thing, before the afternoon sun heats up and lines easily reach 45 to 60 minutes. FASTPASS is available and highly recommended for *Splash Mountain*. On a hot day, you'll thank me as you're speeding past all those sweaty cranks in the standby line.

And *Splash Mountain* is definitely one of those attractions with a high re-rideability factor! You'll catch different little details each time, and the dips and drops never ever get old.

 The official Ears of Steel recommendation: *Splash Mountain* is one of the best rides at Walt Disney World. Plain an' simple!

Pirates of the Caribbean

There is a third mountain at the Magic Kingdom any real man will want to conquer, but for now, let's stay on the ground. When you exit *Splash Mountain*, most of the crowd will probably gravitate back down through Frontierland toward Liberty Square. I say let 'em. We'll catch up later. Hang right and keep hugging the outer edge of the park keeping the railroad tracks on your three. Follow the path around the backside of Pecos Bill's and you can step right into Adventureland through the back door. I do fancy myself the Rick Steves of Walt Disney World!

You'll cross under an archway, past a quick service restaurant called Tortuga Tavern, a good spot for lunch if you're in the mood for a burrito or nachos. Sadly, it's only seasonal—and it's not clear what season. More importantly, you'll be practically walking right into one of the most famous attractions at Walt Disney World. You know a ride is a classic when almost half a century after its inception it can inspire four blockbuster flicks, which in turn re-inspired the ride. Obviously, I'm talking about the one and only *Pirates of the Caribbean*!

This may not be a thrill ride, but you won't find many more scurvy, stinky, testosterone-oozing attractions than this oldie but goodie. For seven and a half minutes you get to experience—from the safety of a longboat—a crew of cutthroats and scallywags committing acts of piracy and drunken debauchery. Who wouldn't want to swill rum in their bare feet and bid a few doubloons for that redhead? Especially with no fear of the gallows at the end! Of course, for legal reasons I cannot endorse such behavior in your day-to-day life, but for a few minutes, you'll love living vicariously through these original bad boys.

There have always been a million things to see around every bend on this boat ride, but a few years ago, Disney added some surprises. With the explosive success of the first *Pirates of the Caribbean* movie, Audio-Animatronics figures of that clown-prince of high-seas crime, Jack Sparrow, were installed, stirring up new excitement throughout the fiery Caribbean port town as well as in the hearts of many unfulfilled housewives riding the attraction!

There are some dark and stormy scenes featuring skeletons and Blackbeard's ghost toward the beginning of the attraction, as well as a drop down a waterfall (but nothing like you just experienced over on *Splash Mountain*). You just might want to give your little buccaneers a heads up. It's all in good fun and even my son, who was not even two the first time he rode *Pirates*, had a great time and by the end was belting out his own "yo ho's" right along with the lads!

The official Ears of Steel Recommendation: Avast! Step lively aboard before all the rum is gone!

Walt Disney's Enchanted Tiki Room

Once you find yourself back on dry land, keep moving through Adventureland. Along with *Pirates*, this side of the park is home to a couple of original attractions directly connected to Walt Disney. That makes them a high priority. Well, most of them. You'll notice a thatched-roof pagoda style building. This is the newly re-titled (for about the 73rd time) *Walt Disney's Enchanted Tiki Room*. The *Tiki Room* at Disneyland is almost exactly as Walt designed it. In their day, those little mechanical birds were top of the line engineering and technology. Nowadays, you'll probably find them about as innovative as one of those singing rubber bass hanging in every good redneck's basement.

The Florida *Tiki Room*, on the other hand, has been changed, tweaked, plucked, and completely overhauled numerous times. You go inside, sit on long uncomfortable wooden benches and watch mechanical birds sing songs even Bing Crosby would've passed on for being too dull. In the nineties, they finally got it right. Banking on the success of two animated feature films, *Aladdin* and *The Lion King*, Disney sank a large sum of money to create advanced AA characters based on two birds featured prominently in those movies. There was Zazu, the hornbill attaché to the king in *Lion King*, and Iago, the fowl-mouthed parrot (see what I did there?) from *Aladdin*, voiced ingeniously and appropriately by the irreproachable Gilbert Gottfried. The show was reworked and re-titled *The Enchanted Tiki Room—Under New Management*. The storyline was raucous and funny and poked fun at itself. I would have definitely recommended you check out *that* show.

Unfortunately, in January of 2011, the Tiki Gods must have been really angry because a fire broke out inside the *Enchanted Tiki Room* show building. The Iago animatronic was reportedly burnt beyond repair and there'd been damage to Zazu and other important show pieces as well. These were pricey birds, so building

replacements wasn't cost effective. Disney made what some ap-
plauded as a return to a classic attraction, but others (like the guy
writing this book) saw it as a disappointing step backward. *The Enchanted Tiki Room* was returned to a truncated version of Disneyland's *Tropical Serenade.* Boring little birds singing awful songs.
The only thing that could save this attraction would be the addition
of an Enchanted Tiki *Bar!* If I could sip a cold Mai Tai and listen to
the birds sing "Tiny Bubbles," I might give it a second chance!

 The official Ears of Steel recommendation is simple: Skip it.

Jungle Cruise

There are plenty of other ways to conserve energy on a Walt Disney
World vacation and still have fun. For instance, how about a nice
river cruise checking out exotic wildlife? We've already talked about
Kilimanjaro Safaris over at Animal Kingdom, but that's a dusty savannah under the hot African sun. Not to mention that, even when
those animals are visible, they're usually just lying around scratching themselves. If I wanted to see that, I'd just set up a mirror across
from my couch!

Along the banks of the Disney attraction *Jungle Cruise,* the animals are comical and adventurous and always putting on a show.
After all, they're programmed to be! *Jungle Cruise* is an opening day
Walt Disney World attraction, and has a twin in California, designed
at the hands of Walt. While little about the attraction has changed,
the scenes are just as funny. Although some of these mechanical
encounters can be harrowing. There's even gunplay! While many
jungle animals are protected, when hungry hippos try to chomp
your marbles, it's a whole different game!

The highlight of *Jungle Cruise* is less the ride than your Captain.
Disney hires the wittiest Cast Members to stand at the wheel and
guide you into the heart of (not so dark) darkness. The moment you
step onto the docks you'll feel transported back in time to the set of
The African Queen. But rather than Bogey, your skipper will more
likely remind you of Bob Hope or Groucho Marx. Even with stale

one-liners and puns the CMs on *Jungle Cruise* keep the ride fresh and funny every time. Between the lifelike AA animal encounters and nearly losing your head to the natives, the Captains will make you laugh, even if you don't want to. It may not be an attraction you'll hit over and over, but take the cruise!

 The official Ears of Steel recommendation: Kick back, laugh, and just enjoy the cruise.

Space Mountain

So far we've hit Frontierland and Adventureland, two sections of Magic Kingdom that pay tribute to eras when men were men. Days when a pistol in your belt, a blade at the ready, and even a whip at your side were just tools of the trade, and whiskey was safer than the water. That's right, the good old days! Now hold on, as we blast forward into the future! Many of us guys love space and technology, especially when it involves warp drive and lasers blasting crap to pieces!

When you see metallic spires, overhead tracks, and spinning rockets, you've left the world of black-and-white serials and rocketed forward into a world of science fiction and technology. Some real and some imagined, but all very cool! Over the next bridge waits Tomorrowland!

Tomorrowland represents an adventurous, exciting future! Disney was smart enough to know an entire themed land representing future technology would likely be rendered irrelevant in a short matter of years. These days it only takes, well, days. So the future tech of Tomorowland was created stylistically with a wink and a nod. Trash cans talk and the trees are made of metal (that's gotta be hell on the landscapers). The industrial atmosphere Disney has created will make your chest swell like a real (cybernetic) man. It's all steel and aluminum, hard edges, lights, antennae, and spires, which we all know is a fancy word for saying spikes!

You won't find soft cuddly creatures and primary-colored boat rides in Tomorrowland. Well, I take that back. There are a few furry creatures around this land, but most of them are monsters and you can't touch them. And then there is a fuzzy blue alien. We'll get there. Tomorrowland is also the Magic Kingdom home of the one and only *HSRIC* (Head Space Ranger In-Charge), *Buzz Lightyear*! There's no *ballsier* Disney character, none with more machismo and gravitas, than Buzz!

As for attractions, Tomorrowland is home to *the* real man's attraction! It's that massive white steel structure visible from far outside the park, second only to the castle itself, *Space Mountain*!

The third of Magic Kingdom's mountains, this attraction doesn't resemble a mountain so much as it does some other-worldly space station. The tranquil, astral queue of *Space Mountain* can lull riders into a false sense of calm. Guests find themselves walking up a dark gangway looking out portholes into deep space as soothing electronic music hums softly overhead. Don't be fooled. When you reach the loading bay, it's sit down, strap in, and hang on! After all, this is a roller coaster!

Space Mountain is no regular carnival dipper racing around in circles. This ride kicks serious *asteroid*! After crossing through a trippy tunnel of lights, your open rocket blasts off into the deepest, darkest recesses of space. In other words, it's a roller coaster in the dark. It is so dark in fact that, combined with the high speeds at which your ship is being hurled along, you can barely see the silhouette of the tracks against the blackness. The only light comes from the stars around you. Now and then, you might catch the outline of a support ahead and it looks like it's headed straight for your forehead! At the last second, you drop into the blackness of another wormhole! More likely it's just a dip in the track, but play along. Okay, Space Ranger?

You race along at warp speed, going up and down, taking hairpin turns, all the while afraid to raise your hands for fear of losing them to a low overhang. Ironically, it's hard to keep your hands inside the ride vehicle if you've left one lodged in the tracks above. In space nobody can hear you scream . . . until the ride ends.

The *Space Mountain* concept was first dreamed up by Walt Disney when he wanted an indoor coaster for Disneyland's Tomorrowland, but sixties tech and limited space in Anaheim caused the idea to be shelved. Turnabout being fair play, when the idea of a *Matterhorn Bobsleds* ride like the one in Disneyland wouldn't fit in the space reserved in Florida, *Space Mountain* rose from the former swampland. *Space Mountain* has the unique distinction of being an attraction that originated in Orlando but grew so popular it was cloned in every other Disney resort worldwide. Make sure you sit up front because you'll have tears streaming backward from laughing uncontrollably from start to finish—along with the intermittent profanity flying out of your mouth as the world falls out from under you and you desperately grab for anything to keep from being sucked into the vacuum of space. I know in the rules I said don't swear, but this might be an exception. In space no one can hear you curse either!

 The official Ears of Steel recommendation: The word awesome has been totally overused since the eighties (as has the word totally) but there's no other description for *Space Mountain* but totally awesome!

Buzz Lightyear's Space Ranger Spin

Now if you're a real man, you've probably got an ugly competitive streak. It's cool. Don't hide your light under a barrel. That need to win is instinctive. If all this Disney happiness and good feeling makes you crazy and you feel the need to get into some heated competition, Tomorrowland is the right place! Directly across from *Space Mountain* is a ride that lets you directly challenge your fellow riders. You get to shoot stuff, son!

Remember *Toy Story Midway Mania!* over at Hollywood Studios? Well, *Buzz Lightyear's Space Ranger Spin* is the original *Toy Story* ride. You're not just pulling some rope or tossing imaginary rings. Each vehicle has two highly powerful space-tech blasters. I can't say much more; you don't have the clearance. Just know it's proprietary stuff. (The CIA doesn't even have it!)

All that matters is once you board *Space Ranger Spin*, you've accepted honorary admission into the Space Ranger Corps and your first mission has begun. The attraction sends riders through numerous spaced-out settings where robots, aliens, and the evil Emperor Zurg have gone on the offensive to evade capture. Fortunately, Zurg and his minions aren't the smartest super villains in the universe. I mean, it's not for nothin' they are wearing targets! Aim quickly and blast away! This might be the only Disney ride where shooting at the characters is actually encouraged.

Space Ranger Spin is a crazy cross between a classic dark ride and a day-glo shooting gallery. Digital tickers on your dashboard keep score as you blast your way through each scene. Just, please, when you do rack up the higher score, don't scream, "In your face, *sucka*" at your wife! Trust me. There's no telling what she might have waiting for you back home, and they remember!

Oh, I wouldn't ride after a big meal either. These vehicles turn rapidly and spin all over the track, hence the name *Space Ranger Spin*!

 The official Ears of Steel recommendation: Definitely give this one a whirl, Space Ranger!

Tomorrowland Transit Authority PeopleMover

As a man, one thing I really love about Magic Kingdom is the balance. You've got your thrillers like *Space Mountain*, your fun exciting rides like *Pirates*, whimsical rides for young and old alike, and then you've got attractions built simply for relaxing. After all, we're men. Aside from food, drink, and sex, what do we love to do more than anything? Nothing. Literally, we love doing nothing! How would you spend a perfect Sunday? Chilling out in your favorite chair with a beer, flipping channels without even noticing what was on. No care in the world, except maybe who's bringing you the chips.

Even on a Walt Disney World vacation, you want to relax while still enjoying the magic. At theme park prices, the last thing you want to do is lay around your hotel room. Tomorrowland has the perfect solution. A ride so smooth and relaxing that, like a hammock in the sky, you could easily be lulled into blissful, infant-like sleep. All the while it gives guests a guided tour of Tomorrowland over the heads of the crowd. Look up! That blue train gliding along like a Zen caterpillar is the Tomorrowland Transit Authority.

Poll any hardcore Walt Disney World fan and he'll probably tell you *TTA* is one of his favorite rides. Why? Because it takes all the work out of having fun! There's even an escalator to the loading platform. You slide into your car, the sides of which come up to armpit level like arm rests when you're lounging. Each vehicle can seat four to six people, but come on now. This ride is for your relaxation! Stick the kids in their own car. Settle into your little blue chariot, put your feet up on the bench across from you, and enjoy as it rockets through Tomorrowland at a blazing six miles per hour.

Originally called the *WEDWay PeopleMover* (trivia: WED stands for Walter Elias Disney) the *TTA* travels around and through Tomorrowland's other attractions, including *Buzz* and *Space Mountain* as well as *Stitch*, *Monsters, Inc.*, and the race track. Yes, there's a race track. Easy Andretti, it's not what you think. I didn't forget. It's just, well, forgettable. You want to hear about a *real* speedway, just keep reading through to the end of the book!

The *Tomorrowland Transit Authority* tour lasts about ten minutes. When you glide back into the loading area, a Cast Member will gently rouse you. Or depending on crowd volume that day, maybe they won't. If you look peaceful enough, they just might let you go around again. I realize the *TTA* may not sound like much, but trust me, after stomping around the parks, your feet alone will thank you. Something about this catatonic cruise above the asphalt and crowds just puts a man at ease. It's proof that those floating chairs from the movie *WALL-E* aren't as far off as we might think!

The only thing that could possibly make the *TTA* better would be a loading bay bar and cup holders. Sadly, no booze on this cruise. Until recently, Magic Kingdom was a completely dry park. In the Florida sun, a bottle of water is probably a better option. You didn't hear it from me, but if you happened to sneak a turkey leg on board I can't see how it *wouldn't* make the experience even better!

 The official Ears of Steel recommendation: Hop on and take a load off. It's like a slowly rolling easy chair!

Monsters, Inc. Laugh Floor

Of all the Disney/Pixar animated films, *Monsters, Inc.* is easily in my Top Three! Being a large, hairy, somewhat scary beast myself, I relate to John Goodman's character, Sulley. So his job requires him to terrify children. What, a guy can't be good at his job without being called a monster? I was a collections agent! Wonder what they'd say about me?

If you've seen the movie, you know in the end the roles get reversed when they learn laughter is more powerful than screams, and Sulley's funny little sidekick Mike Wazowski becomes the top producer at the plant. It's a little high concept, but roll with it. Disney California Adventure has a good old-fashioned dark ride based on the film called *Monsters, Inc. Mike & Sulley to the Rescue!*. It's a blast! It flings you right into the movie! However, for Walt Disney World, they went a different route—*Monsters, Inc. Laugh Floor.*

When you cross through the *Laugh Floor* doors, you've crossed into the world of Monsteropolis. A makeshift comedy club has been built inside the power plant where Mike and Sulley worked. Once inside, the curtain and the stage are actually projections on a screen. So are the monster comedians who stomp, slither, and ooze out to entertain the guests! They not only tell jokes and perform rehearsed material, they banter with the crowd, choosing particular guests to mess with. For kids, it must be astonishing to see Mike Wazowski and other familiar characters single them out specifically. Imagine Al Michaels or John Madden looking directly at the camera and calling you out for the salsa you dribbled on your shirt or the tankard of beer you're sucking down!

The monstrous jokes are kid-friendly. In fact, they're about as offensive as a fifties Catskills comedian. Like Henny Youngman if he had three eyes and scales. Or, actually, just like Henny Youngman.

Stitch's Great Escape!

Directly across from *Monsters, Inc. Laugh Floor* is one of the most polarizing and controversial attraction spaces in all of Walt Disney

World. Here is where the aforementioned, terrifying *Alien Encounter* once stood. There are many who feel what they replaced it with, while not nearly as scary, is horrific in its own right. Where once a horrifying alien beast assaulted guests, a new little space creature holds court and causes mayhem in *Stitch's Great Escape!*

I am not one of the *Stitch* haters. As a character, he reminds me of some of my buddies, confused and destructive but well-meaning! The little blue guy is a favorite with my kid, so I suppose I also have some sentimental attachment. But there are many Disney fan boys and crazed bloggers who constantly rip this attraction a new orifice. I mean, you know, if rides had orif . . . you get what I mean. As for his attraction, I actually find it amusing and the animatronics are incredibly impressive, but man do some people out there hate it!

I don't think you can blame this one on the character. The show is very similar to the original nightmarish version, only *cartoonified* to make it kid-friendly. Instead of a flesh-eating space beast, Stitch, the multi-armed laboratory experiment gone wrong, is beamed into a holding unit in the middle of the theater. Wouldn't you know, he manages to get loose?!? The animated movie *Lilo & Stitch* explained that Stitch was created by a mad scientist for the sole purpose of causing chaos. So you can imagine what he does when set lose among a room full of heavy machinery and tourists strapped to their chairs.

Alien Encounter's old tricks are employed for the new show. The lights go out and soon you hear Stitch chattering, feel him crawling overhead, spitting, even whispering in your ear—which is really creepy! At one point he chows down on a chili dog (where he found a chili dog in space, who knows) and belches into your face. I could do without *that* special effect.

With all the special effects, sci-fi theme, burping—it's gross, but definitely manly—and robotic laser-blaster arms swirling around the room, *Stitch's Great Escape!* fits on the Ears of Steel agenda. I did it once, it was okay, but haven't felt a need to hit it again.

 The official Ears of Steel recommendation: A lukewarm "you make the call" for *Monsters, Inc. Laugh Floor* and *Stitch's Great Escape!*.

Cosmic Ray's Starlight Café

Speaking of chili dogs, by this point you've gotta be getting hungry. One of my favorite Magic Kingdom spots to grab lunch is right here in Tomorrowland. Just around the corner from *Stitch* is a mammoth-sized counter service eatery called *Cosmic Ray's Starlight Café*.

While it doesn't stray too far from typical theme park food, Ray's menu is relatively extensive. Multiple space ports (counters) serve up burgers, chicken, hot dogs, and the like. For the record, the foot-long chili dog with cheese and onions is not bad. Come to think of it, now I know where Stitch got his! The food at Cosmic Ray's is good, but it's the atmosphere that brings in the guests. I've never seen this restaurant *not* packed before 8:00 at night and by that point they're running the vacuums. Since it's a counter service location, you're going to have to send a hunting party out into the wilds of the dining room for a table. People circle like buzzards waiting to strike the minute you throw down your recycled paper napkin. And so must you, or your kids. Once a table is secured, Ray's has activities to keep kids occupied while dad stands in line for food. There are games, hula hoop contests, and so forth.

However, I go to Cosmic Ray's for the entertainment. Ray's dining room doubles all day long as *Cosmic Ray's Starlight Lounge*! The stage features a stellar act, literally, that entertains guests while they eat! Remember Bill Murray's lounge singer character on *Saturday Night Live*? Imagine he was a four-foot green alien with fuzzy red pompadour. This other-worldly entertainer extraordinaire is the one and only Sonny Eclipse, the biggest little star in the galaxy!

Sonny is actually an animatronic alien lounge act who plays a strange, spacey keyboard right out of that *Star Wars* bar! He sits on stage in the dining room entertaining diners throughout the day. This may be the closest you can get to a Disney animatronic if you want to get a really good look at how they work—or ask for an autograph. Sonny looks a bit like a green hippopotamus with bushy hair and a velour tuxedo. The original songs are funny, though admittedly filled with a plethora of groan-inducing space puns. The voice behind Sonny is legit Chicago blues man Kal David. David performed all of Sonny's singing and jokes, plus he played the tunes.

Respect the Eclipse! Of course, Sonny gets by with a little vocal help from his invisible alien back-up singers, The Space Angels. We don't know what they look like, but they sing like true celestial beings.

All right, so maybe Cosmic Ray's hovers a little close to dining at Showbiz Pizza, but it's fun and the food is good. I'm sure the character cost a premium to build and they probably don't see any traceable return, but he's there to entertain guests. It's one more extra that makes Disney the best in the business. By the way, Cosmic Ray's bathrooms aren't too bad either!

Mad Tea Party

We've checked out the manliest attractions Tomorrowland has to offer and only ignored two attractions. Heading out of Tomorrowland, things can get a little dicey. Stay alert! I've been nervous about writing this next section for some time. But it can't be avoided, and it can't be ignored. It's time to cowboy up, put on your Ears of Steel, and pray you're not allergic to pixie dust. We are heading to Fantasyland!

What am I supposed to do? Write a book about Walt Disney World for grown men and just pretend Fantasyland doesn't exist? This is possibly the most popular land in the park. It's likely the Walt Disney World you've always pictured. Princesses, pixies, fairy tale characters, Winnie the Pooh, everything childlike and whimsical everywhere you look! I'm not going to blow smoke up your honey pot! There's nothing very manly about Fantasyland. It oozes syrup and gumdrops, not testosterone. Unless machismo looks a lot like pink and blue cotton candy!

However, unless you are planning to take a trip to WDW by yourself, there's no way in the world (big or *it's a small*) you're going to avoid spending some time here. Don't worry. I'm here to guide you through. Guess what? I think if you man-up and give it a shot, just like quiche, you'll find you actually like it.

Since we're entering from Tomorrowland, the first ride you will come across may appear girly and childish, but it actually requires a set of brass *you-know-what's*! It also requires a cast-iron stomach.

If you're prone to motion sickness or vertigo (secretly of course—I realize it wouldn't be very macho to admit publicly) just keep on walking. I'm talking, of course, about another famed Disney attraction, *Mad Tea Party*.

You'll hear it referred to as "the tea cups." Lots of non-Disney parks and carnivals have similar rides and usually just copy the tea cup design. That's how much this classic has seeped into the amusement industry's DNA. Giant pastel cups revolving around a moving ride floor while spinning independently. Not the most complex ride system or complicated story, but very effective—especially if you're trying to drop a few pounds. I'll just come out and tell you, I don't ride it. I'm not a spinner, period. If I got on *Mad Tea Party*, they'd rename the tea cups the *barf buckets*. This ride requires a constitution I don't possess. For that alone, I'll put *Tea Party* on the Ears of Steel approved list. You'll just never catch me on it—or hovering over a garbage can afterwards!

As you work your way around *Mad Tea Party*, you will begin to hear familiar calliope music, see flashing popcorn lights and colorful banners with familiar characters waving in the breeze. Where once stood Mickey's Toon Town, the circus has set up its tents permanently. Storybook Circus, as the new area is called, was the first phase of the New Fantasyland expansion to be completed and opened to the public. There are people who will try to tell you that this area is just for young kids. I say push those fools in an elephant patty. Storybook Circus is just a fun area to visit. Sure, the rides (of which there are only two anyway) cater to kids, but they are Magic Kingdom classics, new and old. The first one you'll know in a heartbeat, even if you've never been.

Dumbo the Flying Elephant

Dumbo the Flying Elephant has been a staple of Disney Parks since the 1950s. For years, the original simple, round-and-round, glorified carnival ride would have lines for days, in the sweltering Florida heat, making tensions flare in both toddlers and harried dads—allegedly. Disney solved that problem two ways.

The biggest change? Double the fun! They built a whole other twin Dumbo ride, moved the original over and placed the two side by side, this time over water. The little guy with the big ears looks better than ever! And to keep the sun from ruining the fun while you wait, they erected a giant circus tent queue filled with games, interactive activities, and even a play area to keep the kids occupied and your scalp from getting a sun burn. I know, you're probably thinking, "If we get out of line so the kids can go screw around, we'll lose our place." Bzzzz! Sorry, Chuckles. Guests are given a pager. When it's your time to fly, trade in your buzzer for a magic feather and soar.

Look, is Dumbo a manly ride? Not in this universe. But it's a classic and it represents Disney and specifically the hand of Walt himself. More importantly, your kids will want to ride it. It is a rite of passage as much as their first set of ears. So suck it up, buttercup.

 The official Ears of Steel recommendation: You may have seen about everything, but you ain't a real man till you've ridden on an elephant that flies!

The Barnstormer

Just past *Dumbo* you'll notice a twisted jumble of tracks going up, down, and around. That's right pal! A roller coaster! See, there's a payoff to being a good dad and doing the gravity-defying pachyderm thing. Go on, get in line quick! Okay, so I admit it. It may be a roller coaster, but yes, it's a kid-friendly coaster, too. The good news is, it's a blast! Why else would this be the only piece of the old Mickey's Toon Town area that survived the wrecking ball? Welcome to *The Barnstormer*!

The Barnstormer has been in this area for the last 17 years in one form or another. Originally, the idea was that Goofy was a test pilot and this strange airplane-train hybrid was his latest creation. In 2012, after a bit of retheming to fit the Circus motif, *The Barnstormer* became the domain of The Great Goofini, the death-defying stuntman alter ego of Goofy. The ride is fun. It doesn't reinvent anything, it does just what you expect. You whiz around the track, taking twisty, high-speed (somewhat) corners, and the whole thing is over in a matter of seconds. But you'll laugh the whole time. It's a good old-fashioned carnival roller coaster. What I really love are the remnants of Goofini's other attempts at feats of derring-do scattered all around the queue! The crashed rocket, the Wheel of Death, the human . . . er, dog cannonball target.

 The official Ears of Steel recommendation: Take the flight with Goofini! This is one stunt that works out in the end!

Pete's Silly Sideshow

Storybook Circus is also home to one of the three stations of the *Walt Disney World Railroad*. So if you feel like taking a railroad trip around the park, this is one of the places you can catch it. Across from the station is *Casey Jr. Splash 'N' Soak Station*. It's a water play area for kids. Not for you, although if nobody's looking and you want to run through those colorful train cars as the elephants and camels spit at you, be my guest. Just take an extra set of dry skivvies.

But the main attraction of Storybook Circus is *Pete's Silly Sideshow*. It's a meet-and-greet area where guests can meet Donald, Daisy, Minnie, and Goofy, each wearing some form of circus attire. You've got The Amazing Donaldo the Snake Charmer, and his ol' lady Madame Daisy Fortuna. Goofy is there in character as the Great Goofini and he does have his manly motorcycle! Don't worry, I'm not trying to convince you there's anything manly about having your picture taken with Minnie the Poodle Trainer—and no, I'm not making that up! I bring this area up for one reason, its namesake.

As a fellow swarthy big guy who, okay, maybe sometimes pushes the limits of decency to make a buck, I feel it's time for Pete, a.k.a. Pete the Cat or Black Pete, to get his due. He is one of the oldest Disney animated characters, after all, predating even a certain mouse in red shorts. I was happy to hear they were naming the joint after him. The outside features a huge talking cutout of Pete the Carnival Barker. Ironic, since he's a cat. Think about it. I'll wait. Even entering the tent, guests pass through Pete's giant, smiling maw! Personally, I'd like even more Pete in the parks. More merchandise, a walk-around character, even his own meet-and-greet area. Okay, so yes, what I'm really doing here is bucking for a new job! Look at me, my costume wouldn't even need much padding! And I can bring my own cigars!

Whether you go into *Pete's Silly Side Show* or decide to skip the photo ops and head back out of Storybook Circus, make a stop at *Big Top Souvenirs*. I know, you're thinking, "Another gift shop?!" This hippodrome of gift shops (no, that's not like *Thunderdome* for hippos, although that would be amazing) may rival the Emporium on Main Street. Inside it continues the circus theme as the display shelves are all circus-train cars. They even sell cold drinks from the penguins' *refrigerated car*! Big Top Souvenirs is one of the few gift shops to sell area specific souvenirs, with Storybook Circus T-shirts, dishes, shot glasses . . . I'm sorry, toothpick holders, please! There are kids around!

The thing you might love most about this particular circus tent is right there in the center ring. Direct your attention to the one, the only, *Big Top Treats* snack counter! Here Cast Members are selling fudge, cookies, and Goofy's Glaciers (think fruity, slushy drinks similar to those served in that convenience store with rhyming numbers for a name!). The star of this particular sideshow for me, however, is another staple treat of the Magic Kingdom, and it seems fitting that once you leave the Circus area you'll be heading to a princess-themed land. Check out the candied apples!

These bad boys won't cause anybody to fall into a deep, death-like slumber. In fact, they're coated with enough sugar to guarantee nobody will be sleeping for a long time. These aren't those limp, caramel-dipped, peanut-rolled taffy apples you see in the grocery every fall. For starters, I think Disney might be crossbreeding Granny Smiths with softballs. These things are huge! Disney is particularly famous for its character-themed apples. There's a Mickey apple, dipped in some sugary adhesive and rolled in red sugar to match his shorts. There's also a Minnie, a Goofy, and the Cheshire Cat. Heck, I even saw a red and yellow Lightning McQueen apple! However, for me there is one particular apple treat here that should have its own cult following. This monster is dipped in chocolate and then rolled in crushed up peanut butter cups! It's no secret I've never met a peanut butter cup I didn't like. I'd never considered pairing them with a sour apple before, but I'm telling you, using a green apple makes sense because this treat will forever be my *kryptonite*! It's a little rich, obviously. I had to eat half right away and wait five minutes before attacking the rest! Rest assured, I left no gooey slice behind!

The Many Adventures of Winnie the Pooh

Fantasyland is home to a number of classic Disney dark rides based on popular properties. It used to house *Mr. Toad's Wild Ride*. If ever there was a "kiddie" ride that catered to men, it was *Toad*. Guests rode runaway roadsters crashing through the streets of Merry Ol' London town, narrowly escaping collisions and chaos at every turn. Perfect! In the end, you even got hit by a train and went to Hell. How that ever got off the concept table is a mystery, but it was awesome! Sadly, in the nineties, Mr. Toad's Florida license was revoked and he took his last wild ride. Toad is still up and running at Disneyland, but his Florida manor was taken over by that silly ol' bear with the ill-fitting red shirt. Where you'd once find Toad Hall, guests now line up for *The Many Adventures of Winnie the Pooh*.

The famous Pooh cartoons we grew up with come to life as guests ride along in giant honey pots. Manly? Not really—unless facing down a Heffalump is a test of courage. But it is cute. What do you want from me? You'll have a good time. Especially when the rain, rain, rain comes down, down, down and you begin to bob up and down though the attraction! Disney threw a lot of money into the characters and scenes and there are lots of little details to catch. In 2011, the outside of the attraction was redone and there are now interactive games and activities to keep the kids occupied while you wait. And you will wait. You may roll your eyes at cutesy rides, but Pooh gets packed! That's really a terrible choice of words, isn't it?

 The official Ears of Steel recommendation: If you've got kids, you're gonna ride! Fortunately, it's actually fun!

Mickey's PhilharMagic

In the middle of Fantasyland stands an enormous carousel. Keep moving around to your left and you'll notice a marquee that reads *Mickey's PhilharMagic*. It's a musical 3-D film featuring some of the best Disney movie songs of the last two and a half decades. The animation and special effects are very cool, although those songs can get long and a bit tedious. If I can be a mush here, seeing your kid reaching out to grab The Little Mermaid's jewels (no, that's not code) floating in the water is one of those great moments you never forget. It's a nice cushioned seat in an air-conditioned theater. Plus you're wearing dark glasses so if need be, catch a commando nap.

A lot of hardcore Disney fans are probably burning me in effigy! I didn't say it's bad. I said it's nice and the effects are cool. But come on, watching a medley of love songs from Disney movies isn't exactly *mancentric!* Just remember, at the final scene, turn around or you'll miss the final effect!

 The official Ears of Steel recommendation: Is *PhilharMagic* manly? No. Is it still cool? You bet a duck's ass!

Enchanted Tales with Belle

When you exit *PhilharMagic*, you are looking at what Disney has been calling "New Fantasyland" for the past few years. New Fantasyland is actually made up of two different lands, the first being Storybook Circus. The second, completely new area is Enchanted Forest. You might as well call it "Princess Land" and buckle up. The good news is, from an architectural and design perspective, the whole area is pretty cool and, dare I say, pretty *man damnly!* Er, uh, reverse that. The buildings are rustic and gothic, surrounded by thick forest and rock and stone and rushing water. On the other hand, this place is Princess-heavy.

As soon as you pass through the medieval gates, which incidentally look like they were built from pieces of Cinderella Castle itself, you are in the realm of *Beauty and the Beast*. Your eyes will immediately lock on to that new castle perched atop a brutal, dangerous-looking mountain. That is Beast's Castle. It is a pretty impressive sight to behold way up there, especially at night bathed in purple light. Where the Beast got purple flood lights in eighteenth century provincial France, I don't know. *Le Depot de Home*, maybe? Courageous adventurer though you are, I suggest you resist the urge to climb up there and explore its vast and mysterious hallways and catacombs. Not only would Disney security frown upon it, but you'd be disappointed when you reached the top to learn it's about the size of a Starbucks. It's that crazy old forced perspective playing tricks on your eyes. Rest assured though, you may be able to explore parts of the castle later . . . sort of.

On your left as you enter this new, mythic land, you'll see nestled among the forest growth a rustic cottage and garden. This is the home of Maurice, Belle's slightly off-kilter inventor father. It would be a heck of a fine fishin' cabin up north, hey? What it really is, however, is an interactive show called *Enchanted Tales with Belle*. Great for little girls and their mothers, but us tripods are best advised to keep on walking and hope the gals don't see it. Otherwise, you're going to find yourself holding a cutout of a teapot in front of a crowd of laughing kids. I will say the effects are actually top-notch, next-generation creations on the part of Imagineering.

 The official Ears of Steel recommendation: Not made for a man, but if your little ones insist, you'd better do it. Just try to stand toward the back!

Be Our Guest

As I mentioned, if you really want to poke around the high hairy one's domain, you will have your chance. As long as you booked an ADR 180 days in advance! You will come to a long bridge, lined with gruesome, golem gargoyle light fixtures. At the other end, a wrought-iron gate waits open, inviting you to queue for the dining experience of a lifetime—dining in the hall of the Beast at the Magic Kingdom's newest table service restaurant, Be Our Guest. As you make your way toward the doors leading inside the mountain underneath the castle, you'll be greeted by two menacing stone lion-bull-baboon creatures and, scarier still, the maître d' who will be checking for your reservation. Be Our Guest began taking ADRs long before it opened and it's been booked solid since. After all, never before have guests had a chance to dine in the sets of a classic Disney animated feature. Inside Be Our Guest, Imagineering has brought actual rooms of the castle to life in painstaking detail. From the corridor of haunted suits of armor, to the grand ballroom made famous as the place Beast busted his dance moves on Belle and swept her off her feet, to my favorite of the dining rooms, the West Wing. No, Martin Sheen isn't here! This room, the forbidden chamber of Beast's castle in the movie, looks as if a surly monster tore through on a particularly unsettled day. Torn tapestries and slashed artwork hang from the walls as a thunderstorm and lightning crash regularly outside the windows.

Look, I'm doing my best to sell a real man like you on the ambiance of a *Beauty and the Beast* restaurant. Trust me, it sells itself. But let's talk about what really counts to guys like us—the food. Remember this is a French menu, and some of the items . . . okay, let's be honest, Clouseau, most of them might be foreign to you. My suggestion, go for lunch. During the day, Be Our Guest is counter service, which also means if you're on a Disney Dining Plan, it eats fewer credits. Plus, you'll find a few more familiar selections on the menu, even if you don't know the names. For example, *Croque Monsieur* sandwich—a fancy (and I might add delicious) hot ham and cheese. If I may simplify the menu for you even further, as a guy, three words—grilled steak sandwich. If I can add three more words to that—garlic butter spread. Done and done.

However, don't be afraid of that dinner menu. There's always a grilled strip steak, but be adventurous! This is France—not really, but go with it! Plus, the most important offering on the Be Our Guest dinner menu isn't food at all. Be Our Guest made Magic Kingdom history the day it opened to its first guest, as the first and—to date—only restaurant in the park to serve alcohol. And a choir of angels sang "Hallelujah . . . Hallelujah!" What's a fine dining French restaurant if it doesn't pair its delicacies with regional

wines and beers? Remember, this ain't Epcot. You can't get a traveler and take it out into the park. But Be Our Guest is a great spot
to split a bottle of Burgundy or sip a couple of Belgian beers over
a nice dinner. This is one of those experiences you will not be able
to replicate anywhere else. If you can somehow arrange it for just
you and the wife or girlfriend (or both if you're really man enough),
it will definitely impress. My only word of warning, the kid's menu
doesn't offer the standard chicken fingers and fries. If your little
ones aren't adventurous eaters, this might make for a very expensive and unpleasant hour and a half. Maybe you can leave them
with somebody. There are plenty of smiling, trustworthy folks milling around the parks.

Gaston's Tavern

For me and any chiseled-jawed, barrel-chested real man who finds
himself stomping around New Fantasyland, there is only one destination that qualifies as a manly must-do! Just beyond the Be Our
Guest restaurant, you'll come to a little village square where stands
a bronze fountain erected in tribute to that icon of masculinity,
sport, weaponry, and expectorating, Gaston, donated of course by
Gaston. This also marks the entrance to my favorite little watering
hole in the Magic Kingdom, Gaston's Tavern.

    If the term "man cave" existed in the late 1700s, Gaston's Tav-
ern would be the personification. Actually back then the term
man cave most likely meant, well, a real cave. But I digress. When
you walk into Gaston's, you'll feel right at home. Stone walls,
wood floors, and stools everywhere. None of those wussy vinyl-
upholstered booths! There are antlers everywhere, mounted heads
of all sorts of critters. Weapons hang from the walls, as well as a
dartboard that seems to have been missed more than hit to judge
by the alarming number of stray darts embedded in the walls, ceiling, and no doubt some poor sap's skull. But that's only one side.
When you look to the right, you'll see Gaston the man's preferred
party room. His portrait hangs in a place of respect over the glowing hearth. His mighty chair is upholstered in leather and the hair

of some mysterious yak-like beast. It waits dutifully for the master's return from another hunting and/or wenching expedition. Fortunately, that means you can sit in it for as many photo ops as your wife will tolerate!

Let's get straight to the one tiny, disappointing detail. Yes, the name says tavern, but no, there is no booze at Gaston's. Fortunately, they've created a beverage that will ensure you never miss it. In fact, it might even trick your brain into thinking you're having a frosty, foamy brew anyway. Because, well, lack of fermentation aside, you are! The first thing you'll probably notice when you walk into Gaston's Tavern are the barrels behind the counter. These hold the house special, a frozen beverage called **LeFou's Brew**. While non-alcoholic, it is tasty! The brew consists of frozen apple juice and toasted marshmallow flavoring, topped with a surprisingly thick passion fruit foam. I know, it doesn't sound like your first choice of drink combinations, but trust me, LeFou's Brew is delicious, and more important it's fun to drink. Opt for the souvenir mug! You feel like even more of a man just gripping the handle as foam drips over the top and down the sides. It helps to slam it down on the table when you're done and wipe your mouth on your sleeve, but you didn't hear that from me.

To complement the icy apple drink, Gaston's offers a "snack" that very well might dethrone my beloved turkey legs at Walt Disney World. For just under a ten-spot, you can get a hot, juicy, roast pork shank to go along with your LeFou's Brew. At first, maybe an odd pairing, but it's actually genius. Remember the old standard, pork chops and applesauce? Gaston's Tavern has ratcheted it up a few notches with this combo. I realize ten bucks might seem like a bit much for a "snack," but believe me when I tell you that term is a misnomer. This hunk of steamy, meaty goodness is almost as big as Piglet himself! Okay, bad example! And aside from the fact that it's delicious, you look so badass sinking your fangs into swine right on the bone and washing it down with LeFou's Brew, sticky foam and pig pieces running down your chin! The only thing that would make it better is a little side of barbecue sauce to dunk the meat in. Otherwise, this may be the perfect snack (that eats like a meal) for a real man. And I won't even bother bringing up the warm cinnamon rolls the size of a tissue box they sell here. That's not really an exaggeration. They're bigger than a roll of toilet paper, seriously! A buddy of mine ordered one and it looked and smelled like Heaven in the form of a pastry, but I was too stuffed to get my own. If, after a pork shank and a brew, you can force down one of these doughy, frosted pillows of deliciousness, you, sir, are indeed a man's man! I salute you!

Under the Sea—Journey of The Little Mermaid

The final and perhaps most popular piece to New Fantasyland's Enchanted Forest is a long-anticipated, movie-based attraction that's been in the plans, on and off, since this author was a teenager. Disney's feature *The Little Mermaid* changed the landscape of animated movies, and by many accounts, brought Walt Disney Animation back from the brink of extinction. Some kind of ride based on one of Disney's most popular films and characters seemed like a no-brainer. It just didn't happen. A few years ago, Disney released virtual footage, hosted by the great Imagineer Tony Baxter, of a *Mermaid* ride that had been designed in the early nineties. But for whatever reason it never came to be. Finally, after 20 years, Disney announced that *Under the Sea—Journey of The Little Mermaid* would be built as the centerpiece of the New Fantasyland expansion.

I'm not gonna lie to you, I was very happy to hear this. Yeah, I hear you screaming *"Whoa, whoa, whoa! What do you mean you were excited about a Little Mermaid ride?"* Listen, I'll argue any time that *Little Mermaid* is very much a guy-friendly movie. The opening scene shows a huge sailing ship out on the open sea, old salts singing a sea shanty, battening down the hatches in the face of a hurricane! It doesn't get much manlier than that! You've got a shark attack. You've got singing seafood and borderline Jimmy Buffett music. And you've got a cute redhead washing up on the beach, and oh, by the way, she doesn't talk! This is a man's fairy tale come true! Maybe I should delete that last line! I should also mention I was 14 when the film was released on home video (yes kids, on a VHS tape) and I was in a very "serious" relationship with an older woman. She was 17, and that was her favorite movie so we watched it every weekend one summer. And by "watch it" I mean sometimes we actually saw the movie. So yes, I'm a *Mermaid* fan!

The attraction is very much like the classic dark rides over on the other side of Fantasyland. Old Fantasyland, maybe? How about *Classic* Fantasyland? It's almost a combination of *Peter Pan*, *Winnie the Pooh*, and a touch of *Haunted Mansion*, but all with the latest generation technology. Listen, it is what it is. It's fun, but yes, it's for kids, and specifically for little girls. So why am I selling it so hard in this *real man's guide*? You have to check out the quéue. Trust me, it makes the ride worthwhile. The designers really created something impressive, between the rockwork and water and the castle they erected over it. As you wind your way through some coastal cave, there is detail after detail to catch your eyes. Shells, jewels, and wreckage abound in every crevice and around every craggy corner. You've heard of "hidden Mickeys?" If not, there's a guide you can buy (available in fine retailers everywhere) from The Intrepid Traveler, natch! Make sure you keep your eyes peeled for the hidden *Nautilus* carved somewhere in the rock. Remember Captain Nemo's squid-skewering steampunk submarine from the Disney classic *20,000 Leagues Under the Sea*? There's an effigy hidden somewhere for you to discover while you wait. I'll give you a hint. Right before you enter the cavern part of the queue, turn around and look behind you at the shallow pool.

From the cave, you wind your way into the bowels of Prince Eric's castle. The architecture is astounding. Once again you might forget you're in Florida. You might even forget what century you're in. I felt like I had been granted access to the areas of the *Pirates of the Caribbean* attraction I'd always dreamed of exploring. Or at least parts of the set from *The Goonies*! At least until we reached the loading area and the pastel-colored seashells came rolling by as a Cast Member bade me climb aboard. Is this a ride for a real man? No. But as you've come to expect from this straight-talking guide, I'm telling you straight up, you're going to have to ride it. Fortunately, the *Journey of The Little Mermaid* is visually incredible. There are more animatronics here than in any other Disney attraction. Much like the queue, there's something different to see every time your eyes dart around. That will, hopefully, be enough to keep you engaged in the attraction. Even if there's nothing new to the story.

 The official Ears of Steel recommendation: Come for the impressive queue, stay for the ride.

Seven Dwarfs Mine Train

There you have it! After more than three years of hype and anticipation, that's New Fantasyland. Well, almost. I know, I just spent the last few pages telling you about all this Princess stuff. Almost discredits this whole book, doesn't it?

Not so fast. After all the tiaras and fluffy dresses, Disney is throwing the dudes a bone! There is one more attraction coming to New Fantasyland that, even now, when it's just a mountain of twisting, turning metal, already looks like it is going to rock! And by rock, I'm talking diamonds! Walt Disney is the ultimate real man, changing every industry he touched. Remember how he changed the feature film with a little movie called *Snow White and the Seven Dwarfs*? Well, for decades Snow White had her own attraction over on the other side of Fantasyland. Things are changing. Those seven little dudes who saved her skin, even faced down a witch after busting their humps down in the mines, are finally getting their own featured attraction! The *Seven Dwarfs Mine Train* looks like it's going to change the roller coaster game. While Disney has promised it will be family friendly, featuring music from the movie as well as AA versions of the familiar seven, the ride system will be unlike anything you've ever ridden. Twisting and turning inside the mine and out, the individual cars will swing side to side. Imagine flying down a coaster track with the added sensation that you might spill out sideways with every curve and turn! Having only seen it in skeletal form, I can already imagine the official Ears of Steel recommendation: *Awesome!*

Peter Pan's Flight

The final attraction in Fantasyland fit for a vacation warrior like you is another movie-based classic located in the older part of the land! It also involves pirates, and as we've already established, pirates = manly! So have no shame lining up for *Peter Pan's Flight*! This really is a fan favorite, dare I say a man favorite! Board a pirate ship and rise into the air, soaring over London into that mythical land where beer doesn't cause a gut and you'll never lose a hair from your head (but miraculously it all disappears from your back)—*Neverland!*

Of course, Captain Hook features prominently throughout the ride. Hook gets a bad rap for being a villain. I say he's just misrepresented. Sure his fashion sense is a little flamboyant, but cut the guy some slack! He faced down a crocodile, who I might add *ate his hand*, and he's still running a tight ship! That's a real man. So Hook won't suffer the shenanigans of some dandy in tights who won't grow up? Does that really make him a villain or just a determined leader? You tell me. At any rate, you know the story. Peter Pan flies in and saves Wendy and the Lost Boys. Hook ends up balanced precariously between the jaws of that same obsessed crocodile.

 The official Ears of Steel recommendation: *Pan* is a good time, no matter how grown-up you fancy yourself.

Haunted Mansion

Here's the good news, when you step off your ship, you're officially done with Fantasyland. Just hang a (King) *Louie* and follow the bend to Liberty Square! What's that? What music? Good feelings? No! Ignore it! Keep walking! Do not let that strange tractor beam of happiness pull you to the right. Yes, I know it's a boat ride! Trust me! It's not that kind of boat ride! I know it sounds happy and cheerful! I know there are smiley-faced puppets singing about a unified world! Fight, man! Fight! It's a trap!

Phew! That was close! We almost got sucked into "*it's a small world.*" Stronger men have gone in and never come out. At least not with their mental faculties intact. That song will bore its way deep into your ears and latch on to your cerebrum for all eternity. Let's forget this happened and move on. Besides, do you smell that? Deep-fried battered fish and hush puppies at 9 o'clock. You've reached Columbia Harbour House! That means you've crossed safely into the land of Paul Revere and Washington Irving. Sorry, you know, the guy who created the Headless Horseman? Just checking. It doesn't get much manlier in Walt Disney World than Liberty Square.

Certainly it is one of the smaller lands in Magic Kingdom, but by no means unworthy of your time. There are two highlights in Liberty Square that make it an absolute real man's must-do! First and foremost, it is home to one of the Top 10 Disney attractions in all the parks. Home being an interesting word, as the attraction itself is home to 999 permanent, or at least semi-permanent, and wholly transparent residents. Our destination, if you're man enough (after all, real men don't believe in ghosts), is that spooky old manor on the hillside, *Haunted Mansion*!

This is one of the greatest theme park attractions ever conceived, conceptualized, and built! I will go so far as to say the Walt Disney World *Mansion* is better than the Disneyland original created by Mr. Disney himself. Inside they're pretty much the same, but the Disneyland *Mansion* is much smaller and quainter. The *Mansion* at WDW is spectacular. It's large and looming, rising up out of the hill toward the heavens (ironically). A little like a castle, a bit like a mad scientist's lair, *Haunted Mansion* starts to set the tone for what you're about to experience while you're still walking up to it. You catch glimpses over rooftops and through trees. You hear the chilling organ music. You see the riderless carriage with a phantom horse hitched to the post. This place is ominous and creepy and awesome all at once! Something calls to your darker nature, compelling you to investigate further . . .

𝔐an's 𝔍ournal

Journeying up Main Street toward the castle, I noticed crowds forming and Cast Members redirecting guests. There were lights and speakers and a group of tight-T-shirt-wearing pretty boys prancing around the stage in skinny jeans and too much hair product. Turned out they were some B-grade bubblegum pop group tapped to record an ad campaign for Disney Parks. To avoid the crowds and the terrible caterwauling coming from the speakers they lip-synched to, I ducked around the castle.

It was early and, aside from the gawkers at the castle stage, there weren't many guests here yet. I found myself in a deserted Liberty Square. To my right stood *The Hall of Presidents*, a long-standing show featuring every President from George "Ol' Wood Teeth" Washington to the current Commander-in-Chief. On a hot afternoon, it's a great spot to catch a cool nap, but I wanted adventure. I wasn't in the mood for a lesson from some old ghosts of the past. Or so I thought.

Across a lagoon, I saw a tall brick mansion set against the trees, looking out over the Rivers of America. It looked like maybe it was some exclusive property for VIP guests. As I approached the covered walkway to the house, a gaunt-looking fellow in a green tuxedo bid me come in. I followed the green awning until I made a somewhat grim discovery. There was some crazy cemetery in the courtyard of this morose manor.

All these pervious residents had met untimely and unusual ends. Someone's poor parakeet-loving Auntie took one in the back and was discovered face down in birdseed. A sportsman Uncle was taken out by a reticulated reptile, another reason I don't let my kids have a snake. Farther in, the family mausoleums were no less twisted and fantastic. One relative was a retired sea captain who ironically drowned in the bath.

Remind me not to join this unlucky family should the opportunity ever arise. The service entrance opened and a maid ushered us inside and into a strange rotunda. I don't know what the master of the house is paying his staff, but she wasn't exactly chipper. I wanted to ask if it would kill her to smile, but soon realized anything was possible around this nuthouse. Once a small group of us were corralled in the parlor, the door slammed shut and some unseen voice began barking at us. Look around, look up, and look at the artwork on the walls. Maybe I was still feeling the time-change but I swear the paintings were getting longer. I watched as more details began emerging. A young lady precariously pirouetting on a tightrope over a hungry alligator pit. Three unlucky chaps sinking slowly into sludge. A suicidal society type standing atop explosives holding his last words on paper.

That's when the lights went out and up above we saw the landlord, dangling overheard from a rope around the rafters. At that moment I thought maybe I would go ride those tea cups after all. The lights returned, as much as they ever did in this dimly lit loony bin. Another wall opened and we were again ushered down a corridor.

I've seen houses with lift chairs running up and down the stairs for the elderly, but this guy had a treadmill running through the entire floor plan with crazy black chairs attached. I'd never seen furniture like this. Must be IKEA, I figured. Not wanting to make a scene, I took a seat only to find it wasn't the most cushioned sofa—it was like sitting on a tombstone. A metal bar suddenly snapped down across my gut. I began to think about the unfortunate saps memorialized outside and feared whatever crazy exit this house had for me.

My host referred to this black-domed contraption as a Doom Buggy. Didn't exactly inspire a lot of confidence for a safe return home. But this was an amusement park I reasoned, what could happen? I swallowed hard and went along with the ride. We passed through a series of staircases that were the very argument for why contractors should have to pass drug tests. They went up, down, this way and that. I was later told they were "Escher-like." If I knew what that meant, I'd have to give myself a wedgie.

We ventured deeper into the bowels of the mansion as our unseen tour guide explained a little about the house, specifically its 999 residents who would very likely be floating by to say hello. From behind numerous thick doors came banging, howling, and moaning as said tenants fought to get a glimpse of fresh meat . . . er, faces.

Finally we were brought into a dark parlor where I hoped we might be allowed to loosen the lap bar a little, until I saw a head floating in a beer snifter! This ghastly gal chanted some kind of strange hocus-pocus Ouija-board nonsense. It looked like the marching band from Main Street had left their instruments hanging around the room. Instruments literally floated around, playing without musicians! For a green chick, the lady in the crystal ball wasn't actually half-bad, but we were pushed farther on before I could ask for her number.

For some reason, our host decided we should see the attic, which was littered with paintings. They were all wedding portraits featuring the same bride. But the different grooms suddenly lost weight before my eyes—the weight located right above their shoulders! Call me a little slow, but I began to think something wasn't right in this nuthouse. I thought this park was about singing dolls and balloons, not murderous brides with bloody hatchets. I was starting to enjoy this! Hey, she's not *my* wife!

We came out onto a corridor overlooking a large ballroom. It was dusty and covered in cobwebs, but in its day it probably hosted some major keggers! My suspicions were confirmed when translucent revelers appeared, dancing, drinking, shooting, and swinging from the chandeliers. Every few seconds, more party guests would appear and then vanish. Clearly this place was getting to me. I had to get out before the mansion sucked me in for good!

Someone must have read my mind—wouldn't be surprised in this psycho sanctum! My Doom Buggy spun around and I slowly rolled backward down a staircase and in a few moments was "outside." Talk about out of the frying pan into the *crypt*! I'd been dragged out to the backyard cemetery. It was bad enough encountering spirits inside the house. Now I was in their playground! As if things weren't weird enough, I was suddenly in some George Romero wet dream where the dead were rising to sing and dance and look for warm partners.

Even the marble statuary had been animated by some ghostly force to welcome foolish visitors. I was suddenly reminded of what Barbosa said. It was time I started believing in ghost stories, because I was definitely in one! And having a blast! My eyes couldn't dart around fast enough to take in all of this lively graveyard's excitement. We eventually travelled back inside and down a dark passageway, where our host returned with a final warning.

While the house was always open to new residents, we should watch out for phantoms seeking a new place to stay. More specifically, beware of hitchhiking ghosts!

Sure enough, there were three ghastly fellows thumbing a ride. The real shock came when we turned a corner, safely away from these runaway spirits, or so I thought. I peered into a mirror hung on the old brick wall across from my Doom Buggy to see I was no longer alone in my seat. One of the happy haunts was right next to me. Before I could react, he pulled off his head . . . AND MINE! In the blink of an eye, he replaced our skulls and vanished. I desperately pawed at my neck to make sure everything was back in place. I was sighing with relief as we coasted into the unloading area.

I hopped out of the Doom Buggy and charged briskly for daylight, occasionally peering over my shoulder to see if my new friend was following. The funny thing is, as soon as I was outside in the fresh air, I felt a strange desire to turn right back around and go party with the Netherworld all over again!

Every kid's tolerance for the spooky and macabre is different, but *Haunted Mansion's* haunts are pretty benign and only out for a laugh. Most of them anyway! You want to see something scary, watch the movie they made trying to cash in on the success of *Haunted Mansion*, the ride! That is terrifying, but only in how awful it is and how mystifying that some studio exec green-lit it in the first place. I'd say it's a blessing that the *Haunted Mansion* movie tanked. Otherwise, there'd probably be a bunch of Audio-Animatronics Eddie Murphys added throughout the ride. Disney gets a pass for most of the changes made at *Pirates*. After all, thanks to Johnny Depp, they could rename it *Profits of the Caribbean*! But don't screw with the *Mansion*. Especially if you don't have great flick to back it up—yet.

 The official Ears of Steel recommendation: Face your fears and ride it . . . many times!

Pecos Bill Tall Tale Inn and Cafe

After *Mansion*, there's not much reason to hang around Liberty Square. At least not until dinner time. For now, let's head back to Frontierland. We skipped through it earlier when we were rushing to *Big Thunder* and *Splash*. If you weren't hungry for lunch in Tomorrowland, that's okay. Frontierland is home to my other favorite lunch spot in the park, Pecos Bill Tall Tale Inn and Cafe!

You'll know Pecos Bill's by the bright blue saloon exterior. But the aroma of grilled beef and onions wafting enticingly from the swinging doors will draw you in. Yes, they serve pulled pork sandwiches and a good taco salad—any salad with ground beef and cheese is a good salad—but that's not what you saddle up for. Not the first time you saunter in anyway. For my gold dust, Pecos Bill's makes one hell of a bacon cheeseburger! That's just the beginning. After they hand you your delicious but relatively tame burger, mosey on over to the fixin's bar where you'll find the usual lettuce, tomato, and what not. You'll also discover molten hot cheese sauce, jalapeños (probably for the taco salad, says you), sweet, tangy barbecue sauce, and mountains of soft, savory, *slathering* grilled onions! I like to create a Western monstrosity of a cheeseburger! If you're not wearing it, you aren't doing it right!

Again, this is a popular dining spot and the tables are first-come, first-served. So while you wait to order send the little buckaroos out to scout a table. Tell 'em to show no mercy. Don't fall for the old lady with the walker or the kid with crutches routine! As soon as they see somebody's napkin drop, jump on that table like a buckin' bronco!

Country Bear Jamboree

After you dunk your face and hands in a trough of water, you're gonna need to set a spell. Saunter on down the road a piece. Frontierland is home to one last attraction every cowpoke should take time to put up his spurs and check out. That perennial guest-pleasing, paw-stomping *Country Bear Jamboree*! What man doesn't love a band of singing bears? The Country Bears are a must-see for history alone, dating all the way back to 1960 when they were originally designed to be part of a restaurant. While Walt never saw it built, he approved the concept art, which is often remembered as "Walt's last laugh." When Imagineer Marc Davis showed Walt his crazy bear designs, legend goes he belly laughed at these ridiculous critters. Shortly after approving Davis's artwork, Walt turned to leave, but stopped and said, "Goodbye." This was something he never did. A few days later Walt died. The *Country Bears* may be the last attraction Walt officially approved.

It's a raucous review of country music performed by animatronic bears. All the characters are unique and cartoonish and good for a few laughs, and the down-home Americana soundtrack is infectious. The good news is that Disney recently gave the *Country Bears* a full once-over to make sure the show would go on for a long time!

 The official Ears of Steel recommendation: This Disney classic is definitely a man's show and an Ears of Steel favorite! Two bear claws up! (Mmm, bear claws!)

Liberty Tree Tavern

There's one more good reason for a man to hang around Magic Kingdom. You'll find plenty of snacks all over the place, along with the bakery and candy shop. I already told you my favorite lunch spots. But for my money (and stomach) there's only one place for dinner! If every day on Main Street, U.S.A. is the Fourth of July, then it's always Thanksgiving in Liberty Square! That is, if you've got your dinner ADR for Liberty Tree Tavern.

That's a hypothetical "if" because, if you don't eat there at least once, well, you're dumb! Fashioned after the colonial inns our founding fathers dined in, Liberty Tree Tavern is the perfect location for family dinner. The food is old school traditional American eats. Servers drop off family-style platters of roast turkey, pork, beef brisket, vegetables, fresh baked rolls, mashed potatoes and gravy, and mac and cheese. It's all you can eat and it's all delicious! In some cases even better than Mom used to make. Just don't undo your belt after dinner. That would be weird.

Don't try to walk up and expect a table, either. The staff will, of course, try to accommodate, but plan on being hungry for another hour or more because that's how soon you're likely to be seated. Unless you get lucky and the manager is a bro who takes pity on you!

Man's Journal

I got to Liberty Tree and stood in the line to check in. I'd personally made an ADR for six people to eat dinner at 7:00. The place was already jumping, and my wife and our friends waited outside in the shade. I realize they're going for that old world, pre-central-air-conditioning theme, but man it was hot as balls in that lobby area! Might have actually been warmer inside than out! What really got me sweating though was when I stepped up to the stand, gave my name, and was told no ADR could be found.

Ha, I chuckled, no problem. I was sure he wasn't looking in the right place. I assured him I not only had a reservation, I'd made two—one for 6:45 and one for 7:00 when I realized we'd have more people in our group—but had cancelled the earlier time. He asked for my confirmation number so I began to search through my emails on my phone to find it. Meanwhile I suggested he check again, this time switching my first and last names as that was a common mistake. Still no luck, he responded. By this time, my wife had come in to see what was going on. We had a pack of ravenous children (and adults) in tow. I couldn't tell them we didn't have a seating! I'd never hear the end of it, from either wife. I'd rather just eat cotton candy for dinner!

The Liberty Tree manager stepped in at this point and asked if he could assist. I calmly (through buckets of sweat running down my brow) explained the situation, that they'd clearly mixed up my reservations. He did some rapid fire typing and after a moment gave a knowing, "Aha!" The manager said he did in fact find my 7:00 dinner ADR . . . for Thursday. This was Monday. That was impossible I asserted. We had dinner reservations elsewhere on Thursday. I was certain I'd made it for this day. He again asked if I had the confirmation email and I said I'd have to go back two months in my phone. As I began swiping at my touch screen like a honey badger with a garter snake, the manager cleared his throat as if calling my attention.

"No problem, sir," he said, staring past me at my wife. He was holding a pager in his hand. "Clearly there's been some kind of system mix-up. I've changed your reservation back to tonight as it was supposed to be. Give us a few minutes and we'll buzz you when your table is ready."

I thanked him and more or less pushed the wife back outside. No problem, I assured our friends. It would just be a little longer, as they had a lot of slow eaters inside. It wasn't 10 more minutes before we were seated and only a few more before platters of steaming food were laid out before us like royalty. We had a great dinner and toasted another perfect night at Disney.

Meanwhile, I quietly located my confirmation email from months prior. I indeed had made the reservation for 7:00 . . . on Thursday! I owe that cat a frosty one!

We've made it all the way around the park that started it all. The centerpiece of Walt Disney World. Wasn't so bad after all, was it? If you trust me on this, you'll feel pretty foolish for waiting so long to check it out yourself. You've missed some amazing old attractions. The good news is you can go every couple of years, hell every year, and there'll be something new. Yet you'll never tire of old favorites. I've probably ridden *Pirates of the Caribbean* and *Haunted Mansion* a hundred times in my life, and I'm never bored. There's always some new detail to be discovered and a favorite moment that captures my imagination all over again!

Above all, Magic Kingdom may seem childish to some, but it's the park that helps real men leave behind the real bull$#@% of the real world! Disney Marketing would never put it that way, but that's what Walt Disney World is all about. You can live like a pirate for a few days. All year you have to be a regular guy, balancing the pressures of life on your shoulders. Throw it all aside and let somebody else worry about it for a while.

Don't you deserve at least that much? Haven't you earned it? I know I have. Even if I haven't, I'm taking it anyway, because nobody is going to give me extra credit if I don't!

Yo ho! Yo ho!

CHAPTER ELEVEN

Nothing to Be Scared Of (Right?)

YOU DID PACK EXTRA UNDERWEAR, DIDN'T YOU?

Real men don't get scared easily. Or if we do, we hide it well, right? Many real men like to prove their mettle by looking fear in the face and spitting tobacco in its eye. The purpose of this book is to change the misconception that Walt Disney World is just for kids. Perhaps the strongest argument is how many downright scary experiences it offers!

Talk to any hardcore Disney fanatic about scary attractions and they're very likely to say two words—*Alien Encounter*. In the nineties, Disney teamed up with George Lucas again, but for a very different attraction. They wanted something new and exciting in Tomorrowland. It was not quite a ride, nor could it be called a show. Together that creative brain trust created a sense-slaughtering experience called *Alien Encounter*. Word spread quickly about this attraction. And that word was *"NOOO!!!"*

Encounter was possibly the most terrifying thing ever built in the Eastern United States, let alone a Disney park. I had the good (or perhaps bad) fortune to experience it firsthand before they closed, nailed, and barricaded the doors. The preshow hurtled guests into the future and the labs of an intergalactic corporation called **XS.** I'll wait. *Riiight! **Excess!***

XS was developing exciting molecular transportation technology as the future of travel. Probably a bad sign for an attraction when a cute, cuddly alien is teleported between two capsules and after painful squeals we see the poor critter's been scorched to cinder! That's fun for kids! That was nothing compared to the big dance inside.

The main theater-in-the-round locked guests into crazy mechanical jump-seats facing a central stage area. The second red flag for *Alien Encounter* should have been the nail marks in almost every seat.

In the middle of the futuristic, Ridley Scott-like set was a giant glass cylinder surrounded by hoses and machinery, like the smaller preshow version on steroids. Only this time something goes horribly wrong and a large, carnivorous alien monster is beamed into the room. The narration assured us the monster was contained in the capsule, which as you probably guessed meant a moment later it burst out and, in total darkness, began terrorizing the audience.

This was a 4-D attraction! When the capsule shattered, you felt "glass" raining over you. When the alien prowled through the room, you heard its growling and breathing right in your ears (thanks to speakers in the headrests). You felt hot breath on your neck. When it was stepping over you, weight came pressing down on your shoulders (and it was not comfortable). This ride jacked you up physically as well as mentally. Of course, the *pièce de résistance* came when the creature caught hold of an unseen XS employee and began eating him alive. We heard his cries, the snapping of bones and ripping of sinews. And if that didn't drive the point home, warm water began dripping onto your face and arms simulating the blood presumably running down the beastie's chin. All to the tune of *it's a small world after all.* Just kidding!

Every Disney story has to have a happy ending and eventually we were saved. The monster was sent back to its hostile home world. I was a little too busy wetting myself and praying it really was *make-believe* to take proper script notes. Laugh if you want, but I assure you *Alien Encounter* could reduce hardened criminals into hyperventilating puddles of humanity.

This is exactly why you'll never experience it. There were so many complaints and negative reviews (and forwarded therapy bills from irate parents) that Disney pulled the plug. *Alien Encounter* was replaced with another *Alien*-themed attraction, scary in its own right (not necessarily intentionally). When you are passing through Tomorrowland, you'll now see *Stitch's Great Escape!* where *Alien Encounter* once stood. The same effects are in place, but tweaked to be comical rather than horrifying. Instead of splattering blood, it's a six-limbed fuzzy blue genetic experiment spitting on you. Oh, and he belches chili dog in your face. Something even the flesh-eating arthropod never did.

Still, in the spirit of frightening attractions such as the gone but psyche-scarring *Alien Encounter*, I give you the current . . .

Ears of Steel Top Ten *Scariest* Attractions at Walt Disney World!

Keep in mind, this is Disney. Scary is relative. We're not talking scary as in actual life-threatening mayhem like axe murderers, rabid animals, or the music of Justin Bieber. Disney tends to keep even their most horrifying chills family friendly. I've listed them in reverse order, from mildly chilling to a little intense for small children to pretty damn frightening!

10. Haunted Mansion

This one seems so obvious I wasn't even going to include it here. Quite frankly, once you're a Disney pro, there's little scary about the *Mansion*. The spirits inside are far more comical and good-natured than evil or malicious. However, there are a handful of scenes discomforting and creepy enough to still send a few shivers down the spine. Nothing reaches out and grabs you, but there are a few ghouls on this ride that *pop up* to say hello. Not terrifying per se, but they will give your heart enough of a jolt to remind you you're alive . . . at least for a moment.

9. Splash Mountain

This and the *Mansion* are interchangeable on this list. While *Splash Mountain* is charming and fun, it is still a log flume. They don't try to hide it. You see the 40-foot drop as you're approaching the attraction and you hear the screams of riders all the way down.

Inside the mountain, Disney disarms you at first with a handful of innocent mini-drops and singing forest critters. But eventually you find yourself climbing. That's when reality sets back in. It doesn't help that above you sit two vultures, dressed as morticians and talkin' smack about how you're about to bite it. If you've got an issue with heights and more importantly plummeting from them in a log, you could experience an existential moment. See you at the bottom!

8. Ellen's Energy Adventure

I can deal with sulfurous volcanoes. I can handle being attacked by robotic prehistoric beasts. I've even sat through Ellen's afternoon dance party chat show. But a face-to-face encounter with an animatronic Ellen DeGeneres during the ride is almost more than my beefy heart can handle. Heed my warning!

7. It's Tough to be a Bug!

On its face, this 4-D flick (pun somewhat intended) based on Disney/Pixar's *A Bug's Life* seems innocuous enough. You're probably thinking what's scary about a kid's movie? It's humorous and interactive, for the first half. Some of the bugs are intense but still funny, like the one that shoots darts out of his ass. The real panic (at least for little ones) generally hits when Hopper, the nefarious grasshopper animatronic appears. Not only is he a large, articulated, straight-up threatening six-foot insect, he summons his hornet and spider minions to attack the audience. The room fills with smoke and an army of arachnids falls from the ceiling, at which point I've witnessed many a small child completely melt down. Then there's that *special* effect involving the seat and your tailbone when the hornets "appear." This one will startle more than just kids.

6. The Richard Petty Driving Experience

Not just a clever name, this one is very much what it sounds like. Anyone daring enough can reserve a seat in a real NASCAR-certified stock car. No rails, no chains, no button back at the loading area to shut it down in an emergency. This is fuel. This is combustion. This is rubber and pavement. High-speed with little protection from a fiery crash, just like the real thing. You might think driving the car yourself gives you control and there's little to worry about. Interesting. Professional drivers lose control on those turns at 80 miles per hour more regularly than NASCAR officials (and Disney attorneys) would probably like me to say. Go ahead, big guy, start your engine!

Speaking of driving, honorable mention goes to riding the Disney buses to and from the parks. Disney's bus drivers all seem sensible and alert and I've never feared for my life at the hands of any of them. It's the tourists in rental cars navigating those Florida roads I worry about. The last time I was down, I was standing (as you'll find you do quite a bit) and some buffoon in a rented hatchback cut in front of us and then decided to brake as he figured out where he was going—and by "he" I mean she of course, but I'm trying to be politically correct! Our bus driver had no choice but to slam on the brakes and lay on the horn until the idiot finally looked up in his (her) rearview, saw his (her) life flash before his (her) eyes, and gunned it out of the way at the last second.

My grip on the nylon ring tightened until I lost circulation to my fingers as I braced for the presumed impact. For a moment, all of us riding the bus exchanged looks as if to say "this could be a *less than magical* vacation memory." Once again, I'm glad that Disney strives to hire the best of the best for every position. I'd definitely ride shotgun in a race car with that particular driver.

5. Summit Plummet

This one's at Disney's Blizzard Beach water park. *Summit Plummet* is a 12-story "ski jump turned water slide" and it's a dead drop. You can find videos online of young daredevils with a healthy disrespect for electronics who recorded their own misadventures on the slope. The view is straight down nearly all 120 feet. Well, until you slip into the dark tunnel halfway down. The audio? Screaming.

Disney boasts that *Summit Plummet* is the tallest, longest, fastest water slide on record. Is it the scariest? I suppose if they wanted to secure that *most terrifying water slide in history* badge, they could throw in a few hungry sharks at the bottom of the pool. Aside from that, I'd say they're good.

4. Mission: SPACE

When *Mission: SPACE* first opened at Epcot, it was much hyped and everyone couldn't wait to get on it. Since then you will see the lines don't tend to be all that long. It requires a certain amount of gusto, courage, or straight-up *huevos*. The attraction itself isn't so much scary as it is unusual. It's a high-tech flight simulator. You're strapped in and launched into outer space en route to the red planet. Your mission is faithfully narrated by Gary "*Lt. Dan*" Sinise. Doesn't sound scary, right? In fact, I know it sounds exciting! Well, before you start wagging your tail like a Labrador at the door with a tiny bladder, let me drop a little real science on you . . . PEOPLE HAVE DIED ON THIS RIDE!

Not in the story. I mean in real life, people have died from riding it. And not died like they slipped out of the restraints of a roller coaster and knocked their melon on a rail. I mean hearts have stopped. And I'm not making light of those sad situations. Truth be told, if I dropped dead having fun at Walt Disney World, I'd consider it an okay way to go. The point is that you could conceivably *not walk off* this attraction (*Ding-dong!* Oh, hello there, Disney lawyers! No, no, it's okay. I'm done!) Just let that swim around in your brain while boarding the attraction.

3. Expedition Everest

Animal Kingdom's high speed roller coaster was practically guaranteed a top spot on this list as is. But it isn't simply the intense speed, or flying backwards inside a pitch black mountain, or coming face-to-face with a snarling, roaring Yeti. Let's face it, the projected shadow of the Yeti in the cave is more frightening than the 0.3 seconds you might actually lay eyes on him. Even then he's bathed in disco lighting. Scary, but for a whole other reason. Let me tell you about real, panic-inducing fear I actually experienced aboard *Expedition Everest*.

Man's Journal

I arrived at Disney's Animal Kingdom park shortly after noon. The crowds seemed pretty light as the tropical Afro-Asian sun was high and hot! I didn't need the signs directing the way. I knew where I was headed. I spied the snowcapped mountain on the eastern horizon. Upon approaching the standby line, the wait sign said 20 minutes, which given the immense popularity of this attraction seemed like nothing. And nothing was right, for in truth there was little wait at all. I was through the outdoor queue and the Yeti museum in about five minutes. Sooner than anticipated I found myself boarding that tea train, ready to ascend the Forbidden Mountain.

I was seated near the front, a coveted spot for many thrill seekers. Not this adventurer. I prefer the back for more speed, less lag, and a full view of all the little extras hidden along the journey. It also provides you an extra second or two to spy the Yeti himself. But it was the front of the train this fateful day. I was seated next to a woman a bit older than me who, I learned quickly, didn't *habla mucho* English. Her preteen kids sat in front of us. We all smiled and nodded, ready for adventure. None of us knew the extra dose of unplanned peril waiting ahead.

The train pulled away and soon we were on an incline, climbing higher toward the mountain's peak. I was enthralled, taking mental notes of the artwork and props in the temple as we climbed onward and upward. We kept chugging higher and I admired the panoramic view of the park and the green landscape all around. I was oblivious to how high we actually were or to the fact that we seemed to be slowing down. At the highest point of the track, where it felt like I was staring straight up into the heavens, our train came to a jerking halt.

"That's not good," I said aloud.

My neighbor looked at me with a nervous smile. My eyes met hers and then, past her confused face, shifted to the view of the entire park beyond—and far below. We were indeed high. Very, *very* high. The track reaches 112 feet into the sky. I am 6 feet tall. So I'm guessing my eyeballs were roughly 116 feet over Florida. There was little around me but an open coaster car, a flimsy lap bar, and a breeze. To my left I was pretty sure I could see Pensacola. I wouldn't say I'm "afraid of heights" but then again, I rarely find myself so high in the air with so little *airplane* around me. I started to feel uneasy to say the least. We sat there another 30, maybe 45 seconds. An announcement was made to remain seated. As though I might be thinking about hopping out to grab a churro! *Mmm*, churros!

I then made a crucial mistake. In every disaster movie involving unlucky characters in a precarious position high above the nearest patch of land some chisel-jawed, blue-eyed adventurer winks, "Whatever you do, don't look down!" There's always some idiot who immediately looks down. In this instance, the idiot was me. I looked over the side of the car, through the tracks, to the ground far below. Another train that had just pulled out of the loading area squealed to a stop as well. At least those people could easily climb out and jump what was maybe four feet to safety.

Suddenly I remembered a news story I'd read recently. The problem was I couldn't remember if it really was *news* or Internet rumor or something my mind was concocting in that precarious position. I was certain in the last year I'd read of *Everest* breaking down and guests having to be harnessed to maintenance workers to climb down the service stairs. I glanced over the edge of the tracks at what apparently passed for service stairs under Florida code. Naked steel grates, complete with plenty of holes to see your impending *flattening* below. Not a handrail in sight. Could that happen to us? What if the announcement came that we were *s.o.l.* up here and they were sending up maintenance workers with harnesses. No way! They'd have better luck releasing the wheel locks and letting me roll back down.

As I sat in the ride vehicle, gripping the lap bar with my eyes shut, I felt my heart start to race. Irrational thoughts began flooding my head. I could see myself completely panicking and going right over the side. So this is a panic attack, I thought? The lady next to me had her eyes closed but her lips were moving in whispered prayer. Probably something along the lines of *"Lord, please don't let the brakes on this thing release due to the strain of the fat gringo next to me!"*

Honestly, I was praying the same thing.

Finally, after something like 10 or 15 minutes (okay, probably 3 or 4), the train lurched forward. We began to climb again, up and over the cursed mountain. There was a sigh of relief all down the train. I managed to wring out my underpants and enjoy the rest of the ride. We actually broke down again a moment later, inside the peak of the mountain, staring at the broken track. For whatever reason, I was completely fine. Even though we were actually higher than before I wasn't bothered at all. Maybe it was because I'd already conquered terror once. Or realistically, because we were surrounded by fiberglass rock and snow so I couldn't see how terrifying it really was. Plus I convinced myself that even if we did have to make the arduous climb down on foot, surely from here we could travel down through the mountain. Not in the open air. Besides, at that level, they had to have a service elevator. I'm probably wrong, of course, but let's just pretend. My book, my imaginary elevator! Savvy?

2. DINOSAUR

This prehistoric fear factory, also at Disney's Animal Kingdom, was originally called *Countdown to Extinction*. The ride might as well be called *Countdown to Soiling Yourself!* It changed to the simpler *DINOSAUR* after the release of the Disney animated movie of the same title. *Dinosaur* the cartoon was mostly a kid-friendly adventure about plant-eating dinos looking for a new, impending-asteroid-free home. Some moments of animated peril, but otherwise safe.

DINOSAUR the ride is terrifying! So much so that every time I'm strapped in and pull away from the loading bay I ask out loud, "Why the @#$% am I doing this again?!?!"

Like in *Alien Encounter* you spend nearly 75% of the ride in darkness. *DINOSAUR* only really lets you see when it wants you to, and it's usually when you absolutely wouldn't want to! But you are whipped and whirled and lunged, feeling your tires fighting the swampy terrain. You hear every bone-chilling wild sound in the forest primeval. You also hear the irritating narrator who sent you on this wild dino-chase announcing that you're stuck or lost or stuck *and* lost. The ship's computer announces the arrival of each new dinosaur just before it appears. Good thing too! That way you know for sure when that gigantic red scaly monster with the dagger-like teeth and horns appears that it is, indeed, a carnivore. God forbid you thought perhaps he wasn't there to eat you!

These animatronic versions are the most realistic, lifelike monsters ever created. Well, in the last ten million years or so. I can say that now because, after riding at least a dozen times, I can finally keep my eyes open (and tear-free) long enough to see them. Laugh all you want, *DINOSAUR* is scary as hell! Tell yourself a thousand times the creatures aren't real. When that Carnotaurus (who makes a T-Rex look like a cock-a-poo) makes his final attempt to rip your head from your shoulders, you will squeal.

1. The Twilight Zone Tower of Terror

Between *Tower* and *DINOSAUR* it was difficult to decide which should be crowned "Scariest Attraction." *DINOSAUR* might be more frightening in the whole "I've been obsessed with these monsters since I was a kid and now here they are to eat me" kind of way. At the end of the day, if something inside *DINOSAUR* breaks, you're sitting in a relatively safe dark room, at ground level, waiting for maintenance. If *Tower* snaps a cable or two, and you find yourself rapidly falling from great heights in a steel box, maintenance will be scooping you up with a shovel. Climbing almost 200 feet in the air before dropping like a lead weight, numerous times, defying gravity over and over, wondering if today's the day the park experiences a casualty (or a box full) earns *Tower* the number one spot!

Besides, if a robotic dinosaur suddenly turned sentient and attacked you, it would be quick. If *Tower* malfunctioned and, like a twisted *Twilight Zone* episode, your elevator came crashing down to (and through) the lobby, you'd probably be wide awake until the final stop. That, as they say, would suck. I know that's a sick, horrifying thought. Trust me, those thoughts and more will be running through your mind as you're clicking your seat belt, preparing to be jerked up and down, and then back up and back down, and then back up . . .

There it is! The Ears of Steel Most Frightening Walt Disney World Attractions. But before we move on, let me lay a sentimental favorite on you.

Snow White's Scary Adventure

If this ride were still around it would have been number 10 on the list, so maybe it's just as well it's not, because I have a feeling if you saw the words *Snow White* you'd just bail. As a grown-ass man you would not have been scared on this ride, even with the word "scary" in the title. As a kid, however, I was terrified of this one. In fact, the name is kind of misleading because you hardly saw the little German princess at all. This ride was all about the Wicked Queen-turned-*Wickeder*-Witch! And she made a couple of startling appearances, along with some angry living trees that turned on your vehicle and chomping alligators that snapped after you.

Maybe that's not so scary for a strapping buck like you, but a good parent would've thought twice before dragging young kids on it. Luckily, you won't have to worry about it. The attraction was dismantled in 2012 and many of her props stored away for all eternity. *Snow White's Scary Adventure* is no more, but she earned her spot on this list.

CHAPTER TWELVE

When Nature Calls

WHAT'S A MAGIC KINGDOM WITHOUT AN ENCHANTED THRONE?

When I was preparing for my research trip to find the best Walt Disney World had to offer real men, I was given a suggestion by a fellow fan. She said to me (yes, *she*): "Are you going to write about the best places to *use the bathroom*?"

Actually she worded it a different way. Her words rhymed with "rake a pit" or "shake a snit." I cleaned it up for your delicate pixie ears. (This book is for men, but we can still be *gentle*men). The question, however, was valid. After all, during any trip to the World there will come a moment, I assure you, when you're out and about having a great time when nature will come a-callin'. I'm not just talking "Number One." I mean a ride on the dump truck. El Lebowski Grande! Huey, Louie, *and numero Dewey!* Well, all I can say is *vaya con Dios* and may the Force be with you.

Anytime the kids are knockin' in public you start to wonder about the conditions of the facilities. I mean, have you ever had to go at an airport? I once had the spirit come upon me in a Walmart. A *Walmart!* Without getting too graphic, even Houdini would have marveled at my powers of levitation!

With Disney's reputation for cleanliness, you would expect to have a little better luck in the parks, should you find yourself in need with no chance of making it back to the hotel! Not so much. I visited a number of bathrooms on my last trip, taking mental notes, glancing around a little longer than normal (not long enough to get my nose broken, or any phone numbers). Overall, I was surprised by how disappointing many of the bathrooms inside the parks were, once I was actually paying attention to them. I suppose it should be expected. They're theme parks. Guests want to get in, go, and get back to the fun. Proper hygiene and everyday courtesy might get overlooked. So be it.

I will try to keep this chapter short, succinct, and productive (as you should the act, because prolonged sitting can cause painful fissures). I'm not going to cover every bathroom in every park. That would be gross. And weird. I'm just going to hit the highlights of the *heads*, as it were!

For instance, Hollywood Studios keeps a nice bathroom right up front by the main gate. Just veer to your right when you walk through the turnstiles. (Although I didn't have need of it when I was in the vicinity.) I ended up finding facilities later, near Pizza Planet, a restaurant inspired by *Toy Story* yet inexplicably located across from the Muppet Theater. This bathroom seemed to catch a lot of traffic, which I can only attribute to its proximity to a pizza joint.

Not to mention nearby you have *MuppetVision* and *Lights, Motors, Action!*, attractions that hold guests hostage for longer periods of time. As guys the first thing we do after being held in place for any extended time span is make a pit stop. This bathroom wasn't anything to write home about, but it was noticeably clean. Sparkling in fact, and I discovered why. The attendant on duty seemed never to leave his post. Or leave the guests alone as they were doing their business. I sat in my own little cubicle . . . *er*, stall (if you work in the corporate world, they're easily confused) and listened to this guy chat up every gent who stopped for a quick number one. I didn't catch his name, but I learned where his sister works, what he thinks of the Florida weather, and that he's a big Gators fan! This bathroom would have received very high marks, if not for this major violation of Guy Code. Talking in the men's room is strictly *ver-*

boten! Unless done at a concert, in which case you're all probably drunk and it's forgiven.

Animal Kingdom being the newest of the parks seemed to have a plethora of clean bathrooms, as you might expect. None really suffered from an excess of space, although they were vividly colored! I imagine that somehow aids in relief. It's nice to sit down in a pleasant environment (especially if there's nothing to read). Personally I liked the bathroom across from Flame Tree Barbeque. Then again, I just like the Flame Tree so it makes sense I'd end up in that particular facility. However, I did find it strange that the entrance to these particular bathrooms was right near the *Tigger and Pooh meet and greet*. Strange and, of course, a little funny. I mean, come on—*Pooh*? Don't groan—that won't be the last Pooh/poo joke! Either way, you don't want to make a wrong turn there!

Magic Kingdom being the most magical place on Earth, one might expect they'd have the most magical bathrooms. Sadly, I was vexed by disappointment. It was pretty much (s)hit or miss. Sorry, couldn't resist! Tomorrowland actually has a decent, spacious bathroom near *Space Mountain*, hidden behind the Tomorrowland Terrace stage. It's not overly fancy, but again, it was clean with a good number of stalls. Due to its secretive location, hit it early enough and you'll probably find this clean latrine pretty empty. It's not as if during peak hours you'll have to double up with a stranger, of course. It's just preferable to do what you're there for in relative peace and quiet, am I right?

I was advised to check out the bathrooms behind Columbia Harbour House, a fish and chip joint at the corner of Liberty Square and Fantasyland. My friend, that same girl who inspired this chapter, assured me that particular location was the finest place to drop a deuce (and a half) on property. I don't know how she could say since ladies don't do that, of course. Either way, I can only assume the janitorial staff gives the ladies room a little more time, love, and tenderness. After all, that close to Fantasyland and *"it's a small world"* in particular, there are going to be lots of mothers changing diapers in that spot. I'm not making any sexist implication. If anything, I'm saying women are more proactive about complaining to Guest Services about bathrooms littered with hygiene products and un-scrubbed public surfaces.

Men are animals. We let more slide in a bathroom. Nine times out of ten we're standing anyway. I don't know why they even bother installing toilets. Dig holes in the ground and hang a mirror to check our hair and we're good. I mean, how dirty can our hands get? Usually men are in and out without touching anything but the precious tackle God graced us with. And let's be honest, we wish there was even a chance *that* might graze public porcelain.

The men's room in that corner near Harbour House did not earn the gold-star raves my friend gave the ladies room. It was pretty filthy, and I mean by a guy's standards. Toilet paper and trash littered the floor, which didn't appear to have been mopped since they opened . . . *in 1971*! Throw in multiple unflushed toilets to complete the picture. In all fairness, the latter is not necessarily the park's fault since they are self-flushing. Even then, the department I'd blame in that instance is *concessions*, not maintenance.

The finest men's room I encountered on my self-guided tour, *Commodes of the Magic Kingdom* (which I'll be offering for a nominal fee in the near future—book now!) was back near Main Street, U.S.A. In fact, it's wedged between two fine eateries not far from the central hub. Just behind Casey's Corner, where you can grab a foot-long hot dog, and next to The Crystal Palace buffet is a little door marked **Gentlemen**. I went in anyway (thank you...try the veal!). Now don't get too excited thinking that I'm about to describe a pooper's wonderland with the finest in marble, stainless, and chrome. There's no attendant with warm cloths and mints or free chair massages. In fact, at first glance it is pretty underwhelming. Boring beige and brown tile with only a few stalls.

However, it is immaculately clean. I imagine it benefits from being somewhat hidden away. The bathroom hooligans probably don't even know it's there. However, it's not the cleanliness or reduced traffic that rate it a bathroom fit for a real man. There's an added dimension. These creative types at Disney are always trying to create full sensory experiences. Due to sharing a building (and it stands to reason a ventilation system) with a hot dog joint, the entire bathroom smells of freshly brined sauerkraut! Not only is that an intoxicating aroma—and it is!—it also masks any other smells trying to assault your olfactory organ. That's an air freshener for a real man!

If you did feel the urge coming on in Magic Kingdom, there's also a very nice down-home commode just a boat ride away in the lobby of the Wilderness Lodge. Just around the corner from Whispering Canyon Café awaits a clean latrine with rustic decor, the smell of cedar, and pleasant frontier music piped in to help you relax as you're cutting logs.

I love Epcot. I always make a point to spend at least one full day there, on some trips two. I just hope I never have to spend time on Epcot porcelain. I've visited numerous Epcot latrines, specifically in World Showcase. It was Food & Wine after all! Most of the bathrooms were unimpressive and a good many were so disgusting they violated the *Geneva Convention*! Forget waterboarding. Trying to hold your breath long enough to pee was real torture! Fortunately, there was a bathroom in Epcot across from *Spaceship Earth* next to the photo shop that was clean, relatively roomy, and worthy of a good "rest stop." It would be a long power walk if the need hit when you were all the way across the lagoon in World Showcase. Just clench your cheeks and get shuffling! If you're really prairie dogging, commandeer an old person's scooter in the name of sanitation!

However, as this is *Ears of Steel* and the goal was to find the best bathrooms for real men, I did in fact find a toilet that exceeded all criteria! The best bathroom on property *period* is not inside a park at all! However, it is within spitting distance of Epcot—but remember the rules, no spitting! If you happen to be in Epcot and don't want to two-step it all the way to the front of the park, you're in luck. Clench with all you've got and get on a Friendship Boat ASAP! If you can hold it through minor rolling waves, relief is just one stop away. It's the greatest place I could imagine to go to the bathroom. Even if you don't have to go, go in anyway.

This is the Coliseum of crappers. A bastion of manly comfort and pleasure. A restroom where a real man can lean back and rest! In fact the location that houses this wonder water closet was already getting a chapter all to itself. That I discovered it houses the greatest men's room in all of Walt Disney World is what they call a happy accident, where one needn't worry about having an accident.

You've waded through this chapter on toilets like a sanitation man in knee-high sewage. Now, prepare to be rewarded. The official Ears of Steel Award for *Greatest Men's Room in all of Walt Disney World* goes to a real man's can located fittingly inside the ultimate hangout for dudes! It is a shrine to all things "red-blooded American man!"

A place with menu items named for some of the greatest athletes of the last 50 years! A hallowed hall where every stall in the men's room has its own flat screen over the door so you can drop trou, kick back, and catch which teams are fighting for number one while doing number two! A masculine man cave offering respite from princesses and singing dolls, where you can reclaim your manhood for an hour or two! This is the Boardwalk beacon that summons you, calling out to all hardworking, sports loving guys looking for a break and a cold beer.

When I first walked in (only to do number one, sadly), I felt like I was in a whizzing wonderland. I knew in an instant I had to write about it, to share the gastrointestinal gospel! After extensive and exhaustive (at least on my nostrils) research, I can safely conclude that the greatest place on property for the man in need of relief, as well as in need of a drink and some cool a/c, is the one and only . . .

CHAPTER THIRTEEN

ESPN Club

BECAUSE IT'S THE FRICKIN' ESPN CLUB!

Yes, that's right. Disney's **ESPN Club** on the Boardwalk has the best men's rooms on property. Black, white, and red tiles sparkle around the large stalls, roomy enough to spread out and get comfortable, which is good, with your own private television hanging overhead, which is, let's face it, awesome. I highly suggest if you find you have to go, whatever the distance from where you are at that moment, take the challenge. Obviously, I didn't get to inspect the ladies' room—or did I? I can only imagine it, too, is a pretty spectacular spot to squat.

But as my wife constantly says to my five-year-old son (Okay, and to me) that's enough potty talk.

However, that's only the beginning of Disney's ESPN Club! For years I'd heard other guys proclaim their love of this place, but I'd never had the chance to experience the legend for myself. Finally, while researching this book, I made a point to stop in and see for myself. From now on, I will schedule a trip to ESPN Club every visit! And I may make it a point to schedule it while the wife and kids are doing something else! This restaurant was made for men. I don't mean that in any kind of sleazy, misogynistic way. It's a tribute to all things manly, celebrating athletic tradition, fraternal bonding, and spicy chicken wings.

The first thing that struck me walking in the front door were the hundreds of flat screens hanging everywhere, of multiple sizes, showing every possible sporting event or sports-related program on at that time of day. As you can imagine, this is a popular spot to watch any big game, regardless of whether your team's playing or not. I'm told if you try to go on a Sunday during football season, you better get there early. They have enough TVs that you're likely to see your home team on at least one, even if you're a Packers fan.

I just threw up in my mouth a little.

The ESPN Club really snuck up on me. I expected more of a gaudy, neon Hooters-lite, or some overly themed restaurant with a giant basketball over the entrance. ESPN is located on the Epcot end of Disney's Boardwalk, where the architecture evokes a turn of the century Jersey shore boardwalk. It's what you imagine Atlantic City looked like a century ago, long before spray tans, "juiced-up gorillas," fist pumping, and something called a Snookie infested it. Everything on Disney's Boardwalk exudes class. Even ESPN Club's exterior is subtle, keeping to the surroundings. It's not until you cross the threshold that subtlety gets blown out a cannon! The varnished bar resembles a basketball court. The walls are coated in sports memorabilia, wherever there isn't a television. Even the booths have monitors so guests can watch events or play games between bites and beers.

This is the ultimate eatery (and *drinkery*) for real men. And for anyone with ADHD. The menu selections are on par with the best of fried and hot-sauced bar food, with a few surprises. Can you say "Boo-ya" Chili?!? Wings, burgers, nachos, the usual game-day staples, but kicked up a notch from your average *Thank God It's Cheap and Edible*'s corporate chain sports grill.

I made the fatal error of coming to ESPN Club after an afternoon of foraging my way through Epcot's International Food & Wine Festival. So I wasn't in the mood to eat. But every plate I saw pass by looked incredible. I considered forcing something down, for you, reader. But all I really wanted when I got to ESPN Club that day, the reason to go at all really, was to belly up to the bar, rest my dogs on the stool next to me, and throw back a cold one. Emphasis on **cold**!

ꟽan's Journal

I caught a Friendship boat from Epcot's International Gateway around 4:00 in the afternoon. The boat was empty but I sat outside in the stern. A family sat on the bench next to me, but I heard the husband say "We're going to reek of diesel fumes if we ride back here."

Yeah, I thought, which means we'll smell *awesome!* Diesel is the official aftershave of real men. Mr. Metrosexual tightened his Birkenstocks (I'd bet my first royalty check he's either a real estate attorney or works in online marketing for a juice bar) and moved his family inside on a perfect central Florida evening. Meanwhile I cruised through the lock with a breeze in my hair, daydreaming about rum drinks and mermaids.

The Boardwalk was the first stop and we docked within minutes. I wished I could grab a traveler and get back on the water, sipping a cold one as that big orange ball slipped behind the palmettos. Unfortunately, the nearest drink stand to the dock was touting its seasonal special, *Caramel Apple Margaritas.* The idea of it made me spit up a bit of lobster roll. It was on to the ESPN Club, the original reason for this little seafaring voyage in the first place.

When I first walked in, expecting it to resemble some cross between Dave & Busters and a Norse Mead Hall (where real men drank frothy, fermented beverages, engaged in brutish competitions of strength, and played Skeeball for prizes!). Instead, it was actually pretty quiet. It was that restaurant limbo hour where the lunch rush is long gone and the dinner crowd is still a little while away.

I'll put it right on Front Street. My first impression wasn't great. No one greeted me or offered to direct me through the detritus of a century of professional sports. I made my way toward the most familiar thing I locked in on, the bar. But no sooner had my cheeks hit the stool than a tired, pissy barkeep demanded my drink order and made it clear he didn't want to give me a minute. I blurted out my usual, bourbon and cola. Not necessarily what I wanted, but always a good appetizer. This guy initially soured me.

I'm a dude. I don't need a server to lather my balls and ask me my favorite color, but a simple "How's it going?" never hurts.

Fortunately, I'd learn he was ending his shift and just wanted to go. That I get. Not an excuse, but I understand. Just as I'm sure he understands that I purposely started a tab so I'd be paying (and tipping) the bartender after him. He dropped my drink and disappeared, relieved I didn't want a food menu. I glanced around, studying my surroundings. The place is a lot to take on the first visit. Considering it was mid-afternoon in early November during an NBA lockout, there wasn't anything especially exciting on any of the numerous screens. That didn't really matter so much, as I was here for the drinks.

I'd heard many positive reviews of their specialty cocktails. I happened to notice a monitor across the room from me scrolling through some of their frozen concoctions. What I saw made me think I should step back outside and check the name over the door. A peach martini? Well, I guess, but . . . a pomegranate Cosmo? I say again, a *pomegranate Cosmo?!?* I don't care what you drink in the privacy of your own home, watching *Sex and The City* and fretting over your cuticles. These were not libations I expected at the ESPN Club!

"Drink menu," I demanded, grabbing the surly saloon sweep by the lapel! "***Now!***"

Fortunately, upon scanning the real drink selections, I found plenty of choices befitting patrons with nuts (Chip and Dale, I mean). A few of these served in the wrong glass might send mixed messages (as would sipping with a pinky pointed skyward). But there's a big difference between the chartreuse of a melon martini and the green haze of ESPN's "Tee-Off," a lethal concoction of vodka, gin, rum, and energy drink, about which more later.

A friend kept recommending one PGA-inspired special called the Bloody Mulligan. A spicy Bloody Mary to begin with, but for my friend Bill Burke (one hell of a great writer, fellow Disney enthusiast, and masochistic drinker) the floor model doesn't even cut it. Bill always demands that the bartender make it "extra spicy." On occasion, he's even deemed their most twisted, maniacal, Tabasco-drenched worst as still not spicy enough. Bill tried to goad me into ordering an extra-spicy Bloody. His exact instructions were to order it "so hot you'll regret having taste buds!"

Based on Bill's description of his preferred mixture, I believe the name is doubly appropriate considering a Mulligan (for non-golfers) is basically a second chance to tee off. I have to believe that any drink with that much acidic tomato juice and spicy pepper sauce guarantees you'll be experiencing it a second time the next morning (see the previous chapter)! And don't tell me the celery counts as roughage!

I'm not a fan of tomato juice anyway. I am, however, a big fan of my palate and all six of my fully functioning senses, so while I did aim to try something unusual I opted to take a Mulligan on that particular Bloody and ordered a Tee-Off.

I'm not much of a golfer, but at ESPN I highly recommend the Tee Off, a drink meant to inspire visions of days on the links. It's a mix of top-shelf vodka, gin, rum, triple sec, energy drink, and a splash of cola. It's essentially a Long Island Iced Tea—with a kick of Three Mile Island! It was good. Damn good! May not have given me the urge to grab my bag, er, *clubs* and get on the fairway, but I'd sure as hell be happy to watch a PGA tourney at the bar with a few of these greenish-gold babies. And if I'm away from home and can't catch up with Sports Center, ESPN Club offers a great alternative while lounging at the bar!

𝔐an's 𝔍ournal

The new shift of bartenders had arrived and we began to casually banter. Turned out two were from my neck of the woods, Chicago. My advice: wear a Bears tee when you visit Walt Disney World (or the Blackhawks or Cubs for that matter). Apparently many of my neighbors are expatriating from snow and wind to sunny Orlando. And as you'll learn, we're damn nice people! I got dozens of friendly gestures and greetings just because I was from Chicago. This evening was no exception.

As I was sipping my second . . . er, third . . . okay, fourth Tee-Off, I noticed something about the audio playing over my head. It didn't match the broadcasts on ESPN, ESPN 2, or any other ESPN, all the way up through ESPN 37! It was considerably louder and the announcer was talking about things a bit more local. As in, right next to me! I spotted a face on one of the monitors that matched the audio I was hearing and realized I could see the bar over his shoulder on the screen. And there I could see my own ugly mug! That's when I learned another cool feature of this joint (besides the awesome bathrooms)!

Disney's ESPN Club is a fully equipped broadcasting studio. In the main dining room, there's a stage where the ESPN staple morning show *Mike & Mike in the Morning* broadcasts live throughout the year. However, there's also a radio booth in the middle of the restaurant where a live sports radio personality entertains the restaurant. I spun around on my stool and saw this broadcast was happening right over my shoulder. The host was talking a mix of sports news and special events at the club and around Walt Disney World. Then he said words that hit a man right in the heart (and wallet): "How'd you like to say you came down here and got something for free?"

I know I say don't sweat the money, but hearing the word "free" is rare down there! When heard, it can cause heart palpitations and sweaty palms. The announcer was going to be giving away prizes to anyone who could be the first to answer trivia questions he'd be throwing out. On one of the monitors a series of clues began to appear. Unfortunately after the first three, I still had no idea what or who the answer was. That's where being a Chicagoan paid off, yet again. One of my new best friends behind the bar leaned over and asked if I knew the answer. I informed him I had no clue.

"Wes Walker," he whispered. At least, that's what I heard.

"Wes Walker?" I repeated with confusion. I didn't know a Wes Walker, but then again, I don't pay attention to many other players if they're not on the Bears!

"Just go up and tell him," he smiled. "But I didn't tell you anything."

I nodded, still a little uncertain and headed for the booth. The DJ was in the bar talking to a group of Navy boys around a table.

Great, I thought. Not only was I cheating, I was going to cheat in front this group of REAL real men. I thought about abandoning ship when he and I locked eyes.

"You have an answer for me?" he asked, loudly. I did my best to act like I was recalling a forgotten factoid. I boldly nodded.

"Isn't it Wes Walker?" I answered.

"Wes *who*?" he asked, cocking an eyebrow.

Damn, I was busted! I had better turn tail and run out of the bar, swim across the lake, and catch a bus to Manitoba before he sicced SEAL Team Six on me for cheating.

"Wes . . . Walker," I said again.

"You mean **Welker**," he started with a knowing grin. "Wes Welker of the New England Patriots?"

"That's it," I said, trying to save myself.

"I need to hear you say it," he told me.

"Wes **Welker**," I said again, my **con-**fidence returning with his assist. "You know from the Patriots. Welker, Walker. Look, I'm a Bears fan. I can't properly pronounce a Patriot's name. It's a law."

He laughed. The sailors laughed. I breathed a deep sigh of relief. I'd pulled it off. He ushered me into the booth and handed me a T-shirt. We got to talking and he asked if I really was from Chicago. His name was Joe and his son lives in the Chi as well! The shirt, he told me was one of a kind, not available for sale. Only available to unscrupulous participants willing to lie and cheat for any free swag printed with *Walt Disney World*. Hey, it's like Captain Jack said, take what ya can and give nothin' back!

I have no proof and don't quote me (I'll disavow any knowledge that I wrote it) but I have a feeling this was not the first or last time a guest received assistance from a Cast Member in a harmless trivia contest. In fact, I'd bet it happens every day and management is cheerfully aware of it. This shirt wasn't exactly sewn with golden threads. And besides, they only had size XL. Each of my calves is XL, and I didn't need leg warmers. Still, it made a nice re-gift.

Joe came out into the bar and we chatted some more. This was a big day in Chicago sports. I had flown in early and been pretty much incommunicado at Epcot all day. Joe filled me in with the day's big news that my Cubbies fired their manager. I asked him about his gig and how the crowds got during high sporting event seasons. He smiled and said, to put it simply, if you wanted a table to watch Sunday football, you'd better get there well before they opened the door and line up. Eventually, Joe went back to the booth and I leaned back, ordered another Tee-Off, and finally began to relax. Part of me contemplated spending the rest of my trip right there on that stool. The bartender leaned over and gave me the answer to the next question, but as they say, pigs eat, hogs get slaughtered. And both make bacon . . . mmm bacon!

I gestured to a guy sitting at the high-top table near me and gave him the answer. I instructed him not to say where he'd gotten it, just as was told to me. It's about brothers helping brothers right? His hot girlfriend was impressed when he returned with a T-shirt. He gave me an appreciative nod and tip of the glass. No thanks necessary, friend. This was indeed a place for men to be men. I realized I was suddenly very happy. I wondered, was this Heaven? No. It was the ESPN Club!

You'll hear the term "must-do" quite a bit at the World. Take if from a brother here. Disney's ESPN Club is a definite must-do for any virile American male sports fan! It's a great place for lunch or dinner with the family. If they're not into it, send the wife and kids to the pool, or better yet, Downtown Disney to shop. You deserve some guy time. It's not selfish. There may not be an "I" in TEAM, but there is a "ME!" It's there, trust me. It also spells MEAT backwards (sorta), which is nice. Anyway, take some "me" time. Go to the club that was made for you.

You're a guy. You're already a lifetime member.

CHAPTER FOURTEEN

Transportation and Ticket Center

"TOO LATE TO ALTER COURSE NOW, MATEY!"

arly in this book, I told you that when it comes to *doing* Disney World properly, Rule #1 is always stay on property. There is no place in all The World where that rule rings more glaringly true than when visiting Magic Kingdom.

When you look at a map, you will see Magic Kingdom sits by a large body of water called the Seven Seas Lagoon. If you're staying at a Disney hotel, the shuttle will drop you off just a short walk from the park gates. Your only encounter with that water will be a short walk past it on your way to the fun. However, if for some unimaginable reason you choose to stay in some random off-property resort, you will become well acquainted with this lovely lagoon. Even if they offer you free shuttle service to the parks, when it comes to Magic Kingdom, all non-resort guests get dropped off at the same place—wa-a-ay over there on the opposite side of the lake.

Look across Seven Seas Lagoon from Magic Kingdom and you'll see a large concrete structure on the opposite shore not dissimilar to a parking garage or elevated train stop. It might as well look like the monolith from *2001: A Space Odyssey* because it will make you feel like an ape wanting to smash something! That is the Transportation and Ticket Center or TTC for short. The TTC is where off-property guests line up for their first ride of the day, either a monorail ride around the lake or a ferry across. Whichever means you choose, get ready to wait. Wait to board either mode of transport. Wait some more to get in the park. On busier days, those waits can be unbearable. Every time someone consults me about a trip to Disney and they mention some cheaper off-prop room rate I ask them: "Why would you consciously cost yourself an extra 10, 20, even 30 minutes of fun time standing in another unnecessary queue?" Not to mention, that TTC has a lot of stairs! This is vacation, not aerobics! Not a fun way to start your visit to MK.

I often refer to the TTC as the *Island of Misfit Tourists!* It is a confused and crowded labyrinth of crushed dreams and damaged vacations. You're here to see the Mouse, not to feel like a lab rat desperately searching for the cheese. Even when you are an on-property guest, the TTC can be maddening. When you go to Magic Kingdom, stay there! Park Hoppers be damned! The only reason to leave the park is to go back to your hotel—either for an afternoon swim and a nap or at the end of the day. Do not, I repeat, do *NOT* attempt to visit any other park! Even getting to Epcot, which has its own monorail line, is a dicey proposition that, I warn you, you'll take at your risk! You still have to disembark and reembark at the TTC. Trying to get to Disney's Hollywood Studios or Disney's Animal Kingdom from Magic Kingdom via the TTC is about as enjoyable an experience as being waterboarded. In fact, by comparison, waterboarding could be considered refreshing.

The TTC will make even a valued Disney guest feel like an unwelcome stranger in a strange land. There are arrows directing you (allegedly) to the bus stops. I can't prove it, but I believe every other arrow points you in a different direction, just to mess with your head. It's like being in Wonderland. Only the *wonder* is why you'd ever come back. Even when you've walked for what feels like an arduous mile to find the lot that time forgot, where buses pick up and drop off, you must battle hordes of oncoming mouth breathers from the no-tell motels across Kissimmee.

Like a hobbit amongst trolls, fight past these plastic-visor-wearing, burnt-cleavage-sporting troglodytes knocking into you and hurling spittle and obscenities as they drag their offspring alongside (and that's just the men!). Even the state of the TTC parking lot is decidedly un-Disney. One wonders if they spent extra money to make it look so dilapidated. Broken asphalt, dead foliage, overflowing trash cans. I believe it's a lesson from management to the off-property visitor—*this* is what saving a few bucks a night has earned you!

The TTC is the greatest argument for paying the premium to stay in a Disney Resort. But go ahead, save a few bucks. Have fun getting lost in the Bermuda Triangle of Buses! My Disney hotel shuttle will be dropping me off a few feet from the turnstiles!

CHAPTER FIFTEEN

Breakfast

THE MOST IMPORTANT MEAL OF THE DAY (WITHOUT BEER!)

It's the most important meal. That's what we've always been told. Most of the year, breakfast equals a cup of Joe as we bolt out the door. Maybe a slice of cold pizza clenched between our teeth or a donut from the Gas and Go!

As your attorney, I advise you that act won't play at Walt Disney World. You'll be on your feet moving around all day, expending loads of energy. Three squares plus snacks are essential. You should listen to me, I was pre-med.

Breakfast at your hotel is more than adequate. Every food court offers plenty of tasty, traditional options from cold cereal and fruit to pastries and pancakes to bacon, sausage, and made-to-order omelets. But having just discussed Magic Kingdom, I thought it important to point out a few additional morning must-eats! When you're going to be in that part of the World, these are standards!

The Crystal Palace

The first might be the most convenient, as it's located right inside the park. The Crystal Palace offers a morning breakfast buffet that will remind you of Easter Sunday, without the church part. Your wife will love the classy, Victorian atmosphere with its flowery charm and decor. The vestibule (triple word score!) is filled with floral arrangements representing the characters of *Winnie the Pooh*. I won't try to hide it, it's a character breakfast. The flowers won't be the last place you'll see Pooh and Eeyore. They make hourly appearances around the dining room. Odds are you'll have your snout so deep down in the trough, you won't even notice a six-foot Piglet. If you do, don't ask him to grab you some more bacon. It's hurtful.

The food at Crystal Palace is top notch, especially for a buffet. In fact it's safe to say the buffets at Walt Disney World are all above par, but this one may be one of the best. Great selections abound. As a real man, you'll dig the homemade corned beef hash with its big chunks of corned beef, fresh potatoes, and peppers. I'm a Midwestern boy with Southern roots, and I judge every breakfast joint by its corned beef hash. Crystal Palace is dishing up righteous hash! It's a great way to fortify your fuel tank for the adventure ahead. Even little ones have their own mini-buffet—where I recommend you snatch a slice of the breakfast pizza!

Another great perk of breakfast at Crystal Palace is location. Make an early ADR and you can enter Magic Kingdom before it opens. There is something mystical about getting up early and walking down a near empty Main Street, U.S.A. while mist is still rising off the asphalt. When you finish breakfast, ask a Cast Member to roll you right out into the park—you have already passed through bag-check long before the crowds arrived. You may have to wait for rope-drop (when they allow guests to enter the main part of the park), but you'll have a pretty good shot at riding *Thunder* and *Splash* while most guests are still shuffling down Main Street!

Chef Mickey's

If you're taking children, this next breakfast option is a no-brainer. In fact, attendance is practically mandatory. That is, if you can get an ADR.

Chef Mickey's at the Contemporary Resort is a popular ticket, and with good reason. The food is good, with a great buffet selection as well. In fact, it seemed like there was twice as much food as at Crystal Palace. They had corned beef hash, too, but this was more the consistency of the stuff you might remember from the red can. And some mornings, that's exactly the hash you want! I scooped two mountainous helpings on my plate before breakfast was over.

Hash aside, this dining experience is all about the shorter humans in your group. I mean not for nothing the name of the place is Chef *Mickey's*! They didn't build it for you. Yes, it's another character breakfast. Whereas at Crystal Palace, Pooh and friends visit the dining room, quietly waving and posing for pictures, Chef Mickey's has created a dining entertainment experience! Whether you like it or not!

There's loud music and loud decor. The "Fab 5"—Mickey, Minnie, Goofy, Donald and Pluto (I can't believe any dogs are allowed in the dining room)—dance around, encouraging everyone to sing, clap, and twirl their napkins overhead! A cunning man will time it so he's at the buffet while this circus is going on in his section of the dining room. But who am I kidding? If you're not there recording the whole event for posterity, there's a good chance your wife won't twirl your napkin for a while!

It's a popular breakfast so you need to make your ADR as soon as you book your trip, if not before. If you just show up one morning around 8:30 and ask for a table, the normally polite and professional Cast Members are likely to laugh and slap you across the face with a mouse glove!

Aside from procuring a decent seating time, the problem with Chef Mickey's is the location. Chef Mickey's is located on the fourth floor of the Contemporary Resort. One of the first hotels ever built at Walt Disney World, the Contemporary is just around the corner from the Magic Kingdom. Sounds great, right? Wrong! Getting there from your hotel can be a pain. (Unless, of course, you're staying at the Contemporary . . .)

I've been on resort shuttles with light crowds and our driver was kind enough to drop a few Chef Mickey's diners off in front of the Contemporary. That was an exception though, as standard practice is to ride all the way to the Magic Kingdom drop-off. From there, you wait for a monorail back to the Contemporary (the monorail actually runs right through the hotel lobby, which is pretty cool). Your other option, which is often actually faster than the monorail option, is to just hoof it from the bus drop-off point! It is a relatively short walk down the sidewalk and across the street to the Contemporary Resort and Chef Mickey's. Just remember, if you're a musk-oozing water buffalo of a man prone to easy perspiration, even that short walk on a humid Orlando morning can have you soaked to the shorts before you get to breakfast. Make sure you brought your Gold Bond!

Kona Cafe

Finally, maybe you want one good breakfast without oversized cartoon characters sniffing around your pancakes. Maybe you'd like to forgo a buffet and relax, letting a server deliver made-to-order entrees. Get to Magic Kingdom early and catch a monorail or a ferry across the lagoon to Disney's Polynesian Resort.

There's a fancy sit-down restaurant everybody praises called Ohana! It's all you can eat with an emphasis on meat. Sounds great, and in fact it is! It's all you can eat, if you're up to the challenge. A great option for a manly breakfast if you've got time for a nap after. We're not headed there this morning. In an upstairs corner of the Polynesian resort hides what essentially looks like a tropical Denny's. This is my favorite breakfast spot on property, Kona Cafe.

Kona Cafe serves breakfast for men. In ancient Polynesian culture, a big belly was a sign of power and opulence. Maybe that's why the staff stood at attention when I approached. Regardless, I arrived at Kona for the first time with a Kamehameha-sized appetite, and I did not leave disappointed.

Kona Cafe is famous for one particular breakfast dish. Any experienced Walt Disney World traveler will tell you if you're going to Kona, you have to get the *Tonga Toast*. I'm not going to break bad on Tonga. It is good stuff. Imagine a hunk of sourdough French toast the size of a pillow stuffed with banana, rolled in cinnamon and sugar! If you want a starchy, stick-to-the-ribs tummy filler with a side of meat before heading to the parks, there's little better. It's a little sweet though, and I like a salty, savory breakfast to power up! There's one major flaw with the Tonga Toast. It's lacking the proper amount of what every brave warrior needs before a vigorous outing, protein. Charred animal flesh. Don't get me wrong, Tonga Toast comes with your choice of ham, bacon, or sausage. That's the problem. The word "*or.*" You only get one. The word "*and*" is so much better than "*or.*"

That's why, for a real man, breakfast at Kona Cafe is all about one selection, the Big Kahuna! Let me break it down, and I hope you've eaten or you'll be chewing the book by time I'm done. French toast. Yes, regular ol' French Toast, not stuffed but still awesome. Pancakes. I repeat, French Toast *and* pancakes. Pancakes covered in a mound of fresh pineapple and macadamia nut compote so unimaginably delicious you don't need syrup. It's so good, in fact, you'll actually be angry at the syrup for even taking up real estate on your table.

Plus you get a thick slab of grilled ham, a fat sausage link, and crisp, smoky strips of bacon. This is a pork luau! It's *pork-tastic!* This isn't utility food-court fare either. This is tasty, quality meat! There won't be a scrap left on that platter. They also leave a carafe of Kona coffee so you never have to wait for a warm-up. Just recalling my last breakfast at Kona Cafe is bringing tears to my eyes. It is acceptable for guys to cry over great food. And your kids. And your dog.

Just one word of caution about breakfast at Kona Cafe—all that food and your own pot of coffee may come back to haunt you about an hour or so into the park. This is where the chapter on bathrooms may come in handy!

Downtown Disney

REAL MEN AREN'T AFRAID TO GO DOWNTOWN!

sually, the last thing any man worth the salt in the sweat-stained brim of his cap wants to do is shop, let alone lug around souvenir-laden plastic bags. However, each year Disney puts out some really cool stuff even guys will see and think "must have!" There's nothing wrong with wanting a memento of your grand adventure. From warriors to soldiers to explorers, real men have always brought home souvenirs! We've just replaced tusks, stolen swords, and heads on stakes with a cool T-shirt, coffee mug, or refrigerator magnet!

What I do suggest is that you don't buy much inside the parks. With kids it can be unavoidable. They're caught up in the magic. They see it, they want it. If the little one is willing to carry around that plush Donald Duck all day and not drag it on the ground—and when you see the price tag, you'll demand a pristine white duck's ass at day's end—then go for it!

Set one night aside and let the family know that is the night when all souvenir shopping will be done. Downtown Disney is the place you will lead them with those dollars burning holes in their pockets! I promise this will be one shopping excursion you will not only tolerate but enjoy!

Downtown Disney is a waterfront dining, shopping, and night-life district that Disney created as an alternative for guests so they'd never be tempted to leave Disney property, which makes Mickey sad. It is especially popular for the adult guests of Walt Disney World. It's a stretch of property similar to a large galleria with a lot of Disney touches. Even though it's free to walk around and peruse the shops—until you buy something anyway—Downtown Disney feels like a smaller fifth theme park. Part galleria, part amusement park, it even has a Vegas feel, minus the gambling and creeps handing out stripper cards and flyers on every corner—and creeps collecting them. Allegedly!

The best part is, aside from the seemingly never-ending shopping opportunities, Downtown Disney is lined with great restaurants and bars. You could eat lunch and dinner there every day of your trip and experience a new restaurant and cuisine at each meal. Everything from quick eateries and snack (and margarita) counters to moderately priced theme restaurants all the way to high-end fine dining. Some of Walt Disney World's best bars and nightspots are located right here in Downtown Disney. To paraphrase Seuss, oh the places you'll drink!!!

I love Downtown Disney. I love the energy and excitement of the waterfront district. I love how clean and well laid out it is. Plus, Downtown Disney just feels safer than a normal touristy shopping district. When you stay in a Disney resort, your bus drops you off right at the entrance to the shopping district or closer to the night-life, depending on your plans. On a map, Downtown Disney looks like a long, curvy strip, but it's segmented into two main areas.

Downtown Disney Marketplace

The Marketplace is where you'll find the bulk of your souvenir shops, T-shirts, toys, *you-name-its*! There's a store where guests can actually design their own souvenir T-shirt—for a premium! You may want to stick with what's on the rack. There's a large store dedicated to Christmas called, cleverly enough, *Disney's Days of Christmas*, where my wife has done some real damage with a credit card. Her annual Tinkerbell tree rivals the actual WDW Christmas trees. For the boys, there's *Team Mickey Athletic Club* offering sports apparel and accessories with the Disney spin. Any kid (including big kids like you, big fella) is going to love the enormous toy store, *Once Upon A Toy*! Then there's the *LEGO Store*. To call it simply a store is a gross understatement. This building block mecca holds enough Legos to build an entire store made of Legos . . . filled with more Legos!

It's not all kid stuff though. If you're feeling hardcore, swing by the *Harley Davidson* store. You can pick up any number of Harley T-shirts and accessories because black and leather feel great in Florida! Plus, if you don't feel like dealing with TSA or being cooped up on an airplane, you can buy yourself a brand new hog and take to the open road! After all, some say all that Milwaukee power rumbling between your knees and the wind whipping through your hair is the ultimate thrill ride.

The Marketplace is home to the granddaddy of souvenir stores. A mall unto itself, the immense *World of Disney* is the crown jewel of Disney shopping. If there's an item you can think of with a Disney character's fuzzy face printed on it, this is where you'll find it. If they don't have it, it doesn't exist. If you thought you were experiencing character overload in the Magic Kingdom, this store might actually cause vertigo! You can't miss the six-foot Stitch perched atop the main entrance. This entire superstore is covered in Disney imagery and props, like a Disney Store on steroids, then blasted with gamma radiation and made very, *very*, angry!

Some people might think it's a bit much, but of course nuts like me love it. Again, yet another attraction designed to add more bang to your vacation experience. I would say "at no extra charge," but eventually you'll find yourself at the register.

Let's dispense with all this girly shopping talk—not to be confused with talking shop, a very manly endeavor! Real men go to Downtown Disney to eat and eat heartily! And the choices are endless. There are a handful of fast-food options which are great if you're there around lunchtime, but at night you don't want to eat out of a wrapper. Not on vacation. There are great, unique restaurants all over Downtown Disney. Many are really cool yet still relatively affordable. Not that it matters, since we're not obsessing about money at Walt Disney World.

Right off the bat, and because otherwise my Celtic ancestors would come for me in my sleep, I must guide you to **Raglan Road**. Raglan Road is an Irish pub like Walt Disney World is an amusement park! Compared to the cozy little pubs I'm used to around Chicago, Raglan Road is a behemoth. It has to be to hold all the guests who call it a favorite dining spot when visiting WDW. If you're a real man who likes to hoist a real pint, Raglan Road is a must-do. I might miss *Space Mountain*, but I'll never skip a night at Raglan Road! It's easy to find. Just spot the building that looks like an entire Dublin city block. On the inside you'll find a massive open dining room and bar, complete with lively Celtic music and live Irish folk dancers, pretty ones I might add, dancing atop it.

But Raglan Road isn't just about spectacle. Rock star Irish chef, Kevin Dundon, is the real deal, taking traditional Irish food and turning it on its *shillelagh*! He makes an appetizer called the Smoky City that makes me want to weep. Its primary components are haddock, potatoes, and melted cheese, along with toasted bread for dipping. I don't even like fish and thinking about it makes me drool. Of course, you've got standards like shepherd's pie or fish and chips, but Chef Dundon throws his own curveballs with touches of Italian influences, curries, and the like. And the man has mastered the art of cooking with that most important of all Irish ingredients, Guinness Irish Stout. Even the Irish stew is "infused" with it. I must confess, I've been infused with Guinness many times myself!

Speaking of, even if you're not in the mood for Irish pub grub you can't pass by Raglan without popping in at **The Hole In The Wall** bar. On the outside of the restaurant, it's even open in the colder months. You know, when it drops into the mid-sixties! If you're from the Midwest or colder parts, you'll know the locals when you're wearing shorts and they're bundled up, shivering over their pints.

Raglan is absolutely accommodating and kid-friendly, but maybe the little ones won't be so interested in bangers and mash (*bangers, hah!*). What about a trip to the jungle, complete with birds and animals?

There's a good chance you've heard of **Rainforest Cafe** (RFC). The jungle-themed eatery has locations throughout the country. I live within reasonable distance of three Rainforest Cafes and we're big fans. The food has gotten a bad rap in the past, but I've been eating there pretty regularly for a few years now and I've never had a bad meal. I will admit, food is not the primary reason I take my kids to RFC, or even just do a lap through the gift shop when I find myself stuck at the mall. Maybe it wasn't created by Disney, but Rainforest Cafe was definitely inspired by the Disney parks. It feels like a Disney attraction, even when located thousands of miles from Orlando or Anaheim. From the intensive jungle theme, to the sounds and special effects, to the animatronic animals throughout the restaurant, the influence of Walt Disney is blatant. The air even smells like a Disney ride. It makes sense that there are two Rainforest Cafes on Walt Disney World property. There is one in Downtown Disney, undergoing a remodel as I write, that will include the installation of a working volcano! The second is located in Disney's Animal Kingdom. Talk about a brand marriage made in theme park heaven. The DAK RFC even offers breakfast so guests can grab a bite and get into the park early when the critters are most active.

Downtown Disney West Side

Want to take it up a notch? How about barbecued raptor or brontosaurus burgers? Okay not really, but if you want a lot of meat and an exciting atmosphere to keep the kids entertained—or too terrified to leave their seats, which is sometimes just as good—you gotta go to **T-REX**! When Steven Schussler, the genius entrepreneur and real man behind Rainforest Cafe decided to inject his popular concept with reptilian DNA, Downtown Disney West Side became the perfect Jurassic spot! T-REX is enormous, loud, and unforgettable, much like its namesake. The outside resembles a nightclub in Bedrock! The moment you step inside, you encounter an enormous mother Tyrannosaur and her pups. She moves, she roars, she lowers her muzzle and looks right at you. Are you there to eat, or bring harm to her brood? I suggest you make your way to the hostess stand slowly with no sudden gestures. The good news is she's purple, so hopefully the little ones won't freak too badly. Barney was purple. He was also lame, but purple.

The restaurant is sectioned into different prehistoric areas such as the Coral Reef bar lorded over by a giant octopus (but a *prehistoric* octopus!). The Geode Room is cool, or rather hot, because you can watch meteor showers streak overhead and watch chickens slow-roasted on spits over a fiery grill. In the Glacier Room, the Ice Age has hit and hit hard. The entire room is encased in "ice" illuminated by color-changing lights. It's almost impossible to describe, except to say it would be like eating in Superman's Fortress of Solitude! It's an amazing effect but also hard on the eyes. I actually pity the servers who constantly pass in and out, their eyes constantly trying to adjust. Hopefully, T-REX offers a good vision plan!

Regardless of which theme you're in, T-REX is populated by AA dinosaurs of all shapes and sizes. There's even a woolly mammoth . . . in the same room as another Tyrannosaurus Rex. Historically and scientifically impossible, but it looks cool!

Rainforest has its haters, decrying the food as awful even when they haven't eaten there in a decade, if at all. T-REX is not immune to those same slings and errors. I loved the food, as has anyone I've sent there! Now I'm no hoity-toity food snob eating foie gras and roasted bone marrow. Bone marrow? Really?!? Am I a Rottweiler? We started with a huge nacho platter which, while not reinventing the culinary wheel, had everything I crave on a mountain of nachos. Ground beef, chili, sour cream, guac, jalapeños, black olives, and more cheese than Wisconsin! Drop this on a table in front of your buddies during a football game, they'll be at your house every Sunday.

For dinner, I ordered the appropriately named *Bone Yard*. Half a roasted chicken and a half-slab of BBQ baby back ribs, and these portions were not weak. Remember *The Flintstones* opening sequence when the car flips from the rack of bronto ribs? Not far off! The chicken was a touch dry (just a little) but it still had good flavor! I'm digging for something negative just to appease the haters. The ribs were fantastic! I had nothing to complain about and, as previously discussed, I am a rib fan. By the end of dinner, my plate was nothing but bones and streaks of sauce. It looked like two prehistoric beasts waged battle and this was the loser. As I leaned back, patted my belly, and finished off a second Category-5 (an amazing rum drink) I was definitely the apex predator!

Bowling has long been a favorite pastime of real men. It's not so much the game as it is the camaraderie among other guys in short-sleeved shirts and funny wrist splints, sucking down longneck bottles and just getting out of the house for a few hours. In late 2012, Disney answered the call of dudes, maybe even specifically *The Dude*. It's as if Disney knew I was writing this book when they introduced a new destination that definitely requires *balls*. Over on the West Side of Downtown Disney, a brand new dining, drinking, and bowling facility opened in the form of ***Splitsville***.

Though not a Disney creation, Splitsville adheres to that staple Disney company philosophy—take a well-known idea and then reinvent it completely. Splitsville is no mere bowling alley. It's another enormous entertainment complex rubbing shoulders with DisneyQuest and AMC Downtown Disney. Don't worry all you junior Lebowski's, there are plenty of lanes if you get that itch to play a few frames on your Disney vacation. Two floors of bowling in fact, randomly spread throughout the facility. There are also pool tables, multiple bars, music, and flat-screens playing sports everywhere. In fact, Splitsville could almost rival ESPN Club for the key to my manly heart. Almost.

Splitsville's decor has a very retro vibe. Think fifties lounge meets your grandmother's basement. Lots of vinyl chairs on rollers and plenty of booths. Black, white, and red are the colors of the day. I will be honest, at first glance, it felt a little too "hipster" for my Neanderthal tastes. But the minute our server brought me my frozen goblet of beer, I was very comfortable here.

What Splitsville really has going for it, along with bowling, is really good food. The filet sliders are mouth-wateringly good. The pizzas, again a sensitive subject with me, are delicious—a perfect combination of thin crust along the bottom but doughy and soft at the rim. In the name of research I ate two. The Meat Lovers lives up to its name with ground beef, Italian sausage, and pepperoni. It has the right ratio of savory to salty without going overboard and turning your face inside out. I also tried the BBQ Chicken pizza and I can tell you theirs is up there in the top five BBQ pizzas I've ever eaten. Whatever the secret, their barbecue sauce has that perfect balance of sweet and savory that works so well on pizza. What amazed me most is that, even though it was nestled in the gooey cheese of a pizza, the chicken wasn't dry at all. It was juicy and flavorful, complimented by the sauce and green onions. And fear not, because when you order a beer, you get a man's beer. Part of the retro feel of the joint is the old school goblets of brew, so frosty there's literally a layer of beer slush floating at the top! Now that's a perfect game!

This doesn't mean I'm a sucker for every overpriced tourist-trap eatery with robots and flashy lights. Well, maybe robots! Even in Downtown Disney, there are touristy locales that I wouldn't mind see meet the wrecking ball. It's fair to say most of the restaurants in Downtown Disney could be classified as theme restaurants aimed at attracting tourists. That's not a criticism. There's nothing wrong with creating a dining concept with a bit more spectacle and story. The reason "theme restaurant" is often used as a criticism is that some are heavy on concept but lack good food, good service, or good value. The good news is, while I have not eaten at every restaurant, themed or otherwise in Downtown Disney, every one I have eaten in has served me good food, and I've had nothing but quick, friendly service. I've almost never felt I didn't get value for my money. With the exception of one restaurant. Get your coin purse because I'm about to drop a dime.

First, let's take a step back in the Disney vacation process. After booking a Walt Disney World vacation, a number of travel documents will begin to arrive in the mail. One such delivery will be a booklet of vouchers. Specifically, it holds transfers for Disney's Magical Express airport bus service to and from your resort hotel. However, there are also a number of unexpected extras.

There's usually a free video game play coupon for use in your resort's arcade—a bargaining chip to hold over your kids in exchange for good behavior. Or a way to get them outta the room for a few minutes, if you know what I mean! There are discounts at one of Walt Disney World's two mini-golf courses, Fantasia Gardens or Winter Summerland. Both are great little spots to take a break from theme-parking and just have fun together as a family—Ugh, what is this, *Good Parenting* magazine?!? Winter Summerland was actually voted one of the top five miniature golf courses in America.

Another voucher I discovered in my booklet was a $15 food credit at **Planet Hollywood**. I had only eaten at a PH once over a dozen years ago. We had one in Chicago, before the movie star owners jumped ship. I had a burger and seem to remember it being okay. To be honest, the experience was so many years (and so many beers) ago the memory is hazy at best. I do recall bumping into a friend working as a waitress who claimed we'd just missed one of said famous owners. Apparently, a certain Austrian action star had popped by while in town promoting a new flick. Having just missed the future *Governator* stuck with me much more than the food.

Regardless, on this trip to Walt Disney World I was purposefully looking for ways to save money any way I could, short of packing lunchmeat in my socks. Yeah, I know I say don't worry about the money, but this was different. I was going for work, not fun. I would be embedding myself like a journalist, doing intensive hands-on research for the book you now hold. Any deal I could find was a bonus. Being a man, I know how to stretch a buck, so a $15 credit would go a long way. It was possible, I reasoned, they'd owe me money when I was finished. What I didn't realize at the time was Planet Hollywood spelled backwards reads "Prepare to be ripped off." Don't write it out. Just take my word for it.

₥an's Journal

My second night in town, I was heading to Downtown Disney to pick up a little something for my wife and kids, so it seemed the perfect night to score my cheap meal at Planet Hollywood. That afternoon I'd had a couple of beers at the hotel, took a combat nap, and grabbed a quick shower before heading out. It was already coming on 7:00 by the time I found myself approaching the first host stand at Planet Hollywood. The joint isn't hard to find. It's literally a giant globe rising over the rest of Downtown Disney with the words Planet Hollywood in bright red lights. You really can't miss it. If you do, ask someone to point you towards the Down-town Disney Lens Crafters!

I encountered two younger, spiky-haired employees with clip-boards and radios as I walked up to get my name on a list. They gave me an askew glance when I said it was just me. They told me to head on up the stairs. The restaurant is actually in the middle of the giant globe, so there's a metal staircase to climb . . . ugh, more exercise?!? At the top of the stairs another little dude with slick black hair (and, I'm pretty sure, eyeliner) wearing a tight black T-shirt asked me again how many were in my party.

When I said "just one" I got a roll of the eyes and a faint noise like steam escaping. The area outside the entrance looks like a red carpet event in Hollywood. There was also really loud club music pumping overhead like we were about to enter some L.A. hotspot. Me, with my graying beard and man-purse (yeah that's right) clearly didn't fit the definition of "cool clientele."

I was directed inside to prepare for my third check-in. Fortu-nately, being a table of one, I was ushered through pretty quickly and taken to a small two-top wedged in among a row of them. I was sitting under Jim Carrey's bike from *The Truman Show*. The thumping, bumping house music was even louder inside. It seemed to me this Planet Hollywood was suffering from a bit of an identity crisis—a movie-themed restaurant that wanted to be a trendy nightspot. My waitress did appear quickly and was friendly, always a plus—although she, too, gave me that "oh you poor thing, eating all alone" voice a few times. She pointed out some specialty drinks and my eyes zeroed in on a margarita-like concoction called the Iron Man. Works for me!

My head was spinning from the music, so I quickly said go ahead and bring me one of those. I flipped through the menu while waiting for my drink. It didn't take long (or complicated math, thank God!) before I realized that my $15 credit would be but a drop in the ol' bucket. Still, I was bored with burgers and this place was definitely something different. After all, if the food was good, at least they'd earn their attitude.

Planet Hollywood's foodie claim-to-fame is their lasagna. It's truly like no other I've ever seen. They use these cylindrical noodle/

shell creations stuffed with lasagna ingredients and served standing straight up on their ends. Being a movie-themed experience, I will say if I were directing a sci-fi flick set on some distant planet, I might use it as the model for an alien city!

I finally shot for the middle and ordered fajitas. It felt like an uninspired choice, but again, I didn't want another burger or their imaginative lasagna. Plus, you really can't screw up fajitas, can you? Their fajitas were, well, fajita-y. Seasoned strips of steak and chicken with grilled peppers and onion—the usual. Not horrible, but not exactly exciting either. What the kids call (shrugging their shoulders) "meh."

By the time I was finished, the place was packed, which surprised me on a Thursday night. Whether it was the loud music or the Florida heat, my head was throbbing. It was time to make my escape. When the bill came, that $15 voucher covered exactly half. I guess I shouldn't complain, except that I was by myself. There were big families in there. I can't imagine what they were paying. I know, don't obsess about money. It certainly wasn't the worst dining experience of my life, but it was disappointing. This is Disney! There are so many other unique Downtown Disney restaurants and for 30 bucks (or less), a guy could have had a much more satisfying experience. As they say, you get what you pay for. Maybe not the first choice for us laid-back dads looking for a peaceful, casual meal, but for the young hipsters out there, Planet Hollywood is probably great.

I spent the rest of the evening milling around Downtown Disney, noting all the restaurants lining the strip. There's great seafood at Fulton's Crab House or delicious Italian cuisine at Portobello. You want Cuban food? Go have dinner at the giant pineapple. Bongos Cuban Café in Downtown Disney West Side is, much like the home of Mr. SquarePants, shaped like a pineapple. Former pack-hunters like us can devour a plate of chorizo and beef skewers (spicy grilled meat on sticks) or an Argentinian skirt steak at Paradiso 37! Sure it might have cost me more than 30 bucks, but I'd have waddled out in a joyful, meat-induced haze!

Even if you insist on going cheap, any guy would be thrilled with the Holiday sandwich at Earl Of Sandwich! It is Thanksgiving smashed between fresh baked bread, right down to the cranberry sauce! It's the most amazing turkey sandwich you've ever lifted to your muzzle! And if you are up for a tasty and still inexpensive burger, I highly recommend Bodie's All-American. It is connected to Pollo Campero, a good fast-food chicken joint. Trust me, keep to the right and get a cheeseburger! It's not my favorite burger on property, but they are good and juicy! Don't skip the sauce bar either. A little of the BBQ mayo on your burger might lead to a re-ligious experience. Just don't get a little down the front of a white shirt (again, you can trust me on this one too!)

The list of options goes on and on. Sure a lot of the other restaurants in Downtown are loud and touristy, but the food and the service live up to the hype. Instead, I'd let my wallet make my decision, going against the very rule I keep spouting.

Fortunately, I soon found myself sitting outside one of Down-town Disney's best-kept secrets, and a refuge for all real men, Fuego by Sosa Cigars. Pinching a nice, relatively cheap Honduran (anywhere outside of WDW that would mean something entirely different) and cradling a cool glass of bourbon. Memories of bang-ing house music and being made to feel like the old man in *Up* faded into the Florida moonlight with a few puffs of blue smoke. Of course, that little treat cost me almost as much as my dinner. Yet I didn't bat an eye. The difference, of course, was value. Qual-ity isn't necessarily cheap, but it's almost always worth it.

It's true what they say. You get what you pay for. And sometimes a voucher is only good for lighting a cigar. So go ahead and spend your own cash and throw those PH coupons in the wastebasket. It's only a deal if it provides value. Real men know the difference.

CHAPTER SEVENTEEN

𝔐anly 𝔅its

A FEW TESTOSTERONE-CHARGED EXTRAS

We've gone through all four theme parks, Downtown Disney, and even a few extras like where to eat, where to drink, and where to go shortly after you've done both. Like a scientist, I've tried to extract the most two-fisted, teeth-baring, manly attractions the Resort has to offer—as well as a few that are just plain cool!

As I've pointed out over and over again, the Disney difference is the extra-mile. The bonus features, if you will, that while maybe not necessary, make the whole experience even better. As Walt used to say, they *plus it*!

While I mentioned Downtown Disney and how in many ways it feels like an extension of the parks and resorts, there are also some great *a la carte* offerings to increase the awesomeness. However, these side orders ain't free! And a couple of them require you to sign a waiver or two. Sure, you can go horseback riding at Fort Wilderness campground or you can get hung off the back of a speedboat in Bay Lake, parasailing like a human kite with a bird's-eye view of *Space Mountain*. Trusting a complete stranger to fasten your harness securely before tearing across the water at 70 mph certainly requires a brass set, but you can do that anywhere. I've hand-selected a couple of experiences unique to Walt Disney World that any guy would consider vacation activities fit for a king!

High-Speed Thrills
This Ain't a Simulator!

Real men have always had a thing for the road. All the way back to ancient Rome, roads were a symbol of power, strength, and how far we could reach. Over time, we turned the road into more than a way to get from here to there. We turned it into an arena for modern sport. We call it the track. And Walt Disney World has one of their own. The Walt Disney World Speedway.

Do you feel the need . . . for speed? Is it just impossible for you to drive 55? Prior to this book, if I had said "Florida," would your immediate thought be *Daytona*? Do you hang your speeding tickets on the wall like nerdy guys hang their fancy college degrees? Then why settle for maxing out at 65 or 75 miles per hour on the expressway? A guy like you wants to white-knuckle the steering wheel, mash that accelerator flat against the floor, and hear the engine roar like Hell's fury making its escape.

There's a place in Walt Disney World where you can do just that. After all, there are few activities in this world more tailor-made for real men than hot afternoons sportin' a tank top, proudly displaying your white and fire-engine-red farmer's tan, sucking cold beer from a foam koozie, watching NASCAR!

The **Richard Petty Driving Experience**, located at the Walt Disney World Speedway, gives you the chance to control a real 600hp NASCAR-rated race car. For a price, of course. In fact, for a couple of prices. The *RPDE* offers several different packages and experiences, depending on how far you want to push the envelope—and how much cash you're willing to drop for this once in a lifetime experience. Personally, I'm more of a drag racing guy—hammer down and three seconds to glory, defeat, or a flaming coffin on wheels. But I can respect stock car racing. If you ever dreamed of suiting up and slipping through that window, trading paint with the likes of

Tony Stewart and Dale Jr., there's no other experience this authentic—except the real thing. Of course it's not cheap, but you get to feel what it's like to be chasing that checkered flag at Talladega. Just you, a roaring engine, four melting tires, and destiny.

There is a ride-along option where you play co-pilot to a professional driver. There's no shame in being a sensible thrill-seeker, especially if you've got kids who depend on you. This ride has no safety rails or tracking systems or emergency shutdown. This is a real deal stock car on an open race track. And these babies hit 120 mph! No matter how brave you think yourself, roll-bars *schmoll-bars*! It takes years of training, not just a ten-minute instructional presentation to learn how to keep a hairpin turn from becoming a fiery barrel roll. With the ride-along option, you still experience high-speed racing inside a car without literally taking your own life in your hands. There's absolutely no shame in it . . . if you're a little girl!

Not all car guys are into racing. Some dudes just appreciate the look, the feel, the lines, and design of a luxury sports car. They admire the precision engineering where luxury and performance meet and create something amazing. Lamborghini, Porsche, Ferrari, and Corvette are just some of the *saints* in the Church of the Motorhead. Well, Walt Disney World heard your prayers and, in 2012, unveiled a new, more sophisticated driving experience without sacrificing horsepower. You may have thought getting behind the wheel of a race car was a dream. Imagine sliding behind the controls of a 2012 Lamborghini Gallardo!

It seems like the prices to drive are tiered by the cost of the vehicle you're taking out for a spin. The aforementioned Gallardo costs $389 to drive, but it can go from 0 to 100 mph in just under seven seconds—all the while surrounded by the intoxicating aroma of fine Corinthian leather. Bear in mind, however, you crack up against the wall, you might have to sell a family member to cover the sticker price!

You might opt to save 150 bucks—and nearly $150K if you break it—and take out the new Audi R8. Audi's not just a banker's car. The R8 does 0 to 60 in three seconds and hits 100 mph almost as fast as the Lambo! Of course, if you're looking for a deal, the Porsche 997 S costs a mere $169 to drive at Disney, and if you like it, you can take one home for a mere $99,000 and change. Prices are always subject to change, but style? Never! My old man always dreamed of owning a Porsche. It'd be money well-spent and a memory well-kept to see him light up one of these babies and let it loose out on the track!

Fore!

Say it with me . . . be the ball! (Na-na-na-na-naa!)

Okay, since it is Disney, I should have gone with "it's a Cinderella story!" If I haven't convinced you yet that Walt Disney World is for grown men, well, I'm a colossal failure as a writer. Fortunately, I'm pretty awesome, so if you don't get it, you've obviously taken a nine iron to the frontal lobe at some point. Speaking of clubs, how long have real men been conducting business, socializing, exercising (sort of), and commiserating about/hiding from their wives on the golf course?

True, there was a time it was only a rich man's sport requiring too much silence and too many flared checkered pants and oversized caps. Those days are over. Especially since a young kid named Tiger stepped onto the tour and schooled a bunch of middle-aged white men on once-restricted courses. These days, golf is an everyman's sport. Even guys who aren't usually golfers will occasionally hit the links on vacation, especially in the Sunshine State.

Walt Disney World has four professionally rated golf courses on property. Choose from Disney's Osprey Ridge, Magnolia, Palm, and Oak Trail Golf Courses. Two of which actually host PGA Tour tournaments, including the *Children's Miracle Network Hospitals Classic*. Recently, Disney turned over management of those courses to living golf legend, Arnold Palmer. Palmer will be personally overseeing the redesign of one course. Presumably with a combination lemonade/iced tea stand somewhere around the ninth hole.

I'm not going to lie to you, greens fees aren't cheap. Plus, you better call early to book a tee time. Rates vary based on season, but you're looking at around $139 a round for peak hours. Rates generally drop in the afternoon as the temperature rises. Hardcore golfers won't mind sweating through 18 holes while everybody else is wading in the pool like hippos on *Jungle Cruise*. These are Mastersquality courses in amazing settings. After all, it's Disney. You'll be playing the best. Even the gators lurking in the water traps whistle *Zip-a-dee-do-dah!*

That was a joke. If you do see an alligator, do not approach. It's probably not animatronic!

If you are a golfer, here's another way that staying on Disney property adds value. You don't need to lug your clubs around with your luggage. When you stay in a Disney hotel, they offer free club rental when you a purchase a round of golf at regular price. Whatever a round costs, I'd say it's worth not having to check a huge golf bag. See how I'm maturing? I really wanted to say ball bag! Nobody ever said a real man has to grow up completely.

Hook, Line and Sinker

A bad day fishing at Disney is . . . pretty hard to imagine.

What's that old adage? Give a man a fish, he'll eat for a day. Teach him to fish he'll eat for a lifetime. Take a man to Disney, you might lose him at a buffet or a churro stand . . . but I digress.

Even after a number of trips to Walt Disney World and finding myself out on the pristine lakes of the Resort, it never occurred to me I could drop a line in the water. Disney offers chartered fishing excursions all over property. From Fort Wilderness Campground on Bay Lake to Old Key West Resort to Downtown Disney, you can schedule a chartered cruise with a professional fishing guide. Imagine spending some quiet time on the water, trying to hook the happiest bass on Earth! Please, for the sake of the kids, do not catch little Nemo!

It is strictly catch and release, but the Disney lakes are well-stocked so your chances of reeling in a big one are pretty good. There've actually been decent catches pulled out of that water, including a 12-pound bass caught in Bay Lake. If you're a serious angler, you owe it to yourself to book an hour or two on a Disney lake. It's a peaceful break from rides, kids, and the constant barrage of calliope music! I'm kidding, it's not all calliope—there's a glockenspiel too! While Disney's great at creating magic inside the parks and resorts, the real magic stuff, the swamp magic, is out there on the water. If you are interested in booking a fishing excursion call (407) 939-BASS. (See what they did there?)

CHAPTER EIGHTEEN

Now It's Time To Say Goodbye . . .

DRY YOUR EYES, LITTLE FELLA.

There you have it. A brief—believe or not, this was brief—tour of the Walt Disney World Resort, *man's style*! My biggest hope at this point is that my book has conveyed what a great time you would have and how recharged you'd feel at the end of a Disney vacation. Still, the end of every trip to Disney leaves you feeling one way . . .

Miserable.

Miserable that it's over! Depressed the fun is over. Distraught that now you must return to the "real world." And after a few days in WDW, you'll dread going back to that dirty, unfriendly, *un-magical* place. Snicker and roll your eyes, but even the toughest, frostiest lumberjack will roll a tear in those last few moments before they board the plane.

However, here's the good news! This was just a book. A low-tech virtual vacation. Now you get to actually plan a trip and go! Even if this book has only mildly piqued your interest, I'm telling you *GO*! Even if you just take a few days. I guarantee by Day Two you'll want to extend your stay—and that's a conservative estimate! I'm willing to bet you'll be planning your next trip before you've finished your

217

first. You can't do it all in just a couple of days. You really can't even do it all in a week! Nor should you try.

Even I struggle with this, but it's true. I have an instinctive drive to hit Walt Disney World like it's my last day on Earth, soaking up every experience. You can't. And if you try, you'll just wind up exhausted and your feet will be throbbing. Not to mention your wife will hate you. Trust me, I know. I've tried to drag mine along as I do Disney "commando style." It's not a pretty picture. I know, as men we want to go, *go*, **go**! Take your time. Force yourself to actually be present (as those tree-huggin' hippies like to say) and enjoy every moment, realizing you are getting your money's worth even if you miss a couple of rides.

It might sound crazy, but some of the best moments you'll have will be sitting on a bench or in one of the many eateries around the Resort. Kick back on a ferry barely making a wake as you cruise leisurely across a lake to the next destination. It won't matter. You won't want the Captain to hurry. You'll be relaxing, hands behind your head, breathing fresh air and watching your family. You'll be watching the expressions of overwhelming joy and wonder in your kids' faces. You'll see contentment and appreciation in your wife's eyes, along with a little bit of exhaustion. But it's okay. It's the good kind. Whether she'll admit or not. You can just smile, knowing, like a general, you led them there! You made this happiness happen. After all, isn't that what being a *REAL* man is actually about?

Oops, did I just tip my hand? You mean I almost got through an entire book without revealing the truth? You see, this whole book has been a set-up. I'm not a so-called "real man" whatever that is. Oh sure, I'm a man. I like football and beer. But I'm not some macho Neanderthal with an overabundance of testosterone who worries about appearing tougher or cooler than everybody else. I couldn't care less about being cool. I drive a minivan, for God's sake! But I'm smart, Mike! *I can handle things!* And I know what's good for you, maybe even better than you do.

You need a vacation. A stellar vacation! And as I said, I am no shill for the Walt Disney Company. What I am is your fellow man. I'm your brother. I see what this world, the dingy, awful, real world I mentioned that we carry across our backs day in and day out, is doing to us. What we need, what *you* need, is a damn break. And yes, tough guy, you need a little ***magic*!

You need some childlike wonder. You need to be in a place where the working stiff is equal to the millionaire. You need to go where every employee's job, regardless of position, is to make sure you have the best day ever! Still not convinced? Let's revisit some other vacation destinations, now that you have a better mental picture of Walt Disney World.

You can bet your bottom dollar (literally) they won't treat you as well in Vegas! Sure, if you're dropping a thousand bucks a hand at blackjack, they'll give you a free buffet. See how nice they are when you're busted—you'll be lucky if they'll call you a cab. In the words of many a fellow dark-haired, swarthy-looking man, *fuggedaboudit!*

There's always that island vacation option. You think they'll treat you like a king in the tropics? I've been all over el Carib more times than Captain Ron! The weather is great, the beach is beautiful. But I've also been spit at for not buying some crappy trinket or shirt that shrinks to doll clothing after one wash. And try getting a decent meal for under a C-note that won't leave you doing the Aztec Two-Step! That mystical oasis Jimmy Buffett sings about doesn't really exist! You're better off sticking your feet in a kiddie pool with a Mexican beer in hand and that song about Margaritas and missing salt shakers playing on your iPod.

Trust me, whether it's Vegas or the Caribbean, they all come with caveats. The nonstop frat party gets old. And the aftermath gets harder and harder to recover from. After the age of 26, aren't you tired of that? Haven't you danced with danger enough? After my first trip back to Walt Disney World as a "grown-up," I was sold. I never wanted to go any place else on vacation. And that was way before I had kids. No, I'm not mentally unstable (not diagnosed anyway). You'd have to be to not get it, once you've been! It's the perfect package. You pay your money and step comfortably into the tender, loving care of Disney. Take your hands off the wheel, Captain. It's time for you to pull up a deck chair and let someone else steer.

Whoa! This analogy is starting to sound like I'm writing about the Disney Cruise Line. That's not supposed to happen until book three or four!

All right already! That's enough outta me! What are you waiting for? Either you're chomping at the bit to go to Walt Disney World because I've convinced you it's the *awesomest* (copyright) place in the world, or you just want to prove I'm a dumbass who doesn't know what he's talking about. Whatever it takes, man! I don't care why you go, as long as you go.

My favorite way is the Bob Vila DIY way. Disney makes it so easy to plan and book a vacation even you can do it! *Snooch!* Get online and go to: http://disneyworld.disney.go.com/

The site is completely caveman-friendly (lots of pictures and monosyllabic words with buttons) and walks you through each step. When do you want to go? How many people are coming with you? What resort tier do you want to stay in? You can browse each Disney hotel's individual website, taking a virtual tour of everything from the rooms, to the pools, restaurants, even the lobby! You can even book your flight and package the whole trip into one price. Heck, if I can figure it out, anybody can book an awesome Walt Disney World vacation!

It's so easy and informative, it's kind of addictive. Sometimes late at night, after a few bourbons, I'll go online and price out imaginary trips. Shake your head now, but you'll see! I'm not alone. If Disney monitors my log-ons, they've probably tracked the metrics to the point where they know my "trip planning to actual trip" ratio. I log on and some IT Cast Member shouts: "Take five, people! This guy's a tease!"

However, since you're a newbie and aren't entirely sure about this, you might want to consider a little help. You can always call 407-939-5277 and talk to somebody in the home office. There are also a number of reputable independent travel consultants out there that are as crazy . . . er, passionate about Walt Disney World as I am. Look for the "Authorized Disney Vacation Planner" seal on their website or promotional materials.

No matter how you book your vacation, you will have the time of your life. That's not an exaggeration. Everyone from heavy machine operators to soldiers to auto mechanics have taken my advice and come back thanking me for convincing them to go! Of course, there's no thanks needed! That's why I wrote this book, my brother.

Every trip to Walt Disney World I've ever taken has only been topped by the next one. I come home worn out physically, but the batteries inside, the soul, the spirit, are recharged and I feel stronger than ever. It pumps me up—emotionally. It's something that not only helps me loosen up and enjoy life for a while, but it creates new memories for my family. Disney vacations bond us together even tighter. Trust me, your Walt Disney World vacation will come up in the car or over dinner conversations every week. You'll constantly pore over pictures and watch vacation videos together. And it should come as no surprise the number one topic will always be, "When are we going back?"

What might be surprising is that question will be coming from you!

See you on Main Street, U.S.A.!

Afterword —
One Last Thing . . .

I almost forgot! Give the book back to your wife and point to the next sentence.

Listen, honey, I'm not trying to be a jerk, but he's still waiting for that sandwich! Seriously, go!

Acknowledgements

Writing a book is a solo adventure, but it's fueled by the help and support of many others. My sincerest thanks and two-fingered salutes off the brow go out to the following:

First and foremost, my wife & kids for supporting this crazy dream even if, and especially when, they didn't quite understand it! All of this is for you.

To Kelly Monaghan, Sally Scanlon, & Sally Bahner at Intrepid Traveler. Thank you for your faith, guidance, and shared wisdom. Most of all, thanks for saying "yes!" This book rocks because of you!

To Stu & Sue Greenberg for finding me room at the inn. To Stephen & Judy for your dedicated assistance in this mission. To Ashley Ahr, for inspiring an entire chapter (all complaints will be forwarded!).

To all my family & friends as well as the incredible online Disney fan community for your friendships, encouragement, and inspiration—your names would fill a chapter, but you know who you are. To Lou Mongello for cracking the code and showing us being a Disney fan can in fact be a career. To Ron Schneider, who has inspired me since I was a kid to chase my dreams and keep my imagination ever sharpened. To Jeff Kurtti, the brilliant author & Disney historian for inspiration and input and just being a man I look up to.

A very special fist-to-chest thanks to my friend, my kindred pirate poet and my liege, Bill Burke. You advised me to tilt and charge when you could have told me to retreat and leave the books to the real writers!

Finally, all my thanks, admiration, and respect to every Cast Member at Walt Disney World, from maintenance to food service to the performers and artists to Imagineering and executives. You are the ones who make the magic real and worth writing about!

Above all, a heartfelt thank you to the "real man" responsible for all the parks, places, and characters I love—Walter Elias Disney. I hope you've been reading this over my shoulder and chuckling.

About the Author

BART SCOTT declared Walt Disney his hero at age seven and has been an avid student of all things Disney ever since. He is an ardent fan and will take on anyone who says the Disney parks are too this or not enough that.

Bart majored in theatre for two years at a Baptist liberal arts college before being "invited" to leave. The details are hazy. He has held management positions in the banking and financial services industry. Today he is a freelance writer and blogger living in the Chicago area with his wife and three children, who are being raised in a "Disney-heavy life."

Aside from his love of adventuring through the Disney parks, Bart's other piratical appetites include good rum, barbecued animal parts, and the occasional fine cigar. He is, in short, a real man. He is also the author of *Balaam*, a young adult novel inspired by the Bible story. He would like to do voice-overs for animation so the whole world can hear the voices in his head, too.

Connect with Bart on Twitter @BartAScott or through his website, earsofsteel.com.

Index

Note: To conserve space, Index entries drop "Disney's" from the names of Disney's parks and resorts. For example, Disney's Animal Kingdom is indexed under Animal Kingdom.